Humanizing the Web

Technology, Work and Globalization

The Technology, Work and Globalization series was developed to provide policy makers, workers, managers, academics and students with a deeper understanding of the complex interlinks and influences between technological developments, including information and communication technologies, work organizations and patterns of globalization. The mission of the series is to disseminate rich knowledge based on deep research about relevant issues surrounding the globalization of work that is spawned by technology.

Also in the series:

MANAGING CHANGE IN IT OUTSOURCING
Albert Plugge

ADVANCED OUTSOURCING PRACTICE
Mary C. Lacity and Leslie P. Willcocks

ENTERPRISE MOBILITY
Carsten Sørensen

GLOBAL SOURCING OF BUSINESS AND IT SERVICES
Leslie P. Willcocks and Mary C. Lacity

ICT AND INNOVATION IN THE PUBLIC SECTOR
Francesco Contini and Giovan Francesco Lanzara

EXPLORING VIRTUALITY WITHIN AND BEYOND ORGANIZATIOINS
Niki Panteli and Mike Chaisson

KNOWLEDGE PROCESSES IN GLOBALLY DISTRIBUTED CONTEXTS
Julia Kotlarsky, Ilan Oshri and Paul C. van Fenema

GLOBAL CHALLENGES FOR IDENTITY POLICIES
Edgar Whitley and Ian Hosein

E-GOVERNANCE FOR DEVELOPMENT
A Focus on India
Shirin Madon

OFFSHORE OUTSOURCING OF IT WORK
Mary C. Lacity and Joseph W. Rottman

OUTSOURCING GLOBAL SERVICES
Ilan Oshri, Julia Kotlarsy and Leslie P. Willcocks

BRICOLAGE, CARE AND INFORMATION
Chrisanthi Avgerou, Giovan Francesco Lanzara and Leslie Wilcocks

e-GOVERNANCE FOR DEVELOPMENT
Shirin Madon

CHINA'S EMERGING OUTSOURCING CAPABILITIES
Mary C. Lacity, Leslie P. Willcocks and Yingqin Zheng

GOVERNING THROUGH TECHNOLOGY
Information Nets and Social Practice
Jannis Kallinikos

THE OUTSOURCING ENTERPRISE
From Cost Management to Collaborative Innovation
Leslie P. Willcocks, Sara Cullen and Andrew Craig

COLLABORATION IN OUTSOURCING
A Journey to Quality
Sjaak Brinkkemper and Slinger Jansen

SUSTAINABLE GLOBAL OUTSOURCING
Ron Babin and Brian Nicholson

Humanizing the Web

Change and Social Innovation

Harri Oinas-Kukkonen
University of Oulu, Finland

and

Henry Oinas-Kukkonen
University of Oulu, Finland

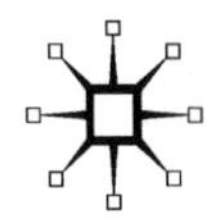

Softcover reprint of the hardcover 1st edition 2013 978-1-137-30569-5

First published 2013 by
PALGRAVE MACMILLAN

Palgrave Macmillan in the UK is an imprint of Macmillan Publishers Limited, registered in England, company number 785998, of Houndmills, Basingstoke, Hampshire RG21 6XS.

Palgrave Macmillan in the US is a division of St Martin's Press LLC, 175 Fifth Avenue, New York, NY 10010.

Palgrave Macmillan is the global academic imprint of the above companies and has companies and representatives throughout the world.

Palgrave® and Macmillan® are registered trademarks in the United States, the United Kingdom, Europe and other countries

ISBN 978-1-349-45488-4 ISBN 978-1-137-30570-1 (eBook)
DOI 10.1057/9781137305701

This book is printed on paper suitable for recycling and made from fully managed and sustained forest sources. Logging, pulping and manufacturing processes are expected to conform to the environmental regulations of the country of origin.

A catalogue record for this book is available from the British Library.

A catalog record for this book is available from the Library of Congress.

Transferred to Digital Printing in 2013

For our families

Contents

Preface

Both of us have had a long-term, profound interest in understanding human-centered technologies, in particular the web. Since this has been the focus of our scientific research for quite some time, we wanted to get some fresh and new ideas. We came to think that our diverse academic fields, one being a computer scientist and one being a historian, could be made to meet, and that as brothers, co-authoring a book would make a nice job. At that time Harri was on a sabbatical, being a visiting scholar at Stanford University, and Henry came to visit Stanford's archives. We saw this as an opportunity to interview Silicon Valley based web innovators in order to deepen our own understanding of the web as a phenomena and how it changes the way people think and innovate. The journey that ended up in this book had just begun.

This meant a multitude of discussions on a myriad of issues, approaching them from various perspectives, reading and thinking, and writing and re-writing about the topic (and again and again and again). Because of our other obligations we often had practically no time to work on the book project, which of course caused delays, but we were persistent. At times we had to escape to hide-away cottages in Hailuoto and Vuokatti to be able to concentrate and push the project forward. But in spite of the huge workload the work was enjoyable and intellectually rewarding. We had a wonderful time during our data gathering trips to Silicon Valley and Napa and we felt that doing the background work and authoring a book of this type was an innovation process in itself.

A special feature in the book is that it draws upon 20 longish first-hand interviews of highly recognized world-class web innovators, who are Silicon Valley specialists and influencers, including founders, entrepreneurs, system developers, and managers from companies and organizations such as LinkedIn, Wikipedia, Flickr, MySQL, Google, Mozilla Corporation, Cisco Systems, and Yahoo! The interviews are a compelling resource. All references to our interviewees as well as to their quotes are from the first-hand interviews unless otherwise specified. The interviews have been listed at the end of the book.

Yet, the book essentially builds upon rigorous scientific research carried out by the authors over the past 20 years in various contexts and development stages of the web. In addition to these, it also uses primary sources, such as official documents, blogs, and other online material, making the reference base exceptionally abundant and versatile. The book can perhaps also be described as a European interpretation of the future of web innovation, because of the Scandinavian authors of the book. Furthermore, two scientific fields, such as management information systems and history, rarely are integrated by two brothers who both have long-term academic experience in the way it has been done here.

The book is structured around the important issues regarding the social and future web with many illustrative cases and examples; these are not, however, presented in a case-by-case manner. Rather, the book could be described as a discourse in four ways. First, it is a discourse between two voices: Computer Scientist and Historian. Second, it is a discourse between the interviewees and the authors: the interviewees being Silicon Valley related visionaries and the authors being Scandinavian researchers. The topic is also such that for many of the issues raised no definite answers can be given; thus, the third type of discourse. Fourth, even though the social web as business is being debated much online, the discussion is scattered around in different forums, such as Twitter and blogs, and this book makes a coherent argument about the social web as a business ecosystem.

Acknowledgments

One of the most remarkable things during the journey of making this book was the opportunity to talk with the world's best web and innovation experts. It was intriguing to see how their stories compelled us think about the phenomena from different angles and to amalgamate a new conceptualization. We wish to sincerely acknowledge all of our insightful and inspiring interviewees for sparking our thinking: Vint Cerf, Henry Chesbrough, Douglas Engelbart, Judy Estrin, Caterina Fake, B.J. Fogg, Hector Garcia-Molina, Mark Granovetter, Reid Hoffman, John Lilly, Mårten Mickos, Ted Nelson, Tim O'Reilly, Paul Saffo, Neal Sample, AnnaLee Saxenian, Ben Shneiderman, Jimmy Wales, Bebo White, and Terry Winograd. In hindsight, we marvel at how we were able to gain access to all of them.

Working with the book was rewarding also because of other bright people around us. Some of our doctoral students read and commented on the manuscript: Pasi Karppinen, Sitwat Langrial, Tuomas Lehto, Salman Mian, Katarina Segerståhl, Donald Steiny, and Agnis Stibe. There were also specialists, who commented on some specific portions of the manuscript: Mika Erkkilä, Tuomas Jomppanen, and Al Kovalick. Sarah Weaver assisted in sharpening the language. We wish to thank all of them for their help. We also want to thank research organizations for enabling and supporting parts of the research that made this book possible: the Academy of Finland, the Finnish Funding Agency for Technology and Innovation, Stanford University, and University of Oulu. Finding Palgrave Macmillan as the publisher was essential at the final steps of this journey. We wish to thank kindly the series editors Leslie Willcocks and Mary Lacity and our commissioning editor Virginia Thorp, editorial assistant Keri Dickens, and production manager Vidhya Jayaprakash for their contribution to getting this book published.

The making of this book would not have been possible without the loving support of our own families. We wish to express our sincerest and loving thanks to our wives Niina and Tiitta, to our kids Henna, Joel, Elisa, Anton, Tiia, and Nea, and to our parents Heikki and Salme. Thank you for putting up with us through this project. We are now happy to bring the long writing process of this book to the very end and finally make the result of our journey visible.

Harri Oinas-Kukkonen and Henry Oinas-Kukkonen
Oulu and Muhos, 2012

Part I
Introduction and History

1
A Shift in Thinking about the Web

The web has become an integral part of business, work and general culture. With an amazing pace, it has transformed from being an esoteric computer application used by academics and tech-savvy youth into being an ordinary household tool and important communication vehicle for people of all ages and professions, and its role in modern society only seems to keep growing. Most importantly, the web has shown the capability to change people's lives.

Just as contemporary cars are different from their ancestors in the late nineteenth century, the web is different from what it used to be in its early days. When the web was introduced in the early 1990s, it was a collection of text, pictures and hyperlinks in relatively simple form, but the web has become a vehicle for media consumption, rapid communication and social engagement. Much of this was envisioned a long time ago by hypertext and multimedia researchers, but some of the things that we find on the web today nobody was able to forecast. Moreover, the web has been and still is a changing object. In order for companies and even individuals to be able to cope with and compete in this setting, it is important to understand the change that has already taken place in the web arena, to identify its mechanisms and to recognize the direction and pace for its next steps. Our claim is that the change of the web is resulting in the humanizing of the web and thus, in a matter of fact, fulfilling the web's original promise.

There is a term which came about to denote a second generation of Internet-based services – *web 2.0*. The first known use of the term dates back to a magazine article in 1999 targeted at web designers primarily in relation to design and aesthetics.[1] Later, Vice President Dale Dougherty of O'Reilly Media used the term in 2003 for characterizing the survival of the web industry after the dotcom burst.[2] In the following year, Tim O'Reilly used it as the theme of the first Web 2.0 Conference, referring to it as the second generation of web-based services that feature openness for collaboration and interactivity.[3] After that the term became widely attributed to him.[4]

Mark Granovetter, Professor of Sociology at Stanford University, explains that people who are using the term web 2.0 rarely have a clear view about what it means. In typical Silicon Valley style, the term has a loose definition. It is first and foremost a catchphrase which catches people's imagination and makes more venture capital flow. Yet, sometimes giving an entity a label may also accelerate the process of actually making it happen.[5] According to Paul Saffo, technology forecaster and futurist in Silicon Valley, generally innovations are named first and invented later. Therefore it is not surprising that the term web 2.0 is overused in many ways. Everyone also wants to be part of the future and the change rather than being part of the past. The implication is that whereas there is "web 1.0" which is old and not as interesting, there is the "web 2.0" which is the new exciting version. Of course, people have already iterated on this and there has been discussion on "web 3.0" developing even now. However, this discussion has been premature and the second generation of the web is still happening.

Still, web 2.0 is not only a catchphrase or a flagship leading in a maritime fleet. It is also a bandwagon onto which people jump at their own time. Indeed, the term is a way of creating awareness that we are moving in a certain direction. The slogan as such came out at a time when people were looking at the shift from primarily a broadcast version of the web with major providers, big networks and big players such as universities, schools and companies to a more distributed web made up of people who put material on the web for everybody else to see. Terry Winograd, a computer science professor at Stanford University and one of the originators of Google's success, explains: "If you think back to the early web, the model that people had of the web user was a sort of serious scientist, so comments would be like you wrote a paper and I want to add some footnotes to your paper. It wasn't a kid who wanted to say that his dog was running around. That just wasn't who they were thinking of. The mechanisms in those early days were not tuned to the audience that became the web 2.0."

Not being able to tell exactly which things belong to the second generation of the web and which do not may be frustrating for those who are longing for exact and uncluttered definitions. But this is not a unique situation. For instance, one would need to think about the labeling of the cultural movement called Renaissance. It began in Florence, Italy in the Late Middle Ages and then spread across the rest of Europe. Its varied versions were not uniform but rather they took slightly different forms in different parts of the continent, and yet there is a general use of the term which refers to it as a historic era. In an ever-changing business environment, it is even more important to allow a little bit of uncertainty. It does not make sense to nail down every definition to the finest detail to keep one's senses open for rapid changes. Yet, the relatively big changes in the web's makeup and façade also require some more terminological and conceptual clarity, and there is an explanation as to how the second generation of the web is different than the original web.

The social web

A widespread adoption of networked information technologies[6] has made the second generation of the web possible, but the most essential change that has taken place is not about particular technology but it is rather a shift in thinking about how the web may be and is being used. This dramatic change is very meaningful irrespective of what label is given to it.

In technology transfer expert Tim O'Reilly's vision, the essence of the second generation of the web is really about the Internet starting to become a *platform for applications* rather than an application itself. In a way, this enables a new kind of an operating system for applications to be created. This implies that rather than developing a multitude of new stand-alone applications and technologies, what we are starting to observe more and more is the coordination of the existing information systems. A simple example of this is provided by devices with geographical positioning linked with a location database. So when you say "pizza," you don't get the Wikipedia entry for pizza, but you get the three local pizza places with exact locations. This is the equivalent of hand-eye coordination between information systems.

The web as a platform also means that data rather than applications become the key driver for competitive advantage – and not just any data but specifically data that are generated by users and user activity. Thus, the web as a platform gives user-generated content much greater prominence than ever before. In addition to treating the web as a platform and encouraging users to participate, a key concept is providing a rich user experience. This has multiple meanings.[7] The basic meaning of rich user experience refers to the web-based applications' capability to offer graphical user interfaces familiar from desktop computers; a deeper sense refers to the provision of positive user experience on a more profound psychological level.

Yet, it is not only user-generated content and activity or rich user experience, but the social activity around content generation that epitomizes the current era. The term *social web* refers to a pattern of thinking in which the end-users jointly create or generate much or perhaps even most of the content for the web, whereas companies try to harness the end-users with tools with which they can participate and engage themselves in content production and sharing. For this reason, the term social web describes the phenomenon in a more detailed manner than the term web 2.0.

The term social web was used already in the 1950s in the context of historical research even if this was not in relation to information technology. In 1955, historian August C. Krey published a book *History and the Social Web: A Collection of Essays*.[8] In Krey's vision, the social web or social network that people form with each other, was to be elevated as one of the central elements in explaining a historical phenomenon. He considered the Renaissance as a prime example for understanding the need for this kind of approach to understanding history.

As described above, the early web was essentially the delivery of services from a centralized source to an individual customer. Even with the state-of-art technologies, it was principally that the user had to enter into a special electronic place and interact there. Of course, it was not that there wasn't any social interaction. There were chat rooms and message boards, for instance, but the degree to which social constructs were supported by technology was much lower. All of this changed with the appearance of the social web. An essential feature of the social web phenomenon is that social web is not only a virtual world; what is remarkable about it is its *interconnection with one's own life*. It is not just that one is connected to people on the web, but one is actually closely connected to people in one's real-world life be it professional or personal connections. Indeed, the web affects the user's life rather than their virtual life only.

The social web is a reconstruction in the World Wide Web of people's lives, and yet this reconstruction by no means is the whole matter. The social web comes down all the way to who you talk to and who within your family or friends you are in touch with. Even if pseudonyms are still common, for the most part, the social web encourages people to use their real identities rather than to act through pseudonyms only. Millions of people establishing identities and connections online are actually changing how we think about the web. What makes this even more interesting, challenging, and even threatening is that when there are hundreds of millions of people establishing a presence through profiles and other kinds of mechanisms and interacting with people, new kinds of applications that can transform people's lives may be, are being and will be developed. Some effects may be for better and some for worse.

Co-creation of value by social web users

People in general tend to think of the social web as literally the platforms and applications that connect them with other people no matter what they happen to be at a given point of time. Well-known examples of services in the social web are, for instance, Wikipedia, Facebook, LinkedIn, Twitter, Flickr, YouTube, FourSquare and Groupon. Wikipedia is a major encyclopedia in which almost all of its content is created by end-users. The rockstar company of the era, Facebook, provides opportunities to keep in touch with one's friends via the platform it provides; LinkedIn is an application to establish and manage professional connections; and Twitter enables tagging and sending short text messages to one's network both via mobile devices and on the web. Flickr provides social photo sharing, and YouTube enables the same with video clips. More recently, many other social web services have gained popularity, too. Yet, the social web is not only about these applications; it is first and foremost about a broader phenomenon that is going on: *connectedness*. We are highly – often overwhelmingly – connected with other people when our devices are connected, our applications are connected, but also the data that we generate is connected with lots of other data. In addition to this, there are many kinds of applications that take advantage of such relationships, which form the broader social portrait.

Understanding this tight coupling is an essential part of understanding not only the contemporary web but also the future web. The change that has taken place in the web as an information and communication environment is similar to the shift that previously took place from old-style character-based software applications to graphical user interfaces. Everybody was able to see it, but the changes were more profound and radical than they appeared at first sight. Many new features were developed after users got the computer mouse and multi-window displays. A similar change happened when we moved into the social web – a data-driven platform in which people are finally considered as more important than technology.

Hundreds of millions of people today not only recognize social networking sites but also actually use them on a regular basis. The social web, including blogging, tagging, wikis and many other facets of communication, has enabled web users not only to use these services but also to start to *contribute* to the services and *interact* with each other through them. The content which they may generate can be text, such as in Wikipedia; photos, such as in Flickr; videos, such as in YouTube; location data, such as in FourSquare, or something else. But the format of the media is not the important characteristic; more important is that users can link these pieces of information together and share them with their friends, acquaintances, business contacts, and others. Many new kinds of tools for knowledge sharing and online collaboration have been developed, which in a true sense take advantage of high-speed Internet technology and its global scope and enable users to contribute to collective intelligence. This denotes a big change from the situation in which content providers, such as news corporations or educational institutions, formerly put material on the web, which in practice was one-way communication only. Although interaction between the users and the producers of information and even among the users was possible in this older model, it was still very limited.

Even if many of the technologies in wide use today were invented decades ago, for the first time in history they are available not only for teams or a limited number of colleagues but to a multitude of users. Many of the social web services have been able to arouse interest in millions of users and in social web applications the number of users really accounts. A mere dozen videos provided by a dozen enthusiasts on most hobbies may not be much, but 10,000 or perhaps a million is a whole different story. This is also why the number of users creates value for web companies in the current era. At the launch of a new service a young company does not probably have very many users and the amount of content available for its users may be small. However, by producing content and via this creating value, users are able to play a key role in the development, and even success, of these companies from their early stages on.

Not all content is good content, of course; sometimes users are just spouting random opinions. But rather than from one single opinion the social web's power comes from understanding the opinions as a whole, realizing what the masses of people think.[9] Nevertheless, because of this inherent idea that users co-create value[10] through active generation of the content, the social web applications have the capability of improving along the way as they are able to attract more users. This incremental view towards web applications is natural and similar to human growth in which one doesn't wake up as a baby simply thinking, "Ok, there seems to be this big sign that says mama and the big sign that says dada." Rather we start making associations over time.

Social web innovation

It is important to understand that the web has different meanings to different people. A technologist may think of the web as a system of protocols; someone else might think of it as the world's largest shopping mall, while some would treat it as a way to socialize and to manage their shared social space. In a similar manner, adults and children, boys and girls, retired and working people use it for varying purposes based on their tasks, interests and needs. Some people use the web only as a broadcast medium, downloading videos from it or watching live sports broadcasts as if it were a television. For the most part, people are just trying to get their work done, to communicate with their friends and relatives or to entertain themselves.

Clearly, the social web can lend itself to many possible perspectives. However, according to sociologist Mark Granovetter, people understand the web only in terms of their own experience, but they do not necessarily have any larger picture of its role in the society. Ordinary people cannot really comprehend what the web as a whole looks like or even what it actually means for their lives. Nothing in their everyday experience gives a hint of what the overall picture might be. In fact, many ordinary people do not even understand what the address bar or the browser is; they just type in the http address into the search box which works, and because that is how they have always done it they do not enquire further. They do not understand how to distinguish the web infrastructure from its applications or from the Internet, and in their mind, Google and the web is the one and same. The users' mental models regarding technologies may be different from what designers originally had in mind or they may just be inaccurate in some other ways, but if they work there isn't any big need for them to question or revise them. And yet, in spite of the form of use, people easily become intoxicated from their new learning experience, possibly losing their judgment and capability to assess themselves. A pitfall in this is that learning basic web skills may lure people to think that they now know the web very well as a vehicle for information and communication when they really only know a tiny slice of its capabilities and opportunities. Moreover, lack of understanding about how the web *really* works or how it is governed does not matter very much for average user in most of their daily settings, but it should for managers and designers, and also for laymen when they need to decide upon matters regarding identity, privacy and other similarly important things.

Another important aspect about the social web's popularity is to understand the role user behavior plays for it. According to Jimmy Wales, founder of Wikipedia, one of the reasons why Wikipedia became so popular is that the way users find information in it is natural for most people. People who type a name of a football team into Google find a Wikipedia entry about the team. The associative connections are made visible for the user. Going to the front page of a news service and then hierarchically clicking on the sports section and looking for the same information would take much more cognitive resources, and in most cases people are not willing to sacrifice much of their convenience if there is no other benefit from doing so. Yet, in the social web the mutual effect of the value people perceive getting from it and the oligopolistic position of the major service providers overrides most requirements for higher usability or further ease of use. For instance, the developers of Facebook – which in fact is a much more complex system than it appears at the surface level – have been constantly trying to make the service more usable, but the need for connectedness is so great that users are willing to go through the trouble. Nevertheless, the importance for web developers to have a deep understanding of user behaviors in the web has become evident.

In our definition, anyone who significantly contributes towards creating an innovation by actively encouraging, promoting or leading innovation processes or in the deepest case directly creating disrupting innovations is an innovator. At an era where there is a growing pressure for any worker to be able to act like an entrepreneur, most knowledge workers could, and should, consider themselves as innovators. At the same time, when the roles of information producers and consumers have radically changed from what they were when the web first appeared, the web has become a spearhead for businesses to satisfy their hunger for breakthrough innovations[11] whether for the web or through the web for non-web environments. A web innovation is first and foremost social innovation because the web forms a social tie between people, using its own more or less clear and distinct social rules and codes of conduct. Indeed, the *social web innovations* may have a larger impact on the quest for innovations than anything since the harnessing of electricity for industrial use.

The social web's capability to change people's lives – ideally by and large for the better – has opened up many new ways to innovate, to provide ways for doing something novel whether in the form of incremental, emergent, radical or revolutionary changes in thinking, products, processes or organizations. Economist and political scientist Joseph Schumpeter defines invention as a manifestation of a new idea, whereas in his view innovation happens when ideas are applied successfully in practice.[12] Management theorist Peter Drucker defines innovation as something that produces a new dimension of organizational efficiency or a new dimension of productivity to customers or consumers.[13] One common view of innovation following Drucker's approach is that if one takes an invention and commercializes it successfully, only then is it an innovation; this would mean that something is not an innovation until there is a business built on it. No matter which of the aforesaid views is adopted, social web innovations are needed. The era of social web innovation has only seen its beginnings.

Structure of the book

In this book, we portray the history of the web as an inherently social medium, though this sociality, of course, varies with time, and we move the reader through that time from the web's beginnings (and before) to today. All of this is important for anyone to understand how the web really works. Based on this, we discuss the social web related phenomena and make suggestions of how to take advantage of those social features.

Part I describes the transformation of the web from a one-way information delivery channel to the socially rich communication vehicle it is now. Our claim is that this change process is still continuing, resulting in the humanizing of the web and thus, in a matter of fact, fulfilling the web's original promise.

Part II discusses the social web's promise and how it keeps changing businesses and software design as well as how we perceive people and what skills are required of them. The social web's key challenges are defined as a series of paradoxes.

Part III reviews the challenges related to the search for breakthrough innovations, which we call Zero-to-One innovations. It introduces the role of the web as an innovation ecosystem, emphasizing the consideration of the social web as a software platform, user experience and business ecosystem. It describes the key strategies for discovering Zero-to-One innovations for the social web or through the social web for non-web environments.

Part IV investigates emerging issues regarding the future web, both transformations that are already ongoing and visible as well as new expectations. Envisioning the next generation of the web will be largely based on the interviews of successful Silicon Valley web entrepreneurs and innovators. An important message for companies and organizations is to adopt a set of core business values that will facilitate innovation processes in this future humanized web. These business values are very humane. Finally, challenges in this next generation web will be discussed.

2
Waves of the Web

A ripple in the water does not raise much interest or cause much concern, but breaking waves on a coastline call surfers for the ride, while an ultimate surfing wave, a killer wave, makes people consider how to survive the extreme challenge caused by it. In a similar manner, the web's development can be described through the ripple, the breaking wave, and the killer wave.[1] But before explaining these "waves," we need to understand that the web is an inherently social medium and that it had social origins from its very beginning, even though the amount and type of sociality, of course, has varied over time.

Social origins of the Internet and the web

Some people consider the World Wide Web and the Internet as being one and the same or at least conceptually distinguishing between them being cognitively burdensome. In reality they are distinct technologies, and yet there would be no web without the Internet technology as its backbone. The emergence of the web was possible because of the Internet of the 1980s, which had its main roots in the Advanced Research Projects Agency Network (ARPANET) established in the 1960s. One of the origins of what we now call the Internet were a defensive need to create a network that could survive a nuclear strike. Earlier network topologies had a central hub; if the hub was destroyed, the whole network would go down. For this reason, defense system developers considered it necessary to create a decentralized network so that if anyone knocked out any one portion of it, the rest of the network would continue to work. Much of this infrastructure was initially built at university supercomputing centers that received funding from defense agencies. In the 1960s, the Defense Advanced Research Projects Agency (DARPA) of the United States Department of Defense backed the development of the first operational packet switching[2] network known as the ARPANET.[3] In May 1974, the network made huge progress when two participants of its development, Vinton G. Cerf and Bob Kahn, published a paper entitled "A Protocol for Packet Network Interconnection," which described a set of network communication rules named as Transmission Control Program (TCP). In 1978 they split their protocol into two: TCP and Internetwork Protocol (IP). The latter protocol was later named as Internet Protocol. The pair of protocols has become known informally as TCP/IP.[4]

With this defense system and technological background, it might seem that there was no thought in those days of what we today would call the social web. But in spite of most of research funding for years having been focused on technological aspects, there were strong social dimensions from very early on in the historic roots of what later became the Internet and the web. The researchers and programmers knew one another, they went to conferences together, and they shared code with one another. There was quite a lot of openness in how they interacted. Moreover, the social nature later inbuilt in the Internet appeared already in the early years of its precursor network. In April 1969 the Request for Comments (RFC) system was launched. Steve Crocker, who was part of a team of graduate students at the University of California Los Angeles, wrote a memorandum carrying the same name and asked the ARPANET community for suggestions for improvements. Computer scientists adapted this RFC system for exchanging their ideas. This sharing of ideas promoted the culture of collaboration. A couple of years later, when there was already 19 nodes in the ARPANET, this collaborative way of working got a further boost by engineer Ray Tomlinson at Bolt, Baranek and Newman Inc., an ARPANET contractor, who created a new method of communication called electronic mail in 1971. Email was soon integrated as a significant feature of the ARPANET. Larry Roberts, ARPA Director, began to use it for his correspondence, the researchers followed, and it became popular within this network.[5] Other social aspects emerged very rapidly. Google's Vice President and Chief Internet Evangelist, Vinton Gray "Vint" Cerf, who is often called as "father of the TCP/IP protocol," notes:

> Very, very quickly after basic network e-mail was implemented people started building distribution lists that were related to social interests. For example, one of the first distribution lists on the ARPANET was called 'Sci-Fi Lovers' for people who enjoyed reading science fiction. Another one was called 'Yum-yum' which was really just restaurant opinions that people shared. So it was very apparent even before the Internet that this computer-mediated communication was very much a social thing.

Vint Cerf further explains that ARPANET allowed a multi-party interaction, and it supported groups and people interacting with each other. This kind of social idea could also be found outside ARPANET. The Community Memory of Berkeley at California was the world's first known community network, created by Efrem Lipkin, Lee Felsenstein and Ken Colstad in 1974.[6] Most of the early community network projects started as Telnet projects,[7] but this one was established utilizing public terminals in Berkeley. In 1978, a Bulletin Board System (BBS) by Ward Christensen and Randy Seuss appeared in Chicago utilizing standard telephone lines.[8] This enabled access to any community network via a computer modem and users could then promote social collaboration. Such early public online communities and public discussion forums were structured by topics or according to topical hierarchies. Similar type of development took place also with the Usenet,[9] which was conceived by Duke University graduate students Tom Truscott and Jim Ellis in 1979 and which became established in the following year, in addition to which it also enabled the transfer of user-generated files.

In a social sense the Internet was fairly progressive already in the late 1980s and early 1990s. This sort of "pre-web" had social dimensions, such as text-based multi-user real-time virtual worlds in the form of Multi-User Dungeons (MUD); these had taken off already in the 1970s, enabling multi-way real-time text chat.[10] These systems tended to be used for supporting communications between people who did not know each other, but they knew where to meet with like-minded people. There were also TCP/IP based tools like the Archie search engine for FTP[11] archives and the Gopher system for distributing documents as well as the "talk" and "write" commands for live text one-on-one communication in Unix machines.[12] Thus, it can be said that the Internet has been social since its origins.

A computer scientist Tim Berners-Lee, working at the European Organization for Nuclear Research in Geneva, Switzerland, better known as CERN,[13] tried to convince his managers that a global information system, the World Wide Web (WWW), build upon the Internet as a backbone would greatly benefit CERN's interests. From its very beginning and following the social origins of the Internet, Berners-Lee's proposal *Information Management: A Proposal* to CERN's DD/OC group in March 1989 included a strong social component.[14] This document described the web's connection with computer conferencing systems such as the chat-type systems Usenet and IBM GroupTalk. The idea was to use the web to consolidate people rather than just being a simple document distribution system. The web was to become a platform for communication, a tool for physicists and potentially the whole physics community to share data. The first WWW server outside of Europe was installed at the Stanford Linear Accelerator Center (SLAC) on 12 December 1991.[15] Via this, SLAC researchers got in touch with the World Wide Web at a very early phase. And the rest is history. As well known, the web quickly became a more general information vehicle than for the physics community only. A major reason for people being interested in going online in the early web was because there were other people there; they did it exactly because of social reasons, whether related to work or private matters. Thus it is safe to say that the original intention of the Internet and later also the web always was to be a social way for people to share their work, communicate and collaborate. The social aspect was not mature enough in the original web, in spite of the fact that after two decades, it has finally truly manifested itself. But many developmental steps would happen before getting at that stage.

The ripple: hypertext

The roots of the web are in fact much deeper than the late 1980s at CERN or even at ARPANET. Many consider its prehistory to start with "As We May Think," an article of President Franklin D. Roosevelt's science advisor and the Director of the

Office of Scientific Research and Development, Vannevar Bush (1890–1974), that was published in *The Atlantic Monthly* and *Life* in 1945.[16] Bush suggested that to coordinate the work of thousands of scientists, an "extension to memory" would be needed that imitates human associations and operates through them rather than synthetic indices. In his vision, human associations would form these webs of trails, which would be the most essential feature of this requested future memory device for personalized use. State-of-art technologies of that time included analog microfilms, which Bush had in his mind specifically, when he wrote these articles. His conceptual sketch, "the memex," however, was never implemented.

An inspiration from Bush was received by Dr Douglas C. Engelbart,[17] the inventor of the computer mouse and many other user interface tools that are widely used today, who published a research agenda known as *Augmenting Human Intellect: A Conceptual Framework* in October 1962.[18] In his agenda, Engelbart introduced the H-LAM/T conceptualization, denoting "Human using Language, Artifacts, Methodology, in which he is Trained." The suggested means for designable artifacts, languages, methods and training were to augment human capabilities and to improve problem-solving and communication capability by using frontline technologies. Based on this framework, he further developed an information system called oNLine System (NLS), which supported hypermedia representation of information with in-file object addressing and linking, and the NLS became the first software application to implement hyperlinks in the late 1960s. The hyperlinks connected specific regions within a document to other regions in the same document or other documents via relationships that were based on human associations; searchable keyword indices were also created, and documents could be worked on simultaneously from multiple places or platforms. Other first debut software features included computer mouse, multiple windows with flexible view control, shared displays, two-dimensional display editing, and on-screen video teleconferencing. Engelbart and his research team at the Augmentation Research Center at the Stanford Research Institute (SRI) presented a 100-minute live public demonstration of the system on 9 December 1968.[19] This demonstration was later nicknamed the *Mother of All Demos* because of its significance for advancing computer sciences.[20] SRI sold NLS to Tymshare, Inc. in 1977, who renamed it Augment.

The term hypertext had been coined by Engelbart's contemporary innovator Ted Nelson in 1965. In his vision, hyperlinks were attached in keywords in the text pointing to other parts of text, thus creating associative "hypertext" – the prefix "hyper" denoting going beyond regular text. In a similar fashion, hyperlinks in richer forms of media, such as voice or video, would create "hypermedia." Bush's article "As We May Think" had also influenced Nelson. He transmuted Bush's analog notion of associative trails and personalized links between different stored records into his newly introduced hypertext concept and global information system called Xanadu.[21] Nelson had gigantic goals in developing Xanadu in the 1980s. His book *Dream Machines* described the system as a storage manager for organizing and reorganizing everything "what is already there" in different ways and for different uses. In another book, *Literary Machines*, Nelson stated that the

Xanadu system is, among other things, "a grand address space for everything," "a linking system for keeping track of anything," "an applicative virtual document system for applying sequential and non-sequential structure to material that arrived out of sequence and unstructured," "a way of tying it all together and not losing anything," and "a way of including anything in anything else."[22] Even though Nelson's view on hypertext was more individualistic than Engelbart's, hypertext still was to be a tool for communication. It was a social vehicle. And even if his claims sounded at the time quite brash, they actually did describe the web's current essence surprisingly fittingly.

One of the early fully operational hypertext systems was NoteCards developed by Randall Trigg, Frank Halasz and Thomas Moran at the Xerox Palo Alto Research Center (PARC) in 1984.[23] PARC was a division of Xerox Corporation established on 1 July 1970, and this productive laboratory later became known among others for its impact in laser printing, Ethernet, the modern personal computer, graphical user interface, object-oriented programming, ubiquitous computing, amorphous-Silicon applications and advancing very-large-scale integration for semiconductors. New and independent start-up companies that had to off-shoot from PARC became the channel for a majority of PARC-invented technologies to advance into the markets, because a closed innovation environment prevailed in the PARC. The plethora of inventions created at PARC helped develop also NoteCards. LISP computer programming language on Xerox D*-machine workstations supporting large high-resolution displays provided the technical environment for implementing NoteCards, which was an electronic generalization of the 3x5 paper note cards as a general purpose hypermedia system. It was originally designed as a single-user system even though it shared the same goals as Engelbart's Augment, which already provided some group support.[24] However, instead of PARC, it was Apple Computer, founded by Steve Jobs, Steve Wozniak and Ronald Wayne in Cupertino, California on 1 April 1976, which was able to bring the concepts of windows, icons, computer mouse and pull-down menus into mass markets.[25] With regard to the later developments of the web Apple was able to introduce to the mass markets a software product known as HyperCard for Macintosh in August 1987. Through providing graphical programmable buttons HyperCard enabled the building of simple hyperlinks between notecards, and it was HyperCard that really popularized the hypertext concept among any larger general audience.

What resulted in the inauguration of the hypertext-based web by Tim Berners-Lee was implementing these ideas on top of the Internet technology. The web was literally placed into the public domain on 30 April 1993, when CERN announced that the World Wide Web was free for everyone. To give it all to everyone for free in the very beginning was a very social action, and it was a result of its social origins and the hypertext being a general-purpose idea. According to Douglas Engelbart, it was the *hyperlinks* that really triggered the rise of the web building a true web of knowledge. This era[26] of navigating the web via hyperlinks was the first wave of the web, and yet it was described already as the "fourth-generation of hypertext."[27] The main interest of individuals and society in the first wave of the web focused on advancing its hypertext features for sharing information. The people putting information onto the web tended to be institutionally trusted. Universities were on the web. A growing number of large companies were on the web. For the most part, it was not just an unknown person from the middle of nowhere who was publishing information on the web. Later, this was to change dramatically.

Decades may have passed by and the areas of acutest interest may have changed, but the idea of hypertext by no means has become outdated. Many of the works and ideations by early hypertext researchers are living in the current web infrastructure and applications. Perhaps the most familiar everyday example of hypertext for people today is the web-based encyclopedia Wikipedia and its texts with associative links attached to hotwords. On a technical level, hypertext has been and still is in steady and routine usage also when utilizing the HyperText Transfer Protocol (HTTP),[28] for example when typing a web site address into a browser.

The rippling victory of the weak links

Already the original web infrastructure and its first browsers provided some software support for reading and writing annotations, which enabled users to publish comments on web pages where they couldn't edit the original content. The Mosaic 1.0 browser developed in 1993 at the National Center for Supercomputing Applications (NCSA) at the University of Illinois Urbana-Champaign supported annotations, but with the rush to commercialize it, many desirable features that would have helped groupwork and other important uses were dropped from the software releases, and for the most part they remained forgotten for years. Yet, not all academic researchers overlooked them. There were a multitude of efforts still in particular in the hypertext research community to build on and off-the-web solutions with sophisticated features such as typed links and annotations. Bebo White, a researcher at SLAC, notes that "a lot of these things [that now can be found on contemporary social web] like mash-ups the hypertext people were talking about long before the web people were."

One of the major concerns in the hypertext research community was the issue of dangling or broken links – hyperlinks that have been damaged over time, for instance, due to the link target being deleted. To the hypertext community, which emphasized the beauty of the full hyperspace and its centermost concept, hyperlink, the dangling links were unacceptable. Bebo White explains the thinking at the same time of web's inauguration as "the web is great but as far as hypertext systems are concerned it's only OK." NoteCards, which was in the late 1980s a state-of-the-art solution and a leader in the area of hypertext systems, offered an ideal link structure. But in fact its very concrete and powerful metaphor of a collection of note cards may have been a hindrance for accepting the existence of dangling links. Most other prominent hypertext systems adopted a similar approach, in which it was important to define elaborate link attributes and taxonomies and to eliminate all dangling links.

Having dangling or broken links in an environment such as the web, however, was found to be more of an academic concern than an obstacle for using the system in practice. The fact that the web ok'd the "Error 404," page not found, became a key strength for expanding the use of the web. Terry Winograd explains:

> When the web first came out, people who were doing things like hypertext said "Well, it won't work, because the links don't have any information, they're one-way, they don't go to a place that's reliable, they can change, and so on." They were wrong. It works and why does it work? It works because when you take the system as a whole, it's got weaknesses in one particular piece of the technology that is compensated for by putting it in other places or by finding the uses where it doesn't matter. The fact that you can have a broken link doesn't mean you can't use the system. It just means once in a while you don't find something.

The existence of dangling links became an acceptable phenomenon in the web community just as dialing to a wrong or non-existent telephone number. With the acceptance of dangling links by the general audience, the whole concept of navigating in hyperspace changed. This development paved the way for search engines to become the leading method for Internet use. Yet, the importance for deep understanding of hyperlinks did not go away even in this new, emerging setting, because search was to be considered as an associative hyperlink generated automatically on the fly. To a great extent the technical success of Google results from understanding the role of hyperlinks for the web. Via their link analysis, founders Larry Page and Sergey Brin were able to demonstrate that there is a hidden layer of link structure and meaning in the web.[29] When Google was released, it was exactly this that made its search engine beat the other contemporary services and led to what is one of the biggest web innovations of all time.

The original intention behind Google was not to make a search engine, however.[30] Page and Brin had a project called BackRub, which resulted in a web crawler that was let loose in March 1996. They began looking for a way to rank links of web pages in order to give a relative ranking to any web page. They developed an algorithm or ranking method that takes into account the pages linked to the page under investigation, as well as the links pointing to those pages that are linked to the page studied. Instead of calling the project BackRub, they created the name Google in the next year. It came from *googol*[31] meaning 10^{100}. Googol is a pretty large number, 10,000,000,000,000,000,000,000,000,000,000,000,000,000,000,000,000,000,000,000,000,000,000,000,000,000,000,000,000,000,000,000,000,000,000,000,000,000,000,000, named by 9-year-old Milton Sirotta (1911–81), nephew of American mathematician Edward Kasner (1878–1955), who was looking for a name for this very large but finite number. Term googol was published in *Mathematics and the Imagination* in 1940.[32] The googol was spelled when BackRub was named Google, but the company's name aptly plays on the basic idea of googol, a very large but finite number. The first version of the search engine was released on the Stanford University web site in August 1996. Stanford's computer science professors Terry Winograd and Hector Garcia-Molina were advisers of Page and Brin, and they also aided in overcoming many early problems from hardware issues to outside complaints. Google Inc. was founded on 4 September 1998.[33]

Despite the fact that Page and Brin understood the deeper meaning of hyperlinks, the way google.com deals with links is blind to link purpose. It basically says that there is a link from page A to page B or that there isn't.[34] It does not say that there is a "definition link" or a "see also" link from page A to page B. Still, it is able to make quite a good an estimation of what is important without actually having that definition information by utilizing the information about existing links. This is exactly why "weak" or simple hyperlinks won over the more complex, semantically rich links such as rich link attributes. There are of course situations in which it is useful to implement links that may contain attributed information about the relation of the link, in particular restricted small-scale applications in which developers know in advance the types of all potential end-users and their specific needs. However, to support specific knowledge activities in a large-scale platform, constructs that are powerful but simple and that can be further built upon are needed. Thus far there seems to be no additional information beyond just raw data about links that would be powerful enough to really challenge the dominance of the weak-link model. The web is also probably too far down one path to expect any kind of major changes in the platform to the way the links are done, and yet it may still be that those who can understand rich meaning of hyperlinks and build systems on top of this understanding may be able to make "the next Google."

Sidetracking from the social path: the expert-based content creation boom

The World Wide Web was invented in Europe, but it really took off in Silicon Valley. The first wave of the web had made it particularly ripe for further development and the Silicon Valley was (and still is) a place where exceptional ideas are always actively sought and built upon. But in addition to the web's ripeness for business, there was also an acute need to take action in Silicon Valley. According to Paul Saffo, there was a hole to be filled with a project relevant to the talents of local software engineers, because the interactive television industry had generated new kinds of expertise and a lot jobs, but it ended in blowing up an excessive amount of Hollywood money.[35] Media researcher Pyungho Kim, who has studied early interactive television systems in the United States, stated that the interactive television "was indeed the wrong technology and the wrong business strategy at the wrong time."[36]

How was it then possible that interactive TV became a buzzword of the time? To be able to answer this question a wider scenario needs to be understood. During the first half of the 1990s the interactive television was an application important to the National Information Infrastructure (NII) of President Bill Clinton administration. The concept of NII was launched alongside the High Performance Computing and Communication Act of 1991. Vice President Al Gore referred to NII as the "information superhighway," which led to information infrastructure hype around the world. The Clinton administration released *The National Information Infrastructure: Agenda for Action* on 15 September 1993 for promoting the ideas included in the concept of NII.[37] The first task was to promote private sector investment in the information infrastructure, and businesses were looking for new ways to make forward strides. The movie industry was active, for example; Hollywood events celebrating the "Information Superhighway" and thematized events like "Silicon Valley meets Hollywood" were organized in the mid-1990s to broaden its cooperation with the computer industry. The focus of the joint endeavor between Silicon Valley and Hollywood was on interactive television. After Hollywood had embraced the computer industry in the mid-1990s a time of many interactive TV experiments had arrived.

At the time Apple Computer co-founder Steve Jobs (1955–2011) became an executive producer of the first ever feature film made entirely with computer-generated imagery, *Toy Story*. Pixar Animation Studios, which Jobs had incorporated, released the film in 1995. The emerging atmosphere affected the cinema in many other ways, too. A wave of cyberfilms hit theaters in 1995, featuring computers, Internet and cyberspace, such as director Robert Longo's *Johnny Mnemonic* starring Keanu Reeves, Dolph Lundgren and Dina Meyer; Irwin Winkler's *The Net* starring Sandra Bullock, Jeremy Northam and Dennis Miller; Brett Leonard's *Virtuosity* starring Denzel Washington, Russell Crowe and Kelly Lynch; Iain Softley's *Hackers* starring Jonny Lee Miller, Angelina Jolie and Jesse Bradford; and Katheryn Bigelow's *Strange Days* starring Ralph Fiennes, Angela Bassett and Juliette Lewis. Hollywood talent agents were hunting after Silicon Valley programmers in order to take the movie industry into a digital era. However, already the 2 December 1995 issue of *Variety* contained an article entitled "Purging the Urge to Convergence" by Rex Weiner, which declared the convergence of computer technology and Hollywood dead: "Major technology companies such as Silicon Graphics appear to be pulling back from the Hollywood spotlight just as Hollywood is retreating to its usual, quite linear, scenario."[38] The computer-effects-driven movies were not, in the end, dead and buried at all, but there was a change after the 1995 thrill of cyberfilms in Hollywood. This, alongside of the vanishing hype around the interactive television, affected Hollywood investments in the interactive TV and the need for programmers. Interactive TV no longer dominated.

Many were left unemployed as a consequence. Paul Saffo describes that this left "a financial crater big enough to be seen from the moon without field glasses." A multitude of media experts who understood the content for new media and the power of advertising were ready and available to fill this crater, and many of the first web companies were founded by refugees from interactive TV business. At the same time, a whole generation of C++ programmers had been trained about the importance of rich media, and they could now start to contribute to a new endeavor. Similarly, Java programming had been planned as a programming language to be used particularly in the set-top boxes for interactive television, but when the original project was abandoned it became critical to find new ways to utilize it. The financial crater had to be filled with something, but the challenge was of merging two diverse communities and cultures. The entering of media experts into web development resulted in a heavy emphasis on creating new media and content, and this caused an expert-based content creation boom. "The Web as Internet Television," a subchapter of the book *Collaborative Web Development: Strategies and Best Practices for Web Teams,*[39] written by Jessica R. Burdman in 1999, explained the change of the future content for Web team members: "Many web sites offer resources for training and development, especially creating content for interactive television." Burdman also described how the development process would play out: "People with experience with television production, scriptwriting, sound design and videography will all become part of the Web team that provides content for interactive television." *Content creation* became the buzzword, and a worldwide boom later linked with the dotcom burst. Although the expert-based content creation boom helped to fill the void created by Hollywood's decreased investment and also encouraged to pursue for faster Internet connections and increased computing power with more customer friendly prices, this one-way provision of digital content was also a side-track from the path which later led to user-generated content and social collaboration so relevant to the social web.

Professor of Information Systems Larry Press at California State University had presented already in December 1993 that there were actually two national information infrastructures, the Internet and the interactive television, and also two amorphous interest groups working around the infrastructure.[40] He named these groups as the Internet community and the interactive TV community, representing two different cultures. These cultures were incapable of fluent communication and understanding of each other. The Internet had supported a community of scholars and communication between people sharing the same interests, in which messaging and information retrieval were the major acts users performed. Within the interactive TV community, the entertainment industry and cable companies relied on improved networks with fiber optics and improved technology for computing and compression, which would enable delivering digital movies on demand and home shopping.[41] This resulted in establishing interactive TV alliances, eventually focusing primarily on video on demand.

In spite of its potential, interactive TV did not succeed at the time and it quickly faded away under the shadow of the Internet. Why? Interactive TV's mode of organizing information and communication with a secure business model emphasized centralized control of access, uses and service of only a few providers' applications, hierarchical structure of organizing information, and in overall a closed system, whereas the Internet utilized a lateral mode where control is decentralized. Interactive TV's vertical mode meant that the Internet would be televisionized losing much of its original cultural dynamics. Interactive TV more or less died out imperceptibly at the time.

Business models start to emerge

The original Internet was not open for business. Even though there were some commercial ventures in the Internet in the 1980s,[42] the entire Internet culture was largely non-commercial. When ARPANET was disclosed, responsibility to oversee its elements was passed on to the governmental National Science Foundation (NSF), which supports fundamental research and education in non-medical fields of science and engineering. The acceptable use policy defined by the NSF prohibited usage of the Internet for purposes not in support of research and education. However, this was reinterpreted in 1993. Founder and CEO of O'Reilly Media Tim O'Reilly was among the first in Internet business with a special dispensation of the NSF before the fully open Internet.[43] Dale Dougherty and O'Reilly Associates built the Global Network Navigator (GNN) information portal in May 1993 making it the first commercial site on the web. GNN built upon an ad model with clickable advertisements, and by 1994 they sold the first banner advertisement to international law firm Heller Ehrman LLP.[44] At the first International WWW Conference in May 1994, GNN was voted the "best commercial home page," and the next year it was sold to America Online.[45] The web became fully opened for commercial traffic on 30 April 1995, and putting advertisements on the web gave a new direction to it. But even a more radical change took place through browser developments.

The National Center for Supercomputing Applications had developed Mosaic, the first graphical web browser that took the HTTP and HTML (HyperText Markup Language) protocols and mapped them into a user-friendly point-and-click interface, facilitating both text and color images to address and connect messaging across computers.[46] The Mosaic version operating on standard Unix had been released in January 1993 and Macintosh and PC platforms in August 1993. But in a larger sense the commercial utility did not really emerge until Marc Andreessen, one of the graduate students from the supercomputing center in Illinois, teamed up with James "Jim" Clark to create what they originally called Mosaic Killer. The software was to be a rewritten and to be "Mosaic to kill Mosaic." They decided to call the software Mozilla as a play on the name Godzilla, a giant monster in Japanese movie and a worldwide pop culture icon. They founded Mosaic Communications Corporation on 4 April 1994, released the beta version of Netscape Navigator 1.0 on 14 October 1994, and then adopted the name Netscape also for the company on 14 November 1994.

A war between browsers,[47] the Browser War I, began between NCSA and Netscape with the release of the beta version of Navigator 1.0.[48] Navigator was better in technical design and usability, and it loaded more quickly than Mosaic. Netscape also adopted a fresh and extremely successful pricing policy with Navigator 1.0, making a free test version available over the Internet. Later Netscape versions differentiated from Mosaic in order to gain proprietary control of the browser standard. The beta release of Navigator 1.1 on 6 March 1995, became a milestone event. Proprietary client Application Programming Interface – *API* – was released which eventually led software companies to enroll into the Netscape camp. There was a vertical value relationship with producers of complementary software, a relationship encouraged especially through making it free for outside companies to create "plug-ins." These plug-ins could be run with the Navigator browser and the platform's functionality was thus extended by third-parties.[49] Importantly, the focus of these independent software vendor plug-ins was increasingly on business applications. Netscape browser became one of the fastest-growing software products in the history of computing. It enjoyed a 90 percent installed user base and a 70 percent share of Fortune 100 companies already on 9 August 1995, when Netscape's successful initial public offering (IPO) took place.[50] Netscape's IPO became a big signal to people everywhere. The stock of a 17-month-old business of the Internet software start-up Netscape Communications Corporation was to be offered at $14 per share, but a last-minute decision priced it at $28 a share for their debut session.[51] Shares of Netscape rocketed as high as $75 and ended that first day at $58.25. To illustrate the change, the valuation of Netscape co-founder Jim Clark's 9.34 million shares increased from $121 million (the midpoint of the indicative price range) to $544 million on the first day of trading. After this extreme rocketing, the web was not only a socio-technical achievement but a hot business activity as well. The Browser War I was over.

Netscape kept pushing hard to secure its position as the undeniable leader in browser markets. On 4 December 1995, Netscape and Sun Microsystems jointly announced JavaScript, an open scripting language especially for intranets and other enterprise information systems,[52] and on 15 December 1995, Netscape released a 90-day free trial of the Navigator's commercial version for corporations and gave it for free for students and educational institutions. Most people downloaded it but never did get around to paying. In the meantime, Netscape sold a number of server tools to people who wanted to put content out on the web that could be read with the Netscape software client. According to Henry Chesbrough, Executive Director of the Center for Open Innovation in the Haas School of Business at University of California Berkeley, it was really Netscape that gets credit for pioneering a business model for the web. What started out to displace Mosaic turned into a company called Netscape that not only improved the browser but created the first native web business model. Indeed, Netscape's charging for the server and essentially giving away the client for free became the first business model that strengthened the web's new role as commercial activity. Netscape had become one of the greatest Internet success stories of its time.

It would be a delusion to take it as predestined, however, that Netscape would be the first browser magnate. Spyglass Inc., founded in 1990 and based in Naperville, Illinois, had been working on data-visualization tools and 3D-rendering engines. Its products Spyglass View, Spyglass Transform and Spyglass Dicer were regarded to belong to the most sophisticated tools for data visualization and analysis of their time.[53] Spyglass Inc. was an offshoot of the University of Illinois at Urbana-Champaign, focusing on the commercialization and support of technologies originating from the NCSA. It had licensed Mosaic in May 1994.[54] By putting its own Spyglass browser, Enhanced Mosaic Version 2.1, into the market on 7 August 1995, it became regarded as a visionary Internet browser company. The Browser War II, by general public much less known than the NCSA-Netscape browser war, had started.[55] Interestingly, Spyglass actually had gone public two months before Netscape in June 1995. It had 11 straight profitable quarters, a healthy stock of $34 per share and robust earnings from licensing fees, and it cooperated with major companies like a multinational computer technology corporation

Oracle Corp. and an early commercial online service CompuServe Inc. Spyglass gained ground in large and influential organizations from Lockheed Corp. to the National Security Agency (NSA), but it quickly faltered under Netscape's hard competition even though, for instance, software company Corel Corporation's spokeswoman Carrie Bendzsa stated publicly that the Spyglass browser was more robust than the one Netscape offered. However, Netscape's innovative business model surprised Spyglass which was using traditional software product sales as its business model. Spyglass had been selling its browser code rather than distributed it for free to end-users, whereas Netscape allowed users to download its Navigator browser for a free-trial period, and after this the price was $39. Many Internet firms that went public in the late 1990s pursued an aggressive acquisition strategy in order to preempt competitors, whereas analysts were stunned when Spyglass decided to withdraw from the browser market and the number two position that it still had in late 1996. It decided that fighting for its market share was too costly and licensed its technology, mainly due to the pressure caused by two companies, namely Netscape and Microsoft Corporation,[56] which had taken the upper hand in the markets. After giving up its position in the general web browser market, Spyglass began to develop specialized browsers for embedded systems in devices other than the PC and those with limited memory capability. This happened during a period when the entire market of embedded software was only about $300 million.[57] New applications were needed in, among others, Xerox copiers, digital television sets and set-top boxes as well as smartphones later to emerge. An interactive television company, OpenTV, ended up buying Spyglass Inc. in 2000. But the Browser War II was far from being over.

Microsoft had been a latecomer into the Internet business. It had licensed Mosaic from Spyglass for $2 million in late 1994, but then in January 1997, it paid $8 million for rights to use Mosaic technology in perpetuity. Program code from Spyglass's browser was at first developed into Internet Explorer 1.0 in 1995 and later integrated into Internet Explorer for Windows 95, the commercial version of which Microsoft distributed for free.[58] After Netscape had displaced both NCSA and Spyglass, Netscape underscored an alliance with Sun Microsystems in order to develop a "super operating system", a Java-based cross-platform browser. This took Microsoft by surprise. The Browser War II, which had started between Spyglass and Netscape and which now was taking place between Microsoft and Netscape intensified in 1996–98. Microsoft fully adopted Netscape's strategy as well as business and pricing models. It was now giving away its Internet Explorer browser for free and made financially competitive product offers to companies. It emulated Netscape's browser features but then added its own proprietary extensions and created an incompatible product with a dense technological dependence, especially on Windows Office, thus building a winner-takes-all competition. Among others it was aggressively channeled to web publishers and PC and retail distributor channels to ensure that its browser was automatically bundled with new deals and packages. Instead, Netscape used a different approach as it utilized the Internet itself to distribute Navigator to compete and enjoyed very low costs. However, Netscape was there too early, because this distribution strategy relied on existing Internet connection and the ability and self-confidence of the user to be able to download the browser, and the general audience was not ready for this yet. Netscape made losses[59] due to Navigator's dropping sales figures and it ended up being purchased by America Online (AOL), which took over its Netcenter portal website in November 1998.[60] As a big surprise, AOL still continued to offer Microsoft Internet Explorer as its default browser rather than Netscape. The reasons for this were expected benefits in marketing as well as complex legal agreements. AOL executives explained that in exchange for their use of Internet Explorer as a primary browser, Microsoft bundled AOL in their online services folder on the Windows desktop. AOL continued with Internet Explorer "partly to get the continued marketing benefits of Windows bundling, and partly to maximize the likelihood of continued 'detente' with Microsoft."[61] AOL's decision to keep collaborating with Microsoft had a remarkable effect on the competition in browser markets.[62] By August 1999, Microsoft had succeeded in capturing 76 percent of the browser markets. The Browser War II was over.

The breaking wave: electronic commerce and hype

The rapid growth of the browser companies assisted many others to get their share of the emerging web markets in the late 1990s. Users were yearning for a starting point for their web navigation. Internet portals, offering linkages to various places on the web, turned out to be a successful approach to support users in their effort to pull out information from the web before the search engines became more polished.[63] Old media companies competed with their offerings, creating a portal craze, which increased the valuations of all web portals, and Yahoo! and a few others were later to become especially successful in this game. During the hype about the information superhighway, the enthusiasm over media convergence and the buzzword of content creation, business managers had started to seek for web solutions that would have organizational impact and that would provide competitive advantage. Businesses started to use the web intranets for supporting internal workings and communication, and extranets, such as web-based inventory and ordering information systems, to support inter-organizational operations. Yet most managers had little or no insight on the web, and they did not understand much about the price tag for developing web applications. New Internet-based companies, commonly referred to as dotcoms, started to appear thick and fast. Problems arose due to quick turnarounds, including critical issues such as security and privacy, however, such problems did not cool the excitement for new web-based services and technologies. When companies began to list their shares on a public exchange, like Netscape had done before, huge IPOs gained attention. Enormous general hype about technological advancements and future profits arose, and money started to talk even louder than before.

The service behind what became to be known as Yahoo! had been started by doctoral candidates in Electrical Engineering at Stanford University Jerry Yang and David Filo in February 1994. They created "David and Jerry's Guide to the World Wide Web," which was an advanced categorization of web sites. Thus, the core content was the web itself. They named their directory as Yahoo!, short for "Yet another hierarchical officious oracle!," in April 1994, and yahoo.com domain was created in January 1995.[64] In April 1995, Yang and Filo convinced Sequoia Capital to fund Yahoo! with an initial investment of nearly $2 million. They also reached a business deal with Netscape through which users of Navigator browser got an icon to link to Yahoo! with a single click. Other pioneering steps included customized and personalized My Yahoo! pages including users' most interesting web pages. Commercial activity increased as they began to sell advertising space on the site. Yahoo! went public on 12 April 1996, and the stock market value of the company was nearly $1 billion within a year. It became the undisputed leader on Internet portals,[65] and the year 1996 became the turning point for the United States high-technology IPOs.

The first e-commerce company, Amazon.com, went public on 15 May 1997.[66] It had been founded by Jeff Bezos, a computer science and electrical engineering graduate from Princeton University, as an online bookstore in July 1995. Revenues doubled in size every 2.4 months and revenues for the first year of operations were $5 million. Within three and half years it reached the position of the third largest US bookseller. Amazon was valued around $500 million during its IPO. Two and half years later, in December 1999, it was valued at 61.70 times its closing price on its first day of trading. None of Amazon's early competitors achieved similar stock market success, and it quickly became a yardstick for measuring all e-commerce. Amazon was also among the pioneers attempting to leverage the medium's capability to develop online social communities. Much of the editorial content was created by customers themselves when they gave space for their registered and potential customers to post reviews. In addition, Yahoo! allowed its customers to be informed before purchasing also by interacting with each other, and selling and giving feedback to each other.

E-commerce bred with interaction within a community was an aim of many in the mid-1990s.[67] A breakthrough for building a community of buyers and sellers was done by eBay.[68] It developed a mechanism that encouraged users to develop trust in each other, although they had never met, because of a self-regulated rating system where traders would leave feedback for each other following a transaction. The background of the company was that French-Iranian software programmer Pierre Omidyar decided to sell his broken laser pointer, which was perhaps worth some $30 when new, on an auction site he had added to his home page in 1995. Bids accumulated until it was sold at a price of $14.83. His website was called AuctionWeb until 1997. In the late 1990s, a myth was fabricated claiming that inspiration for the company's business model had originally been to create a platform to help Pierre Omidyar's fiancé's online trade of PEZ dispensers. These mechanical pocket dispensers of an Austrian confectionery invented originally in Vienna in 1927 are regarded widely as popular culture artifacts and collectibles. The PEZ legend circulated in the media and enhanced the company's visibility for potential users. In 1997, the site had 341,000 users and the listings consisted of 4.3 million items. AuctionWeb became a trading platform for collectors, and collectibles and antiques played a crucial role in its development. During the first few months in 1997 the company could not cope with the volume of its traffic and due to this got in trouble with its protesting community. A new technology platform was launched, and this helped AuctionWeb to rebrand itself as eBay. The domain name had already been eBay.com for some time, named after Omidyar's consulting firm Echo Bay Technology Group, and the company changed the name from AuctionWeb to eBay on 1 September 1997. Competition became harder, but eBay users were loyal to the site thanks to a great extent to its feedback system. The IPO of eBay took place on 21 September 1998, and its stock rocketed to a high of $234.16 in November 1998 from its opening level of $18.

By this time, it had become evident that the dominion over the web clearly had shifted from hypertext to something else. Its hypertext functionality did not vanish, but the web was now better known for something else: e-commerce. The IPOs of Yahoo!, Amazon and eBay were highly successful and many others followed in going public. The stock prices soared, and this yielded a bubble in the stock markets. The bubble period was evident in 1998–99, and the year 1999 has been termed "The Year of the IPOs."[69] During the dotcom bubble of 1999 and 2000, first-day returns on Internet IPOs averaged a stunning 89 percent (median 57 percent). The Internet sector earned over 1,000 percent returns on its public equity within only two years from early 1998 through February 2000. The Internet sector equaled six percent of the market capitalization of all US public companies and 20 percent of all publicly traded equity. But twisted trends had started to emerge around the Internet. Many poor business decisions were made based on hype. The huge business returns completely disappeared by the end of 2000. Dotcom businesses fell apart leading to a fall in stock prices and a massive crash of Internet companies.[70] For example, by the end of 2001, Amazon.com's value had declined to one-tenth of its peak (even if still 6.26 times its initial level). Entrepreneurship and finance specialists and professors Alexander Ljungqvist and William J. Wilhelm, Jr. summarized in 2003: "Finally, it is possible that neither standard rational nor behavioral models can fully explain investor behavior in 1999 and 2000. Suppose, for whatever reason, that investors were simply optimistic in the extreme."[71] And they indeed were. There were insane expectations in the markets, which were based upon greed and opportunism, and the general attitude in the stock markets by so many was to get rich and the quicker the better.

The bubble burst was of stock markets and of financial expectations, not really of web technology. For this reason, it can be said that there never was an "Internet bubble" – it was only a financial market's crash – even though it greatly influenced most web endeavors for a number of years. The hype around the web that brought recognition to web technologies was directed toward content creation and electronic commerce. The burst of the dotcom bubble was a signal of the next major change that was taking place. Of course, e-commerce and e-business applications did not disappear with the burst, but the dominant force started to shift elsewhere. The wave of the first web had broken, and a new compensatory surge began to develop.

3
The Killer Wave: The Social Web

After the dotcom bust, there was in the minds of the general population a question of what the web was good for, and there was a backlash against companies which had built their business around the web to the extent that there almost needed to be a reason to go back to enterprises and justify that web-based business made sense. It was evident that the web should find a new path. This opened the door for emphasizing other facets than electronic commerce or business from the web's rich set of features. In this state of affairs *the web got redirected more towards people*, the process of which is explained in this chapter. The new wave of the web, the social web, started quickly to massively influence human life, business and society. In this sense it is like a killer wave; it transforms people and societies, destroys old businesses, and opens up new opportunities. This is so even though new human-centered applications could be seen as boring from technology and marketing perspectives, refashioning of old technologies to do things that make everyday tasks easier. Because there was already a critical mass of information on the web, a key aspect now became how to make use of that information and leverage user participation from the bottom up, based on what people actually do, rather than the top down, based on what companies would suggest them to do.

One way to pinpoint the start of the social web era is when survivors of the second wave, companies, such as eBay, Amazon and Google, began polishing the social network based aspects of their sites and drawing their strength from their users. They became pioneers of this third wave of the web. But the roots of the third wave, the social web, are much longer, namely they go all the way to the origins of the web, when budding social networking functionality existed although not very many people used it. Let's next describe key events which started bringing also regular people to the web, technical development threads preceding social web's emergence, early signs of it, and key corporations and applications in its takeoff.

Average Joe starts getting access to the social phenomenon

From the early on in the history of the Internet, there were ways through which geographically distant users could have real-time conversations in teletype style.

An example is the "talk" feature in the Unix operating system. A home-based user needed a telephone line and modem connected with one's computer as well as a valid user ID for the Telesys dial-up system and a UNIX system. It was necessary to know the username of the person to talk with as well as the networked machine that the person was logged into. In addition to this, one had to have the knowledge about the command language. At times terminal emulations were needed, which the user had to carry out. Also compatible talk daemon, a backend process software program, had to be installed and had to be running on the other end for the system to operate. Because there were several versions of the talk program there were compatibility problems. Nerds got excited about the "talk," but it wasn't really realistic for the Average Joe, laymen, to start using the Internet technology for conversations or social networking in this way.

Real-time communication between geographically distant users took a giant leap forward in 1988 with the invention of the Internet Relay Chat (IRC).[1] This text-based internet discussion setting developed by Jarkko Oikarinen at the Department of Information Processing Science in the University of Oulu, Finland enabled multiple parties to partake in discussions, and it was easier to use than the previous tools. So in the late-1980s if one was interested in the writer Jorge Luis Borges, they could find a group of Borges scholars and spend time online talking with them through an IRC channel about him. Channels could be controlled by operators who usually were the originators of the channel. Yet there were still high barriers to entry, and primarily only power users were online. Users still had to be quite technically oriented and have access to such equipment that most people did not have; in most cases, the user also had to be associated with a university. But it was IRC that laid the ground for an Average Joe to start doing social collaborations on the Internet, and many modern technologies related to the social web have later build upon the idea of IRC. Also other software started to emerge that provided ways for helping regular people, who could not write their own programming scripts, to participate. Little by little people started to publish their own media, upload photographs, and connect with other people without the need to have access to their own server or know how to do FTP.[2] These technologies became transformative technologies. What was to be transformed took quite some time, because it still had to become user-friendly.

In addition to chat, the sharing of one's pictures played a big role in introducing the social phenomenon behind the web for regular people. Digital images are intensively uploaded into the web today, but it took over a decade for digital cameras to overtake film cameras. The first fully digital consumer camera, the Logitech Fotoman, was released by Dycam in 1990. It was able to accommodate 32 black-and-white images at 376 x 240 pixels. Thus, it was not very powerful for being a nearly $1,000 camera. A color digital camera, Kodak DSC-100, which was released in the same year, cost 30 times more. It took four years until a color digital camera, Apple Quick Take 100, was sold for under a thousand dollars and another two years after that until the first color one megapixel camera, Kodak DC-120, was sold under a thousand dollars. These were not yet laymen's cameras. For several years, they did not have advanced image editing software either. The first version of the software to become de-facto standard for digital photographers, Photoshop, had been released for Apple Macintosh in 1990 and for PCs two years later. Photoshop was originally targeted for professionals and it took years before it became a tool for all, but ten years later the situation had become totally different. Customers were now able to choose from several easy-to-use image editing software and three megapixel cameras that cost less than $30.[3] Even mobile phones integrated sharp digital cameras and the ability to share photos and videos were readily available via web-based services. The table was set for the Average Joe to get into the social web and share one's life with others also through pictures.

Browsers started to provide better support for multimedia. On top of enabling the reading of web pages, Netscape's pioneering technology allowed quite a bit of interactivity and social features, and Netscape 1.1N, which was released in the spring of 1995, led the way also in supporting the use of photos. There started to be much more multimedia around, which moved the web from being based predominantly on text and simple graphics into being a richer media platform incorporating audio and video. This contributed to user experience, and quickly changed the game for what people were there for. This change was to a wider appeal with many more things for people to do on the web, more emphasis on socialization, more games online, and no longer using software systems in a closed sphere of engagement. One could simply fire a browser in a URL and then all of a sudden have access to "everybody" in the world. Average Joe started to get access to the social phenomenon. Caterina Fake, co-founder of Flickr, explains that this was "basically return to the roots of the web, but now you no longer had to be a power user and have technical skills in order to participate."

Technical development threads related to the social web

Before the social web could fully emerge, some important threads of technical development had to take place. Seamless integration of *relational databases and the web,* and development of *web-based software architecture frameworks, web mashups, wireless protocols,* and the *semantic web* paved the way for the social web to emerge.

An important technical progressive step helping the social web to emerge was seamless integration between relational databases and the web. Several commercial and free offerings were available by the late 1990s, but the MySQL relational database, released by a software company called MySQL AB in Uppsala, Sweden in 1996, quickly became the most popular web backend. Its code was made open source and available under the terms of the GNU General Public License. A list of companies that since have become MySQL AB's customers shows its enormous impact and scope on web development. These companies include, for instance, Amazon, Apple, ClassMates, Craigslist, eBay, Google, Groupon, Facebook, Flickr, Friendster, Kiva Systems, LinkedIn, Nokia, Tumblr, Twitter, Yahoo!, YouTube and Wikipedia. In 2011, the MySQL website claimed that it was the world's most popular open source database software with over 100 million copies of its software distributed or downloaded.[4] The importance of MySQL in bringing the next wave of web about can be seen also from the fact that MySQL AB was acquired in January 2008 by Sun Microsystems for one billion dollars, whereas Sun Microsystems was acquired by Oracle Corporation in 2010. In overall, the provision of backend solutions such as MySQL eased the development of more complex customer/user centric web-based services.

In a similar manner with the integration of the web and relational databases, the emergence of web-based software architectures for popular software platforms, in particular the .NET framework for Microsoft Windows, paved the way for tying office and other applications with the web. The original release of version 1.0 of the .NET architecture and the related software development kit took place in 13 February 2002. What had happened before was that in the mid- to late-1990s the world's largest software company, Microsoft, was generally considered to be lacking behind of innovative web companies in their platform's web application development capability. The company launched a project on next generation of web services in order to become a leader also in this area, which resulted in the .NET framework and evidently brought Microsoft into a much better position in the web application game. A key visionary role in this endeavor was played by Vic Gundotra, who after a long career at Microsoft later became Vice President of engineering at Google, bearing responsibility in their social web, mobile, platform and API strategies.

Another related technical development thread is known as web mashup, the idea of which is to enable gathering data from different sources and to put it together in a way that creates previously non-existent knowledge or information. Of course, the idea of web mashups had been around for quite some time already, but it started to become more popular at around 2005. After the release of Google Maps and the development of housingmaps.com in summer 2005, the term mashup became a widely known term to characterize such services.[5] It is sometimes claimed that the mashup concept originated from the DJ music culture, when new digital technology allowed musicians to easily and economically sample and recombine music from multiple sources and create a remix. This music background may have rendered the term used today for the web's mashup applications, but the term's origin in itself is much older. According to the *Oxford English Dictionary*, the first known usage of the term, when it meant "a mixture or fusion of disparate elements," was in Dion Boucicault's play *The Octoroon. A Play, in Four Acts* in 1859.[6] Like there was a fusion of disparate elements in the Octoroon and DJ music culture, a web mashup combines data and services from more than one source. One of the key ideas behind most mashups is the use of the computational power of web services, access to large amounts of real content, and the speed with which they can be created with minimum effort. Mashups show special potential when there is a need for a rapid realization of ideas and content creation costs must be avoided. Through the use of publicly available APIs, various components of the mashup are incorporated as a new application. In December 2012, the website programmableweb.com listed 6873 different APIs, which could be mashed-up.[7] From the technological perspective, mashups created by end-users becoming possible were a precursor for many of the critical features in the contemporary social web environments.

An early attempt to bring the Internet into mobile phones via something known as Wireless Application Protocol (WAP) helped direct attention to the mobile web. It was developed by the world's leading companies in wireless telecommunications, Ericsson, Motorola and Nokia, and Unwired Planet taking the initiative that resulted in the WAP Forum industry association to be founded in December 1997. The WAP Forum cooperated with the World Wide Web Consortium and the Internet Engineering Task Force, and released its first software specification, the WAP 1.0, in 1998. Wireless service subscribers were supposed to get anywhere, anytime access to web-based information from cellphones and palmtop computers via this protocol. It was supposed to become the wireless Internet, promising to be a giant leap in electronic and mobile commerce and generating great revenues for products and services to be offered through it. Network operators got excited, and hype emerged particularly in the European markets at the time of introducing the protocol. Still in 1998, the WAP Forum opened its membership for all industry participants to join. The first WAP software development kits were released in early 1999.[8] After the turn of the Millennium, the Forum claimed that its members represented over 90 percent of the mobile phone manufacturers, 99 percent of the handsets sold worldwide, and over 450 million global subscribers. WAP was expected to offer a new leading paradigm for accessing the web. Yet, there were challenges with the retrieval speed, the size of the screens, navigation friendliness, and the very small number of applications and services available. Also severe competition arose, which was a surprise for the gigantic players in the standard-based oligopolistic telecommunication field. The Japanese i-mode, which similarly utilized packet data technology, became a forerunner and WAP started to be challenged also by Java technology. It soon became clear that WAP could not become the flagship for e-commerce, wireless Internet or the mobile web.[9] The marketers promised much more than what it ever was able to deliver. In January 2002, WAP 2.0 protocol was released, but already on 12 June 2002, nearly 200 world's leading ICT companies formed another standards development organization, the Open Mobile Alliance (OMA), shifting its interest into consolidating all specification activities rather than simply focusing on wireless protocols.[10] The WAP failed to bring the web into mobile phones, but nevertheless it had directed attention to wireless and mobile access to the web.

Yet another powerful web development trend, which has gained much attention is the semantic web. The idea of it is to make the web operate more intelligently through ontologies and specific technologies so that a computer that has no idea what a page is about can better find things. The role of the World Wide Web Consortium (W3C) has been critical in introducing the concept of semantic web. W3C had been established by Tim Berners-Lee on 1 October 1994, with the support of the Massachusetts Institute of Technology, the Institut National de Recherche en Informatique et en Automatique (INRIA) in Europe, DARPA, and the European

Commission. Over the years, the organization of W3C has evolved, but its key goal has remained stabile, namely the development of common technical web standards through its recommendations. For instance, XML (eXtensible Markup Language) and CSS (Cascading Style Sheets) have been among its key recommendations. Since January 2007, the Linked Open Data Initiative has had a goal to bootstrap a set of principles to structured semantic data. The initiative tries to make it easier to connect individual entities in documents to somehow related entities in a global data space or the "web of data" by using typed links, relying on documents containing data in the RDF format.[11] Christian Bizer, Tom Heath, and Tim Berners-Lee describe it as "a Web of things in the world, described by data on the Web."[12] This development has resulted in new applications like Revyu.com and DB-Pedia Mobile, browsers like Disco and Tabulator, and search engines like Sindice and Watson. According to Bizer, Heath, and Berners-Lee, "unlike Web 2.0 mashups, which work against a fixed set of data sources, Linked Data applications operate on top of an unbound, global data space. This enables them to deliver more complete answers as new data sources appear on the Web."

From the social web's point of view, the semantic web has an absolutely correct vision, which is that one can get a lot of mileage by putting more semantics into certain kinds of data so that computers can make more out of it. Yet, the social web builds upon the fact that much semantics already exist through tagging and other semi-formal means. It is not necessarily explicit and neat in the way that computer scientists perhaps would like, but much of the same meaning could still be extracted. A structure needed for the semantic web can perhaps be implemented in such fields of business where somebody has full control or can create a standard. The question is, could the web at large be organized in this way, or would it be too much work. According to Terry Winograd, if we look at the different types of content within the web, there are parts of it that are capable of being highly structured, such as product information or some of the material on Wikipedia. These are amenable for building a semantic representation, whereas blogs and Facebook are not as well structured. They do not have the content that lends itself to that kind of established structuring. Even for the part which is capable of being structured, there is always the question of how much extra effort it takes for the individual to provide that structure and how much they gain from it. There is a collective individual breakdown in that if everybody structured their material for semantic web, it would be very valuable, but if everybody does not do it it is not that valuable. It is impossible to command users to do it. So there is a high likelihood that it is not worth putting one's time into doing it, which, in fact, is the greatest challenge of the semantic web. Indeed, the idea behind it is important, but the applications that have been developed thus far have not proved to be very successful. There is a lot of promise in the semantic web approach, but its *dejure* type approach does not seem to be as nimble and as general purpose as the social web's *defacto* based approach. To sum it up, semantic web is more of a vision by computer scientists than a goal, which is based on observations of human behavior in the real world as is the case with social web.

Early signs of social web

Several instances of the early social web phenomenon took place more or less at the same time: *Social networking, instant messaging, online gaming, blogging and online encyclopedias*.

Web hosting companies started to offer social networking through "community sites" in the mid-1990s, for instance theGlobe, GeoCities and Tripod were launched in 1995 for forming general online communities.[13] Classmates.com in 1995 and SixDegrees.com in 1997 were among the first specific social networking sites, which enabled the definition of more complex user profiles.[14] They enabled users to define their preferences, list their friends and surf the friends lists as early as 1998. However, they still failed to sustain their business, and, for example, SixDegrees closed down in 2000. Early adopters of social networking sites did not have extended networks of friends online at the time and there was little to do in practice in these systems after accepting friend requests. Then in 2002, Friendster was launched to compete with an early online dating site Match.com, originally launched in 1995, and as a social complement to Ryze.com, which had launched the previous year to help people leverage their business networks. Teams behind Friendster and Ryze as well as Tribe.net and LinkedIn believed in collaboration and they were closely entwined personally and professionally. Quite soon, Friendster, which was designed to help friends of friends meet and date, became the most significant of these sites. Three hundred thousand users joined Friendster before press coverage began in May 2003, and the site surged before facing many technical challenges, social collisions and ruptures of trust. The social networking sites, being connected to one's own network of friends in real life, really started taking off only later.[15] Yet, Friendster was the first service that really introduced people to the idea of having a personal identity online.

Another related thread of technologies and applications that started to emerge relatively early on was instant messaging (IM). IRC and, for example, work-focused Zephyr[16] had already laid the basis for and brought this type of technology closer to an average user. Early communication was particularly topic-centered with a large but constrained population of users, but then the predominant messaging shifted to take place with known others. These early IM systems supported, for instance, synchronous text chat between users of the same system and enabled asking and responding to questions without overt interruption. Email was often used to coordinate IM sessions with others, but it still did not replace the more social IM. Some systems made chat rooms public and URLs could be included in the messaging. IM connections could be easily sorted into user-defined categories like friends, family or co-workers. Instant messaging was soon widely adopted by teenagers, and it was rapidly on the rise during the turn of the millennium. In teenage communications, the important visible areas were informal talk or socializing, event planning and schoolwork collaboration, and multitasking became an additional new effect as teenagers engaged more in other computer-based activities, such as completing schoolwork, web surfing and emailing while using instant messaging.[17] The four most popular IM systems that made it through were

AOL's ICQ, released in November 1996; AOL's Instant Messenger, released in May 1997; Yahoo! Messenger, which was originally launched under the name Yahoo! Pager in March 1998; and MSN Messenger, released in July 1999. A few years later, in 2003, Niklas Zennström and Janus Friis founded Skype to enable not only communication by instant text messaging but also by voice, and later also by video. In spite of the rapid growth of instant messaging, stand-alone instant messaging did not encourage and support creating applications on top of it. It was not a software platform yet.

Gamers were among the first ones to discover the social web. What had happened was that massively multiplayer online role-playing (MMORPG)[18] continued the social interaction of real-life players in virtual worlds based on earlier MUD computer games. The honor of being the first multiplayer networked role-playing game is generally given to Meridian 59, which debuted in 1995, only two years before Richard Garriott coined the name for the MMORPG genre. His 1997 game Ultima Online became popular and was a signpost for the whole genre. However, it was Sony Online Entertainment which released EverQuest in 1999 that really gained wide attention in the Western world. It induced communication, interaction and interdependence among players. An epoch-making graphical browser-based MMORPG was RuneScape, released in January 2001. Guinness World Records recognized RuneScape as the world's most popular free MMORPG in 2007 and 2008. In October 2010 Blizzard Entertainment, Inc. announced that the worldwide subscriber base for its award-winning MMORPG, World of Warcraft, exceeded 12 million players.[19] Communication, interaction and interdependence among players have increased enormously within the last decade.

Blogs are essentially micro-publishing and even if these are highly unstructured, the beginning of blogging emphasized more than just personal websites. It restarted the old tradition of writing pamphlets, which was a means of vivid self-expression a few hundred years earlier. Pamphlets then had, and blogs now have, the effect of making people argue about matters discussed in them. From early on, some bloggers used to search for web pages, evaluating their value for readers representing a specific profile, and posted links and descriptions of them. A Swarthmore College student Justin Hall's "Filter log" was an early attempt to give recommendations for surfing the Net in 1994. Three years later in December 1997 Jorn Barger used the term "weblog" to describe his collection of links logged from the Internet, but it was Peter Merholz who first broke the word into "we blog" in 1999, and later shortened it to blog.[20] But the introduction of the first blog-supporting services such as LiveJournal and Blogger, which were launched in 1999, and Movable Type, which appeared in 2001, was really the early sign of this social direction the web was taking. Technologically, it was essential that content management systems became available for managing and updating web pages, which meant that also an Average Joe with only basic web skills could now publish one's own ideas to a global audience. Content management systems offered web pages to which their owners regularly added new entries or "posts," which usually were short and contained hyperlinks. WordPress, a leading open source blog tool and publishing platform built upon a general-purpose scripting language "PHP: Hypertext Preprocessor (PHP)"[21] and relational database management system MySQL, was released in May 2003. Beyond blogging, WordPress also became a hugely popular content management system through which small companies became capable to maintain their websites with low cost and relatively high quality.[22] Bloggers publishing became the web's dominant publishing paradigm, which has since reshaped social collaboration at the level of politics and public relations. Later, the ideas of blogging were borrowed also for microblogging services[23] to support very fast exchange of small portions of data such as short text messages or links to videos.

In addition to social networking, instant messaging, gaming and blogging, online encyclopedias started to gain popularity. Ideas related to open-source encyclopedias appeared even before the reign of World Wide Web.[24] Internet pioneer Rick Gates proposed the Internet Encyclopedia in October 1993 in the PACS-L Listserv,[25] and this idea was later named the Interpedia by a discussions participant, R.L. Samuell. It did not proceed far, however; the advancements in World Wide Web soon made such a project more plausible. It was about the turn of the millennium when there appeared three major free encyclopedia projects. Britannica.com Inc. made free online access to the full text of *Encyclopædia Britannica* available since October 1999,[26] but a shift back to subscriptions took place in March 2001. Richard Stallman's open-source and free content encyclopedia, the Free Universal Encyclopedia and Learning Resource, also known as GNUPedia, went online on 17 January 2001, and ever since a wide range of other open source applications have been developed. But in the encyclopedia markets GNUPedia had to compete with the third project, Nupedia developed by Jimmy Wales and Larry Sanger.[27] Wales knew Sanger from their joint participation in online mailing lists and Usenet discussion groups devoted to Russian–American writer and philosopher Ayn Rand and objectivism, and he recruited Sanger as the editor-in-chief of Nupedia. Nupedia went online on 9 March 2000. The plan for it was to feature expert-written, peer-reviewed content. It was inspired by Stallman's ideas and open source projects, and it switched to the GNU Free Documentation License. GNUPedia, which had changed its name into GNE, and Nupedia were now on a collision course. But in fact none of the early encyclopedia projects worked out in the longer run. *Encyclopædia Britannica* was not free, GNE project stayed as a short lived experiment and also Nupedia gave up. However, the Nupedia project had started to use WikiWikiWeb software, which was a platform for collaborative web applications created by software programmer Ward Cunningham as early as in 1994. "Wiki" comes after a Hawaiian word for fast, and now the *fastness* became a key. With this software users could utilize web browsers to create web pages in a quick and easy manner and then edit them collaboratively. Wikipedia became a successful wiki-based successor of Nupedia by mid-January 2001. It took less than a month to get the first 1,000 articles, and within the first year the number reached 20,000, second year 100,000, and in ten years there were over 3.5 million articles in the English edition only. Larry Sanger left the project in 2002 over questions about the legitimacy of the project's entries. He later established a competing encyclopedia, Citizendium, with more rigorous contribution criteria. Wikipedia itself was transferred in late 2003 from the Bomis Inc. to a non-profit organization, known as Wikimedia Foundation, Inc.,[28] with the foundation's three original trustees being Bomis' joint owners.

Key applications and corporations become visible

In the beginning of the social web, the idea of applications driven by vast databases created by user contribution started to become a reality. Google, which had emerged only a few years earlier, was a breakthrough company in this space, when it started to crawl the entire web figuring out a different way to get meaning out of it and building an ad/monetization system associated with it. The original Page Rank patent,[29] which was filed on 9 January 1998 and issued on 4 September 2001, is about a link analysis algorithm that assigns importance ranks to nodes in a linked database and in the World Wide Web. Most people perhaps would not think of Google's Page Rank methodology as a social web phenomenon, but it takes advantage of exactly the same, namely large numbers of people frequently searching huge databases. Thus, Google became central part of the third wave even though it already had started its success story in the second wave.

There are numerous contemporary social media systems and networking services, and they are evolving extremely quickly, but to get an overall view on the social web services let's focus on the development of some of the popular services during the critical years: MySpace, Facebook, LinkedIn, Twitter, Flickr, YouTube, Groupon and Foursquare.[30]

MySpace, founded by Chris DeWolfe and Thomas "Tom" Anderson, was originally a side project which its parent company eUniverse launched in Santa Monica, California in mid-2003 to compete with sites like Friendster. MySpace was one of the newer social networking systems that took advantage of the deteriorating relations between Friendster and its early adopters, which was exacerbated by rumors of its forthcoming fee-based system. Furthermore, indie-rock bands and rock artists playing in the network of independent record labels and underground music venues were expelled from Friendster due to recklessness in following profile regulations, but they were welcomed to MySpace. Overall, the relationships between bands and their fans aided MySpace to expand beyond former Friendster users. MySpace was also special in that it allowed personalizing of users' pages, and it began to allow minors. Teenagers encouraged their friends to join the site, and there was a flood of new users in 2004. Rupert Murdoch's News Corporation purchased MySpace for $580 million in July 2005, which attracted massive media attention. Unfortunately, a series of pedophile cases took place and safety issues began to plague MySpace. The company had attracted major media attention, but there were several social networking sites gaining ground outside of the United States and also new blogging services with social networking functionality breaking through. These systems started to flourish and they accustomed people to the idea of socializing online in ways that they had not been doing previously.[31] MySpace got rival sites, which attracted first users and then advertisers to the extent that its business eclipsed by them and MySpace was sold just for some $35 million dollars in June 2011.[32]

Alongside open social networking services were restricted networks. In early 2004, Mark Zuckerberg, Eduardo Saverin, Dustin Moskovitz and Chris Hughes founded Facebook in Cambridge, Massachusetts. The service, which was based at Harvard but already available to other Ivy League Schools and Stanford, required its users to have university email addresses associated with its related institutions. Thus, Facebook was about connecting and sharing with people one knew at least partially, "me being your friend and you being my friend" in a symmetric way. The service steadily gained the attention of college students. During the early phases, it got some criticism of being an upper-class, only-by-invitation network. In September 2005, Facebook opened signup to high school students and professionals inside corporate networks. As it was released to people outside of educational networks, it was really competing with the most popular social network system at the time, MySpace. A sign of technological progress was that Facebook users could now make their full profiles public to all users. Then, Facebook announced on 24 May 2007 its new software developer platform with an open application programming interface. Even though MySpace continued to grow very strongly until 2008, Facebook's open API caused a radical change in the scene. The social network of users was now available for all web developers, who were able to create various types of applications allowing people to interact in new ways. This activity began to bloom. According to Facebook, it gained 24,000 applications and 350,000 developers in a year after launching its platform. Since then, also many other web services have started to use people's Facebook profiles for registration and login into their systems thanks to its huge popularity. Facebook has indeed become the rockstar company of the social web era.

Reid Hoffman, who had been influenced by SixDegrees,[33] co-founded in 1997 an online social networking service SocialNet, which was used for dating but also professional networking, roommates, carpool, golf partners, and was an executive vice president of PayPal, an online payment and money transfer company. In 2002, he co-founded LinkedIn with Allen Blue, Konstantin Guericke, Eric Ly and Jean-Luc Vaillant. LinkedIn was officially launched on 5 May 2003, when they invited 300 business contacts to join the network. Close connection to other key players in the social networking scene at the time can be seen, for example, from that their office was right across the hall from Friendster in Mountain View. Yet, it was not an easy start even for them. An early LinkedIn executive described challenges of their team: "They did 26 VP pitches early. Basically, two VCs offered to lead ... So nobody else wanted to invest at the time."[34] Sequoia Capital invested $4.7 million in it soon after its launch, in November 2003,[35] and Nokia Venture Partners became another major investor. LinkedIn grew slowly compared to other major social sites, but later it has become the world's largest business contact and professional network oriented service, which makes money from online advertisements, premium subscriptions of its service and hiring tools for recruiters. In April 2007, a businessman from Belgium who signed up after a former colleague invited him to reconnect on the network became the ten-millionth member.[36] Some five months later, a much better known person, a Democratic Senator from Illinois and then presidential candidate Barack Obama, solicited opinions before the Super Tuesday on LinkedIn about how the next president could help small businesses and entrepreneurs to flourish.[37] Three years later the service reached the benchmark of 100 million members, and one million earliest adopters of the LinkedIn received a thank-you email from founding CEO Reid Hoffman on 22 March 2011.[38] Surely the interest of these one million original users rose again when they received a message with their original member number assigned more than half a decade earlier when the network was a novelty. LinkedIn made the first social network IPO on 19 May 2011. The shares of LinkedIn soared from their offering price to more than double, 109 percent, in the first day of trading on the New York Stock Exchange. At the time it was the biggest Internet IPO since Google Inc.'s debut in 2004.[39]

During these critical years, Twitter, a mixture of messaging, social networking and microblogging, emerged. The concept of Twitter is very different from Facebook, being based on an idea of broadcasting. Twitter users are able to send and read short messages of 140 characters or less, called tweets, and it is sometimes described as the SMS of the Internet.[40] It has an asymmetrical follow model, meaning that if Harry follows Tim, it does not mean that Tim follows Harry.[41] In a way, asymmetric following is much more true-to-life than the sort of "declared friendships" that exist in Facebook even if ordinary people often do not really know how to make use of Twitter. But someone's ideas can be of interest to thousands, hundreds of thousands or millions of people, and it is clear that the person cannot be true friends with all of one's followers.[42] Twitter was created in March 2006 as a side project in Odeo Inc., a company for web-based broadcasting of music, located in San Francisco.[43] Leading and most well-known figures were Jack Dorsey, Evan Williams, Biz Stone and Noah Glass. The implementation was originally to be used as an internal service for Odeo employees. The first message sent was "just setting up my twttr" by Jack Dorsey on 21 March 2006.[44] A full version of the service was introduced publicly on 15 July 2006, and Twitter was incorporated as a separate company on 18 April 2007.[45] It got some public notice, but not until 2009 did it grow tremendously, becoming the third most popular social network, trailing only Facebook and MySpace[46] at the time. It had taken four years for Twitter to reach its 10 billionth tweet. This happened in March of 2010.[47] In contrast to its slow initial development, the total number of tweets doubled in less than five months, passing the 20 billion messages mark in August 2010. With some 55 million tweets a day Twitter plays a significant role in the world of communications today.

While Facebook and Twitter were developing text-based networking, the social nature of photography became evident with the photosharing site Flickr. By using it, anyone could put their pictures online to share with others. Flickr became possible, because broadband was becoming popular, the majority of mobile phones were being shipped with built-in cameras, people were getting used to social networking through sites like Friendster, and the population was ever more accustomed to publishing online through blogging. Flickr was launched by a privately held company called Ludicorp,[48] which had been developing a massively multiplayer online game known as Game Neverending[49] in Vancouver, British Columbia since 2002. The game included an instant messaging functionality, which could be used to form communities and share photographs or other objects. The interface of the game was practically the "early Flickr." Thus, Flickr was actually a side project for a game. Players of Game Neverending first encountered Flickr on 4 February 2004, and its public beta was released a few days later on 13 February 2004. The co-founders were President Stewart Butterfield and his wife Caterina Fake, who acted as Vice President of Marketing and Community. Fake coined the term Flickr after finding that Flicker.com already existed. Later, many other software developers named their online products by shortening the English words. Photosharing became widespread and Flickr became very popular. As with many other fast-growing web services, Flickr was frequently down for servicing.[50] In spite of this, Yahoo! bought Ludicorp in March 2005, and in 2007 they encouraged their static photosharing site Yahoo! Photos users to move their pictures from it to Flickr.[51]

The video sharing site YouTube was launched in February 2005 by ex-PayPal employees Chad Hurley, Steve Chen and Jawed Karim. Hurley had studied design at Indiana University in Pennsylvania, and Chan and Karim had studied computer science at the University of Illinois at Urbana-Champaign. The basic idea behind YouTube is similar to Flickr in that anyone can put video clips online, share them with others and others can comment about them.[52] "Me at the zoo" was the first uploaded video clip to the site on 23 April 2005. This was a 19-second clip of co-founder Jawed Karim at the San Diego Zoo filmed by Yakov Lapitsky.[53] In November 2005, YouTube received funding from Sequoia Capital and officially became a corporation the next month. It became hugely popular and one of the fastest growing websites in the world.[54] It was sold to Google for $1.65 billion in Google stock in October 2006, a mere 11 months after its founding.[55] At the time there were already over 100 million video clips viewed and 65,000 new videos uploaded daily. The viewership for the most viewed videos is measured in billions.[56]

When the majority of other social networking sites were developed by computer experts, one of the growing e-commerce sites, an online coupon company, Groupon Inc. in Chicago, was somewhat different, being run by savvy sales representatives finding suitable deals for its users. Andrew Mason, Eric Lefkofsky and Brad Keywell founded Groupon, which is a collective buying social site for getting an unbeatable daily bargain offer for a subscriber in one's own city. The fundamental idea is that each user gets one group coupon, "groupon," per day. Even though the level of sociality may be considered lower than with Facebook or Twitter, for instance, Groupon still draws its power from the social web through its group coupon concept. It also encourages sharing of deal information between friends, thus building upon the word of mouth effect. Its first trial deal on 22 October 2008 was taken by 24 Chicagoans, who bought two pizzas for the price of one in Groupon's building.[57] The service was launched in November and at the end of the year it had 400 subscribers. However, within two years, it grew by a factor of 110,000. In two and a half years it was offering more than a thousand daily deals, it had some 7,100 employees, and it had received $1.1 billion venture capital. Groupon's IPO strategy was the most closely watched of initial public offerings at the end of year 2011. The three-year-old company raised $700 million by selling a small portion, only five percent, of its shares on 4 November 2011. In three and a half years, it had sold 170 million groupons, and it counted 33 million active users (with many more subscribers) and 250,000 merchants in 48 countries.[58]

Foursquare,[59] launched by Dennis Crowley and Naveen Selvadurai in March 2009, is a location-based social networking service for the web and smartphones. Users check-in at different geographical locations and correspondingly they can see where their friends are at a given moment. They are able to share photos and tips as well as send messages via the service and they get recommendations, advertisements and bargains as well as hints of points of interests there are nearby. Foursquare also offers game-like features based on user check-ins and sharing of location-based experiences through which users can compete with each other by collecting "points" and achieving public recognition such as social badges. A superuser status can be received for helpful contributions to the community. After a bit more than two years, the New York City based Foursquare had over ten million users of whom a half were outside the United States and half were women. Less than a year later their user community included over 20 million people worldwide.[60] Foursquare is expected to keep growing, as the number of smartphones in the world is increasing. Also the fact that big commercial brands have started to utilize Foursquare gives further backing to services of this type. For example, McDonald's participates actively in the 4sqDays,[61] global gatherings of Foursquare application developers. The 4sqDays are being held every year on April 16, 16 being four squared, and celebrated widely around the globe but differently at different places, demonstrating the diversity within this social web community.

The next wave

After many stages in the web's development, the emphasis finally became social rather than business or technical. Tim O'Reilly explains that the social web was "implicit in the Internet all along just like the adult is implicit in the child. Certainly there's nothing different in Web 2.0 that wasn't in Tim Berners-Lee's original web." The waves of the web are not parted nor are they detached from each other, but continuity can be identified. This also applies for the future: The next waves have already been born, and they are waiting to be discovered.

Part II

Social Web as a Transformer

4
The Promise

In the early days of the web there were many technical issues to be resolved. For instance, searching the web used to be often daunting and caused frustration, and Google was a major step forward, providing better search results thanks to its more thorough hyperlink analysis, best practices being soon copied by others. For another example, few users or even developers knew how an online shopping cart was meant to work. There was a multitude of different designs, some of which were good, and some were bad, nonetheless, shopping carts have improved and most designers now know how to build a cart. In a similar manner, there have been many technical matters to resolve in the social web. For instance, it used to be a lot of work to get a web host, set up a database and build one's own commenting system, and many people tried to perform such tasks beginning from scratch. Today, it is all well packaged and much easier to do. Also, if one wants to write a blog, one can go to dedicated web blogging services or install specific software packages for it and the blogging capability becomes ready immediately. Indeed, many of the weaknesses that existed earlier have been resolved, and it is easier now to make the social aspects of this technology driven connectivity as the core of the site. There doesn't seem to be any great technical roadblocks, which would inhibit the social web to be capable of delivering its promise. Let us now sum up its key undertakings.

Establishing online social networks

> *Reid Hoffman:*
> *The [social web] happens when millions of people all express their real identity online and then establish networks with people that they know in fact in real life.*
>
> *Jimmy Wales:*
> *[The web] is a social industry. It's about people and how they interact.*

After the introduction of hypertext information systems[1] and later the web, theorists argued that "hypertext would ... revolutionize social relationships through new forms of communication,"[2] and that the web's capabilities would be experimented with by diverse groups in such a manner that new genres of communication would be created.[3] It was still unclear how much existing communication would be adapted and how much new communication would emerge, but nobody had to wait very long to see the social web in full strength. It quickly became one of the core ways that people interact with each other, a fully accepted form of communication, which really seems to be here to stay. The social web provides much easier sharing of information between friends and acquaintances in terms of staying in touch than the web did before, and it does not seem to even matter much whether the content provided is anything from entertainment to education to business. In line with this, the CEO of MySQL Mårten Mickos[4] claims that "The web is social – that's all the web at the end of the day is."

Philosophically, the individual is vertex, a center point, of one's own community, and the most central facet of the social web is its way of extending one's ability to establish and maintain social networks. Sociologist Mark Granovetter explains that people maintain far more relationships through the social web than they could ever before and that "it [the social web] gives more opportunities to reach out for people that [one] would otherwise have lost touch with and find out about what they are doing." Ben Shneiderman, Professor of Computer Science at University of Maryland College Park, explains that "what's amazing [in the social web] is the capacity for individuals to express themselves, share it with their friends and family, their colleagues and neighbors, and then the broader audience. [It] is a remarkable transformation that we have only begun."

The social web has allowed people to have much broader, more geographically diffuse social networks. One of the benefits related to this is that one may have *ambient intimacy*.[5] For example, for someone living far from relatives, the social web may open up an opportunity for feeling closeness with the relatives in a way that was not possible before, and to get to know little things about their lives that one would not know without the social web. Relationships may perhaps even deepen through this ambient intimacy. When a relative or close friend living abroad is found on the social web, they are sometimes contacted much more frequently than when living next door or in the next town. Most of shared social space also works asynchronously without restrictions to time zones. The instantaneous nature to stay connected with so many people and to have ambient intimacy with otherwise distant friends, relatives, or acquaintances is something extraordinary for this era.

In the early 1970s, Mark Granovetter studied the getting of a job as an element in social mobility. The people that he interviewed repeatedly reported that they had obtained their job through casual acquaintances rather than through close friends. The reason for this was that friends tend to recycle the same information to the extent that they all know the same things, whereas people we know less well are likely to have information that we do not have. The key conclusion was that we are more likely to hear of a new job from acquaintances – weak ties – than from our friends or other strong ties.[6] Thus, broadening of one's own social networks from tight connections to acquaintances could bring additional benefits.

In addition to reaching people one already knows, the social web acts as a bridge builder, bringing people together. Paul Saffo states that "in cyberspace there is no distance between two points." Following Saffo's statement, we call the idea that distances between people's viewpoints are extremely short or nonexistent as *cyberspatial non-distance*. For instance, with the web one can connect over distances by finding people who have exactly similar profile or a buddy who has the same interests, which means that suddenly one is able to find new acquaintances even if feeling a misfit where one lives. The social web can also give unparalleled access to cultures and locations around the globe and a chance to comprehend existing problems of the world in a much broader context than ever before. Kevin Kelly, one of the original editors of the *Wired* magazine, wrote in the late 1990s that technology also closes various kind of gaps.[7] The web, with the social web as its pinnacle, closes information and timing gaps, for instance, now it is possible to find out in more or less real time citizens' viewpoints on a political or societal issue that has only just emerged. The social web also closes quality and distance gaps. Previously, if one wanted to find someone who was located in a far away place and to talk to him or her personally, they often had to travel there to meet that person, whereas now it can be done at a glance from the living room through professional and personal social networks and Internet telephony. John Lilly,[8] the CEO of Mozilla Corporation, proclaims that the social web "finds every gap and it closes it down; I really feel like every day I'm standing on the shoulders of giants."

An example of cyberspatial non-distance is Kiva.org, created by Matt and Jessica Flannery as peer-to-peer microlending site in October 2005. "Kiva" means "harmony," "agreement," "unity" or "approval" in Swahili, and the service aims "to connect people through lending for the sake of alleviating poverty." As a non-profit microfunding organization, it helps people to lend money to small businesses and students in developing countries either directly or through other microfinancing institutions in those areas. Because of its zero-percent interest yield for capital lenders, it can be regarded as social lending. To get an idea about the level of activity, Kiva had more than 840,000 users with total value of all loans more than $180 million at the end of year 2010, an average loan amount to an individual was $382.05, women entrepreneurs received 81.66 percent of these loans, and repayment rate by all partners was 98.91 percent.[9] The social web really seems to make the world shrink.

Perhaps a more nuanced example of these bridgebuilding and gapclosing capabilities is LinkedIn, which provides professional social filtering through one's business acquaintances. In addition to being a problem-solving tool for instance for the task of finding a job, it is also a tool for giving and getting recommendations. Indeed, whether in small or big issues, people are often willing to take recommendations in their lives from their friends and acquaintances very seriously. Following the findings of Granovetter, Reid Hoffman, co-founder and executive chairman of LinkedIn, believes that recommendations can have an even greater influence when people's careers are involved, because with better information through one's own trusted network one may get a more accurate vision of work related opportunities: "What we [in LinkedIn] basically do is we make people's reputations much more discoverable. You're essentially incenting people from being single transactors to multi-transactors, because even though you may only be doing one transaction with them the fact that you can discover my past transactions easily raises the quality of the incentives in the system for me to be a much better transactor within the system." This kind of recommendation-based information services have a huge growth potential because of the fact that they can ease user's cognitive overload in searching for a job or resolving problems.

The professional social networks are also becoming ever more important because of the change that has happened in the labor markets. It used to be that one worked for 30 or 40 years at the same company and the company sent one to professional training in seminars, but it is beginning to head towards two to four years work stints. In Silicon Valley it is considered OK for people to go from company to company, and it is getting world-widely to the same direction. In some cases, one may work in dozens of different companies during one's professional life. At such short gigs, companies don't train their employees anymore. This is simply because the companies only get a couple years from their employees rather than a 30-year arc. Moreover, if a company gives them the training, it has raised their market value, and they may suddenly head off somewhere else. Quite understandably, in most cases the firm doesn't help an employee to find the next firm either. What results from this is that individuals need to start managing training themselves. One will have to tackle questions such as how to manage themselves and their assets just like a small business, how to define what really makes their offering valuable for business, why someone else would want to employ them, and how would they find them.

In this sense, everyone is becoming a small business in their own career, which means that every individual professional will *operate like an entrepreneur.* Reid Hoffman explains that one way to think of LinkedIn is its support for this kind of thinking and action:

> Part of how LinkedIn was founded was every individual was gonna [need] a professional identity on the web. Their presence and identity there will help them navigate everything from long time scales, which is their career, to short time scales, which is solving a particular problem in front of them. People most often started because the old uses of professional networks tended to be job seeking and recruiting [only]. It was hard to deploy your network on the things that really mattered to you. You really need a job, you're gonna use it. You really need to hire somebody, you're gonna use it. If you look at one of the traits of [the] modern economic world, accelerating time frames, global competitions, radically changing job roles in terms of what is competence on what you're doing, actually being able to share information, practice, tips, find experts, etc., is all part of being a successful professional in these compressed time frames and more global environments.

Thus, in addition to finding general information and expertise, the social web can help go outbound and look for the right professionals with whom to connect and from whom to learn. It is also a mechanism for managing connections to professionals and information coming inbound, enabling one to utilize one's various trusted networks and be connected to shared affiliations like university, alumni, or corporate connections. Managing individuals' personal and professional identities is a key part of what the social web can do.

Greater access to diversity of viewpoints

Reid Hoffman:
[In] the Internet you are only a URL away.

Ben Shneiderman:
We have more to do about broadening to reach people who don't have access and giving them capabilities also to express themselves and to provide input to decision-making of governments and of communities.

One of the strengths of the social web is great diversity of information and viewpoints that can be found on it. If one wants to find facts or opinions on just about anything, it is reasonable to assume that it will be available on the social web. Practically all views are represented. This produces a wide variety of perspectives and offers information that users can synthesize. In fact, such access to information and ability to synthesize is extraordinary in the history of mankind.

Before the web, even if there were printed encyclopedias, often there was no convenient way to follow up on some matter if one vaguely wondered about it. One could look up for information in an encyclopedia if fortunate enough to be able to afford one or to have time to go to the library to do so, but now, in contrast, one can immediately search, find out, and obtain the basic background information from the various sources in the social web. This may even result in a very detailed understanding of the issue under investigation. One of the core strengths which already the original web brought about was information gathering based on associative thinking and navigating the web, which is much easier than reading electronic versions of lengthy documents in a linear manner or even via tree-based or hierarchical structures. A reader became capable to swiftly bury oneself deeply in a topic online and learn more quickly than before. Through sharing of notes, links and learning experiences the social web has extended this capability to a whole new level. Another remarkable quality of the original web was the free access to large amounts of information resources for a wide variety of users, the capability of which the social web has extended. This can be seen, for example, in news services and journalism, where the reader has much more direct access to and control over what news he or she receives. We are also seeing that many people, not just the wealthy or scholars, can now access archived materials that otherwise would be hard to find, such as genealogical information concerning a distant relative or a coincidental person of interest linked with some special occasion. Let's take as an example: White Star Line RMS Titanic's "unknown child," a fair-haired toddler, who was found five days after the disaster in April 1912. The neatly and warmly dressed child was found floating, but shockingly frozen to death. Although bodies of two older boys were also recovered, the toddler whom recovery sailors named "Our Babe" became a symbol for all the children who drowned when the ship sank and as a third class passenger also a symbol for the ordinary emigrants.[10] On the web, one can find, for example, Titanic's list of passengers, the original of which is stored at the National Archives in Kew, England; lists of cruise members; lists of allocation of cabins on board; lists of children on board; passenger biographies; pictures of passengers, including even a picture of the known "Our Babe" taken probably in 1911; various kind of information on official traveling documents; identification research and genealogical research. Much of this information has been made available for the large audience by other social web users.

Indeed, the social web provides a wealth of information, much of which is generated and stored by users. Without the user-generated content, much of this nuanced information would not be available for any wider audience. Thus, users have become co-creators of value. For anything one wants to do, from buying a book to fixing up a toilet seat, others have probably done similar things before and have posted advice online. One can start from where they left and at least try to take advantage of their experience. This advantage outlines enormous potential for society's pace of positive progress. In a similar manner, today it is often likely that one has heard a piece of news first from user-generated sources of information rather than news channels. Information access and the ability to get relevant background information instantly have helped people understand world events better and in a very quick manner. This ability to search and find information about almost anything one wants is one of the factors that have had a great impact on human behavior.

One of the directions the web is currently taking is broadening the access to the social web, and even if this advancement is not necessarily because of the socialness of the web, it essentially helps in providing even greater access to diversity of viewpoints. A key aspect of broadening relates to the number and geographical distribution of people who can get to the web. There are countries spearheading expansion efforts such as Finland, which was the first nation to make broadband a guaranteed legal human right to at least a minimum speed of one megabit connection in 1 July 2009.[11] According to International Telecommunication Union, the number of Internet users in the world doubled between 2005 and 2010. More than 2.3 billion people, one third of the world's population, were online at the end of 2011, and developing countries have evenly increased their share of the Internet users. There were already twice as many Internet users in Asia as in North America in 2008, and China alone represents about 25 percent of the world's Internet users in 2011.[12] The web reaching two billion people was a remarkable achievement and a huge expansion from its small beginnings, but much more is likely to be done with this regard.

Another important aspect of broadening access is to better take into account disadvantaged users such as the disabled, the elderly or those with low literacy or low economic status. They need better access to the web, finding of services that fit with their needs, and training that will enable them to really utilize these web services. Yet, the underprivileged users should not only be guided to the sources of information for passively receiving one-way outputs but actively express themselves, and also in this way to ensure that the diversity of viewpoints really is present in the web. Both government agencies and industry may play a role in working towards this goal, but the pressure perhaps needs to come from non-profit agencies and non-governmental organizations. For instance, the National Federation for the Blind in the United States is active in pursuing legal cases to encourage companies to expend more effort on promoting universal usability in their websites.[13] It is important to make companies and government agencies aware of the issue of universal usability and encourage designers to address it, for instance, by putting on the bottom of pages in a website not only a link for their privacy policy as often is the case, but also for a statement explaining what they did to make it accessible. In some cases, increased awareness may even have a business advantage for the companies, because a small additional effort can give them deeper insight into user behaviors.

Capacity to communicate ideas

> *Douglas Engelbart:*
> *The strength of the web is an open communication pathway everywhere in the world.*
>
> *Ben Shneiderman:*
> *Democratizing access to information is actually the early notion of the web. But the second notions are democratizing the capacity to communicate ideas. Blogs and others allow ordinary people, common people to express themselves in their communities and wider ways. That's a historical change.*

The original web facilitated democratized access to information, whereas the social web democratized the capacity to communicate ideas. Of course, possibilities existed previously for people to share their thoughts, but the social web is a highly enabling media through making one's writing and images very quickly available on the web and get them seen by potentially a very large audience. This freedom to express oneself at least ideally means that almost everyone is now able to participate in the worldwide dialogue and publish. Most people do not necessarily want to have an audience or publish their thoughts, but those who do are now able to find people who are interested in what they have to say. According to the *State of the Blogosphere* survey of Technorati, more than a third of professional bloggers received over 10,000 unique visitors per month,[14] and also hobbyist bloggers sometimes attracted a wide audience.[15] Fittingly, pop artist Andy Warhol proclaimed in 1968 in the catalogue of his first museum exhibition in Europe that "in the future, everyone will be world famous for fifteen minutes."[16]

When everyone could potentially write what they wish in Wikipedia, some want to meticulously guard details significant for them, some people write insightfully and helpfully at a high level, and other people write things that are of more common interest and may entertain while offering information. Information is needed for various purposes, and interests may range from basic facts to details to opinions to theoretical discussions to meta-debates. People often express themselves at different levels of abstraction. For this reason, social web users need the ability to move across these abstraction levels based on the task at hand. Yet, it is not only individuals who can communicate their own ideas, but also users jointly can conceptualize and reach consensus. Collaboration among Wikipedia contributors is an example of this, especially the ability of the community to mediate conflict of opinions and interests and to moderate an article's content. Jimmy Wales explains that most people find the contents in Wikipedia convenient because they are just wondering about things in a general level rather than want to debate about details:

> The Wikipedia entry on Iwo Jima is probably not perfect, but it probably is satisfactory, gives you the basic information and an accurate way of what happened there. Maybe a crackpot conspiracy theorist might find it dissatisfying and would like to write their own page, and an academic historian might say: 'Well, it's pretty good but it doesn't really contextualize or properly identify this problematic part of the dialogue.' But I think most people would say: 'Well, that's great. I would love to know more about that if I get interested some day, but basically I just was wondering what happened there.'

An ordinary person can set up Twitter account, be on Facebook or upload a YouTube video, and millions of people around the world can be exposed to it. Ordinary people can reach thousands or millions, which was never before possible. In addition to sharing and publishing personal reflections, the social web has fundamentally changed and expanded the ability to speak out on matters such as consumer or political issues. This empowers consumers to an entirely new extent. For example, the song shared in the web since July 2009 called "United breaks guitars" got more than 12 million views in YouTube in three years. The man behind it is a Canadian musician Dave Carroll, who had brought his guitar on a flight in March 2008. The song tells how he was looking at the unloading of the luggage out of the window of an airplane and saw his guitar being destroyed. He tried all of the means to be compensated for it but nothing happened. The airline simply ignored his complaints. Later he wrote a trilogy of songs, made videos about the case, posted them on the web and got millions of views. Only then the company offered compensation for what had happened, and following Carroll's wish, it was donated to charity. This "guitar incident" further hurt the reputation of the airline, which at the time was struggling with a falling stock price. The losses of the sunken stock price reached $180 million and some experts claimed that this incident had played significant role in it. In any case, it certainly shook the global credibility of the company, whereas Dave Carroll was named 2010 Man of the Year, a Halifax Consumer's Choice Award. Getting a million people to watch your video is an empowering thing.[17]

A concrete and exciting effect of the social web on civilization on the level of everyday life is the opportunity to democratize household economics, enabling the buying and selling of merchandize and services between people. eBay which was an early notion of the social web helped democratize individual trade. Suddenly, it gave the power to the people to sell their own possessions without having to go through an established chain of intermediaries anymore. This transformed the ways that we both sell and shop. Indeed, many people do not go to stores anymore; they simply buy practically everything online. At the same time, another thread of democratization is, according to Caterina Fake, that people also want to get back to meaningful processes, know the people who made their soap and have real market places. For instance, popular craft website Etsy calls itself a "community of artists, creators, collectors, thinkers and doers." Etsians are part of a more global movement, people reacting against big box retail and Walmart-type stores and monoculture.[18]

The social web does not empower ordinary people only on consumer issues. Now that almost anyone can publish it is harder to suppress public opinion or political information. Authoritarian regimes in the Middle East and North Africa faced an Arab upheaval that began as Jasmine Revolution triggered on 17 December 2010, in Sidi Bouzidi, Tunisia, and then spreading to other areas. Since 2007 Syria was blocking access to social media websites like Facebook, YouTube and various blogs, as well as many other websites, for political reasons. Many of those accessing them were arrested. Yet, it did not prevent its citizens to call for strikes and protests, and videos from these eventually were uploaded into YouTube.[19] Qatari-based Arab news channel Al Jazeera paid specific attention to how calls for protests were spreading on the social web to mobilize Syrians, when a revolutionary wave of demonstrations and protests were occurring widely in the Arab world.[20] This became known as the Arab Spring. The social web replenished traditional communications. Indrani Bagchi, the Diplomatic Editor in New Delhi-based the *Times of India*, wrote about this Arab upheaval in January 2011: "Communication technology has proved to be the joker in the pack. Facebook, Twitter, and other social media are playing a crucial role in the Arab protest movements, just as they did in Iran in 2009, and, of course, WikiLeaks. The diplomatic cables showed the opulent lives of Arab dictators that would be unacceptable in any country; their weaknesses, their corruption, and their compromises were all exposed. In many ways, this [Jasmine revolution] could be the first Wiki-revolution."[21] Editor of an U.S. news website *Business Insider*, Gregory White, stated on 14 January 2011 about the role of WikiLeaks in the collapse of the Tunisian government on the very same day of the collapse: "Tunisia's government has collapsed, partially due to food price inflation and unemployment, but also because of WikiLeaks." and "So, while unemployment and inflation were the underlying causes of the revolution, this WikiLeak may have been the spark that turned the public, and the government, against itself."[22] Democratizing effect of the web in society has been widely recognized and celebrated in the world in the twenty-first century, and in spite of any political or authoritarian hindrances people seem to be flocking to the web from all over the world.

The WikiLeaks, mentioned above, is an explicit example of the power the social web's capacity to communicate ideas has on governmental issues. The WikiLeaks was launched in 2007 as a non-profit media project of the Sunshine Press, publishing restricted or censored material. Its operation relies on a network of dedicated volunteers around the globe and monetary donations. It provides different channels for anonymous informants to deliver information to it, namely a secure electronic drop-box, a separate postal network or rendering information in person, and its journalists analyze the obtained material, try to verify it and write a news story the same way wire services do, and both the story and the original leaked material are published through WikiLeaks. When WikiLeaks first introduced its website it was built on top of the Wiki software platform, which had already become familiar to many people through the social web.[23] Later the prefix "wiki" stayed in the brand name "WikiLeaks." Soon after its launch, it was awarded the 2008 Economist Index on Censorship Freedom of Expression award and the 2009 Amnesty International human rights reporting award on New Media.

WikiLeaks became very high profile due to its release of "Afghan War Diaries" on 25 July 2010, and even more so after probably the largest classified military leak in modern history, the release of "The Iraq War Logs," a set of 391,832 reports, which cover the war in Iraq from 2004 to 2009. This was released on 22 October 2010.[24] The third grand size leak was publishing of 251,287 U.S. embassy cables that began on 28 November 2010. This all had challenged the status and authority of U.S. government agencies. On 22 December 2010, approximately five months after the release of "Afghan War Diaries," the Central Intelligence Agency (CIA) launched a WikiLeaks Task Force,[25] a panel led by its Counterintelligence Center to assess the impact of WikiLeaks. After the WikiLeaks anxiety, the United States tried to improve its shielding of classified data. It launched a whole set of new apparatus to be utilized to do so.[26] Several other governments have also attempted to block access to the WikiLeaks site, and legal disputes have been frequent.

WikiLeaks has been rumored even to be a front organization for an intelligence agency and it has been in conflict with some other intelligence agencies. It ardently denies any connections with governments or intelligence agencies and states that it cooperates only with independent people including accredited journalists, software programmers, network engineers and mathematicians, among others. In turn, WikiLeaks itself claims that it has been illegally harassed and attacked. One alleged instance of harassment resulted in WikiLeaks's site going down for some time in December 2010 due to attacks that caused denial of service.[27] In retaliation, hacker supporters of the site began the so-called "WikiLeaks War" or the "Operation Payback" campaign in the same month.[28] They targeted firms that had withdrawn their services, including major corporations like Mastercard, Visa and PayPal. The hackers also bombarded anti-WikiLeaks websites with service requests until they collapsed. They were also accused by former U.S. vice presidential candidate Sarah Palin, who had vocally criticized WikiLeaks, of carrying out same kind of attacks on her website. In any case, from the latter part of 2011 it started to look difficult for WikiLeaks to make much progress because of multiple reasons. A faction detached when competing OpenLeaks project had been founded in September 2010; a year later WikiLeaks confirmed that it has lost control of a cache of U.S. diplomatic cables that it had been publishing, and an encrypted and unedited file was available online revealing names of individuals;[29] its figurehead's autobiography, *Julian Assange: The Unauthorized Autobiography*, which was actually written by a ghostwriter, went on sale in the Great Britain against the wishes of Assange himself; and finally the figurehead himself was alleged for sexual offensives in Sweden.[30] Whatever one would think of these incidents, the WikiLeaks has clearly demonstrated its influence on governments.

Generally, the social web has had, and still has, a chance for democratizing effect through providing a forum for many different voices to express their ideas. This can be done for positive purposes, but it can also be ferment for negative intentions. Indeed, the social web democratizes the *capacity* to communicate ideas – how that is utilized is up to people and their networks.

Fertility for innovation

> *Tim O'Reilly:*
> *Fascinating about the Internet as a technology culture is that people are able to bed it to their will and they are able to make it do things that the creators never imagined. Those kinds of systems are fertile for innovation.*
>
> *Mårten Mickos:*
> *To think that we already have reached some reasonable level of maturity [in the web] is just plain wrong. It will be much bigger. There will be much bigger successes than Google. There will be much bigger fortunes made than we can see today.*

The term social web emphasizes actually doing things through social mechanisms, focusing on collaboration and sharing of web experiences. In the digital economy, where collaboration is central to organizational effectiveness, growing attention should be paid to the relationships that people rely on to accomplish their work. Social network analysis, an approach that has been used in sociology for decades, provides a rich, systematic means of assessing informal human networks by mapping and analyzing relationships among people, groups, teams, departments, organizations, or even geographical regions or markets.[31] For instance, AnnaLee Saxenian studied the rise of Silicon Valley to the position of the largest hi-tech concentration in the United States, overtaking the Boston region.[32] In this study she observed that the dense network of bankers in the Boston area was not as nimble in its reactions as were the networks of the new type of venture capitalists in Silicon Valley, who were able to assess a company's potential far more quickly because contacts existed between the banking and technology worlds and with other networks in general. Saxenian also claimed that many firms in the Boston area tried to prevent their employees from communicating with the staff of other firms, whereas in Silicon Valley this kind of interaction was encouraged.

In the business context, social web based network analysis may help create organizational network awareness[33] of linkages between people and of who knows what, which are important factors for understanding the organization's own collective intelligence and potential.[34] However, working within these networks is rarely well supported or even understood by the organizations concerned. By making informal networks visible, network analysis may help managers to systematically assess and support strategically important collaboration. Moreover, this visibility helps recognize when changes in the knowledge environment have taken place. This is highly important due to the fact that people are learning things all the time and someone may know something that is important at one time but not at another. Some members of an organization are also more central to the passage of information than others, and frequently there are a few people who have a wide range of connections while most of the others have only a small number. Similarly, some managers have better connections than others, and they have access to more sources of information and influence than others. On the other hand, the managing director's secretary exercises considerable power in a large company as the gatekeeper to direct contact with the operational chief. In this case the power is contextual, implying that anyone occupying that position would have the same influence. It is surprisingly often the case that a person's position in an organization is determined by the power that that person exercises rather than by his or her background or experience, and in general it is those who have large numbers of connections that exercise a particularly great influence on the functioning of the organization (either as an especially valuable employee or as a notable bottleneck).

Network relationships are critical particularly for employees whose loyalty and commitment may be more to sets of individuals in their network than to a given organization, and (at least) in their case informal networks are becoming increasingly important contributors to job satisfaction and performance. Network analysis may be a valuable collaboration vehicle also in such strategically important groups as top leadership networks, strategic business units, product development teams, communities of practice, joint ventures and mergers.[35] It can be an effective means of pinpointing breakdowns in informal networks that cross functional, hierarchical, geographical or organizational boundaries or when considering the steadily increasing role of offshoring IT operations and industry to emerging areas. In this way, the social web can give scale, for instance, to new individual contributors entering into the market.

The social web is malleable for a wide variety of purposes. There are, of course, differences in the way people use various social networking systems depending on the type of infrastructure, applications and role they provide. For instance, the 2011 Pew Internet study reports that 52 percent of Facebook and 33 percent of Twitter users engaged the platform daily, whereas seven percent of MySpace and six percent of LinkedIn users did so.[36] Through this malleability for a wide variety of purposes, it, by definition, encourages people to come up with creative ways to use it for doing things in their everyday lives. Users are able to make the social web do things that its developers never imagined – the social web is fertile for innovation.

Another important feature which partially explains the social web's high potential for innovation is that it is a system without central coordination. Jimmy Wales emphasizes the importance of people showing good will in the social web: "One of the big design principles is: 'Assume good faith.' What I mean by that is people are mostly pretty good. A big mistake that a lot of technologists make, particularly those who are socially very computer programmery [*sic*], they tend to think of the world in a very mechanistic fashion." Computer scientists often think in terms of complex security models, such as who's allowed to do what, whereas in the open philosophy of Wikipedia a physicist and a historian may end up debating and collaborating on an article both from their own angles and at their own abstraction levels without restrictions. Jimmy Wales explains the phenomena:

> That kind of openness is counter-intuitive for a lot of technologists, because they can think of a way to have a permission model. They really get lured in by those kinds of structures. Imagine if you're designing a restaurant and you think "Oh well, in my restaurant everyone's going to have knives. When people have knives they might stab each other. So we're going to put a cage around every table." We chuckle, because there's something wrong with that logic, although each step kind of sounded okay, and we realize, "Hey, you know what? We sit next to people all the time with knives, and they don't stab us." And yeah, we do know there's some crazy people out there who will stab each other. This is [the] same in the Wiki. People might come and post spam. Most of them won't. You don't want to deal with that social problem by preventing ordinary good will amongst people. When we look at some of the earlier content management systems and things like this, that was the big flaw.

Relating to social web innovation, Tim O'Reilly explains that "when you try to engineer something in such a way that you can't do anything bad, you often can't do anything good either." According to O'Reilly, the web's being a system that allows anybody to do practically anything with information is actually a characteristic of many humans' systems that end up working well. For instance, we can say good things or we can say bad things. We can use a language well, or we can use it poorly. Early on in the history of Internet, Jon Postel, one of the key figures behind the early Internet and in particular its domain name system, defined a golden code of conduct for the Internet by stating that "be conservative in what you do; be liberal in what you accept from others."[37] A person socialized in a healthy way in a family and in wider circles of society is usually able to show good will towards other people. Joseph M. Reagle, Jr., explains that there has been noble efforts to create a freely shared, universal encyclopedia previously, such as H.G. Wells's proposal for a *World Brain*, but that it was Wikipedia's good-faith collaborative culture in its articles, discussion pages and other software features that finally made it extraordinary and that made it succeed.[38]

Caterina Fake, the co-founder of Flickr, claims that in the social web there is also a culture of generosity where people are publishing things just for the sake of sharing it without a hidden agenda. Fake explains that people in some businesses expect that everything should have exchange value, and that they are trying to book a price tag on the activities that people are engaging in. But the social web, Fake points out, actually works without economic expectations and social web users do not need to be paid for creating content. Most of the people who upload their photos into Flickr are not thinking, "I could get a career as a photo journalist," they are just uploading and sharing their photos from a trip abroad, for example. They are sharing their experiences. Of course, part of the reason is that some people yearn for attention and recognition for what they have achieved, and they use the social web as a personal advertizing tool and ego booster, which can be seen from the fact that in the social web readers seldom can find information about failures or personal mishaps by people. But still, people have a deep desire to share things.

In sum, the support for establishing one's own social networks online, both work-related and private, and the democratizing effect, including both access to diversity of viewpoints and capacity to communicate ideas, hold great promise for supporting collective intelligence. Most importantly, systems that support these kinds of activities are fertile for innovation.

5
The Change

People's lives started to change in a slow but profound way when the original web came into existence. More recently, people even have started to comprehend things that are new for them by comparing them with the web, and the web has become a model for interacting with technology also in non-web contexts. For instance, the interface of games, television screens and ticket kiosks start to resemble the web, which means that technology and application developers already assume that majority of people know how to use the web. Moreover, the social web's breakthrough has made it an integral part of our way of thinking and perception of the world. For those growing up with the web, it is also what they have always experienced, whereas people who grew up before the web have experienced the change in their perception of the world. Skills that are needed to succeed in the modern environment and our view about people, their nature and abilities have changed, and the social web has also dramatically transformed how companies conduct business and design software.

How has the web changed the skills required of us?

The shift into a new information and communication environment requires a new set of cognitive and web skills for acquiring and acting upon the up-to-the-minute information available at the social web. This concerns people of all ages and from different circumstances. For instance, finding a senior citizen paying her bills online via the web is far from rare. Not only have the elderly been able to learn e-banking skills and increasingly want low-cost and easy-to-use web services, but they are also becoming more and more experienced with the social web. For a negative example of ordinary people's web skill level let us consider the misinterpretation that happened during Hurricane Katrina. The application forms for getting assistance were published only on the web and, moreover, a specific advanced version of web browser was required to fill in the forms.[1] As a result, the poorest of the damaged areas in Louisiana had the lowest percentage of applications for assistance. We as a society are becoming ever more dependent on the web, which seems to happen at least partly unintentionally. So the web has been dramatically and extremely rapidly changing the skills required of people, and it even looks like the web skills are becoming as important for mankind as the ability to read and write. Furthermore, there is all the reason to believe that the change that we have seen thus far regarding the social web's influence on the skills required of us is only the beginning.

A way to describe the web users' desired skill set is to think about them as *T-shaped people,* having a broad interest but a deep area of expertise. The vertical aspect of T-shaped people represents depth, competence in a narrow domain and the horizontal bar represents breadth, basic literacy in a relatively broad domain of relevant knowledge. The first known use of the phrase "T-shaped people" was printed in *The Independent,* a world-famous London newspaper on 17 September 1991. In his editorial, The hunt is on for the Renaissance Man of computing, David Guest wrote that "individuals known as T-shaped People ... are a variation on Renaissance Man, equally comfortable with information systems, modern management techniques and the 12-tone scale."[2] An assistant professor at the Harvard Graduate School of Business Administration at the time, Marco Iansiti, further employed the term T-shaped people to academics in his *Harvard Business Review* article in 1993.[3] Bill Moggridge, The British-born designer of one of the first laptop computers, the GRiD Compass in 1982, and the co-founder of the Silicon Valley-based design firm IDEO,[4] continued to talk about T-shaped People, helping to make the concept well-known among IT experts.

A T-shaped person thus has a broad interest but a deep area of expertise. A person who is only a generalist is not going to make much progress, but a person who is only a specialist is going to miss many opportunities. For this reason, in the future, people ideally should be generalists with deep skills in obtaining information, which resembles what was considered "a superior person" during the age of the Renaissance. Our era of transformation is in many ways comparable to the age of the Renaissance. Yet during the Renaissance itself, laymen did not much appreciate or even particularly pay attention to the fact that they happened to be in the middle of a cultural revolution. The difference to our time is our huge self-awareness, because we do recognize that we are living in an era that is radically changing the society around us.

In written communication, it has always been essential to understand who is it that wrote what we are reading and where he or she comes from to genuinely understand the point of view of what is being delivered and evaluate the credibility of the source. However, now in this era being able to *pick up* relevant information has arisen as a core competence on par with source credibility. When publishing its *Standards for the 21st-Century Learner* in 2007, the American Association for School Librarians stated that "the amount of information available to our learners necessitates that each individual acquire the skills to select, evaluate, and use information appropriately and effectively."[5] The current information pool is indeed exhaustive, and in addition to picking up relevant information, the need for being able to *compress* information, as exemplified by Twitter, has become critical. The downside of this compressing is, of course, that messages easily become superficial.

Differences between the generation that grew up with digital technologies and the generation that grew up before these technologies can be described by terms *digital native* and *digital immigrant,* coined by an American writer and speaker on learning and education Marc Prensky. He published the twin articles "Digital Natives, Digital Immigrants" and "Digital Natives, Digital Immigrants, Part II: Do They Really Think Differently?" in *On the Horizon* in 2001.[6] Digital natives have a different set of expectations from digital immigrants. For instance, it used to be that you would make a rendezvous at a particular time of day and a place, whereas now the attitude of the younger generation is "do not worry, we'll find each other." For people who are used to a more rigid way of doing social scheduling, that feels flaky. It is easy to criticize the younger generation, the digital natives, for not planning things well ahead anymore, but they can sync up with their cell phones. For kids it is just a kind of ambient scheduling that happens naturally. It's not that the digital immigrants are incapable of using cell phones in the same manner – it's just not their idiom. In a way digital immigrants have to re-think and re-learn the basic capabilities of how to "read and write" on the web to cope with the new information and communication technologies in this new era.

The original discussion about digital natives and digital immigrants that Prensky started in his articles in 2001 centered on change in education and learning processes. The web applications, such as professional networking, gameplay and virtual worlds, are indeed also changing how we learn. It might even look like that traditional learning has been abandoned and that pupils were skipping their homework, and instead they were just networking and playing games. Jimmy Wales disagrees with this view:

> People say Wikipedia is dangerous, because I wanted to do my homework but I ended up two hours later reading something I didn't even intend to read. But they follow their interest, they follow the passion. They learned things that they wouldn't know otherwise. That's a change. It's a change that's made because humans by their nature do desire to know and do want to learn. Putting the capacity for this amazing, flexible tool for learning and knowledge right at everybody's fingertips really is allowing that to flourish in a way that in the past was harder.

Even though there seems to be no explicit signs currently that the role of formal learning would disappear or to any great extent even diminish, it is evident that informal learning has absolutely exploded. A survey of Internet use among 11-year-old schoolchildren in Finland showed that 90 percent of the children were using the Internet on a weekly basis in 2006, but only one out of five thought that using the web to accomplish their homework actually was part of schoolwork.[7] Thus, when kids are doing their homework by exploring the web, they do not necessarily think they are doing schoolwork but rather they just do it for fun. This is seamless practical combination of education and entertainment, "edutainment," something that has been long requested and hoped for.[8] In fact, people are spending huge amounts of time learning new things, while utilizing these modern information resources. Digital natives can, according to Prensky, spend an estimated 20,000 hours with new technologies in the first 20 years of their lives.[9]

Prensky also states that one reason why the old ways of learning do not attract digital natives is that they have short attention spans and they crave interactivity and immediate responses to their actions. This has been linked by many with the concept of multitasking especially since March 2005, when The Henry J. Kaiser Family Foundation released report, "Generation M: Media in the Lives of 8–18 Year-olds," done in collaboration with researchers from Stanford University. The report suggested that multitasking or consuming different kinds of media all at once was a growing phenomenon in media use. Some people began to suggest that the younger generation has much more multitasking capability, even wondering if this suggested multitasking capability is linked to the rise of attention deficit disorder (ADD), which in a way helps to handle continuous flow of different inputs.[10] Others opposed. Some stated that the humans have always had the capacity to attend several things at the same time or that the multitasking was actually only a habit of dividing one's attention into many small slices or rapid toggling among tasks rather than simultaneous processing. Dr Edward Hallowell stated that multitasking is rather a myth, which makes people believe they can perform two or more tasks simultaneously.[11] The Kaiser Family Foundation's follow-up report "Generation M^2: Media in the Lives of 8- to 18-Year-Olds," which was released in January 2010, emphasized findings of "nearly 24-hour media access" and "much of that time 'media multitasking' (using more than one medium at a time)."[12] Whether the tendency that the younger generation has much more actual multitasking capability is true or not, it could be linked to the number of stimuli to which an individual must react all the time on the web. Attention span is a scarce resource these days. People are currently jumping around from one thing to another in the web and they often have neither possibility nor ability to stay steadily on one path. Under information overload in hectic times, quick, striking and thinly sliced information – easy bites – are requested rather than deep, meaningful information.

Nevertheless, we do not really know yet what part of the increased information flow is good and what part of it is bad as far as there being too many stimuli. Tim O'Reilly suggests that we will need to learn to ignore much of this information overload: "If you're a baby, man, that stimulus [being in the world] is like 'whoa.' The light, the colors, the sounds, it's all coming at you, and you make sense out of it, you order it. That is what we do as humans. We actually learn to figure out what to pay attention to and what not to pay attention to." But how would you just learn to ignore a lot of it and get better at picking out what's important, that's the question. The issue of relevance – how meaningful and relevant the information we obtain really is – is of severest concern in the social web, and the dominant general expectation of instant returns makes this even more challenging in this current era. It can easily happen that we develop patterns of picking out such information that is not at all important, and even more seriously, end up needing 15–30 minutes recovery times after a breakdown of a knowledge work activity or other mental tasks. Much needs to be still worked out.

There is a plethora of social web applications for various technological platforms available today without monetary cost, but users do not, however, get an access to these numerous applications "for free." Starting to use them and then really reaping the benefit from them requires skills, time and effort. In addition to this cognitive overload, people are often overwhelmed by the pace of adopting new technologies into use, and they may lose their personal balance in the face of this massive increase in information technologies. There is a simple explanation for this phenomenon. The web was originally designed by and for people passionate about high tech, who had almost no limits to their ability to learn new things about technology. They were expected not to mind if something was complicated or that one might need to know many types of shortcuts and details to operate it. For the most part, however, high-tech business people tend to think that their designs are natural even when they really are not, and yet there are still only a few truly intuitive user interface solutions thus far. Fortunately, some recent technologies have demonstrated a new way of interacting where one does not need to know all modes of use upfront, which makes the process less intimidating for non-techies.

Users – whether digital natives or digital immigrants – need to spend lots of resources to maintain and upgrade their skill level. Even though the bar may be very different between these two, both face the challenge of potential technological fatigue, when there are so many new technologies and applications that one is supposed to adopt and adapt. Use of smartphones and tablet devices that we carry around with us practically everywhere pose another danger. People can develop a tendency to spend so much time with their mobile devices that they get sucked into the screens and never emerge, or they may end up spending much of their time when visiting their friends fumbling their devices. In spite of the newly acquired skill level, it is important albeit challenging also to be capable of making media choices and tearing oneself away from the social web and have direct interactions with real people. Ideally speaking, the hunt is really on for the Renaissance Man of the social web.

How has the web changed our view about people?

The social web may cause the relationships of both mature people and children to go through an upheaval, but it, on par with other current information technologies, is revolutionizing particularly the early socialization of children. Children traditionally socialize first with their family when they grow up, and then they enter into a school situation, where they move with their peers and simultaneously continue learning certain values, ethics and ways of acting. Proceeding has been incremental. Now, with the social web, this situation has dramatically changed. A serial entrepreneur, CTO of Cisco Systems and Board Member of

Walt Disney Company and FedEx Corporation, Judy Estrin describes this sudden change:

> Historically those kids didn't get thrown into the wide world, the mall, or whatever until they were teenagers. They weren't off on their own. All of a sudden, you have kids at a much earlier age connecting with people in a virtual connectivity and certainly on the social web much earlier. The values, ethics, and etiquettes for how you interact with people are not as baked as they are when kids grow up in this incrementally increasing world. Yes, there are all sorts of ways where we protect kids. Club Penguin doesn't let you openly chat. But it's a fine line between that [and letting to openly chat]. I'm not raising these as "it's bad," but these are the parts that we really need to understand. The same way when we started driving automobiles, we needed to understand that we needed rules and laws, there were going to be some number of people killed. With any new technology we need to be thinking about this.

Judy Estrin has been promoting the advancing of the technology sector in general, but she thinks that the change in people unfortunately has been for the worse. One of the negative aspects of the web is that people are more inclined to "simply say what they wanna say" and "just throw it out there." Even some of the best bloggers seem to be in some ways ranting. Prensky's digital native definition revealed the trend that people tend to think in shorter units along with an increased desire for instant gratification. This can also be noticed from the tendency to immediately search for an answer from the web instead of first stopping to think whether or not a problem can be solved right away by oneself. According to Betsy Sparrow, Jenny Liu and Daniel M. Wenger, particularly when people face difficult questions they are primed to think about the web, and when they expect to have access to the web in the future they do not recall the information itself but rather recall where to access it. They describe the web as "a primary form of external or transactive memory, where information is stored collectively outside ourselves," and the people as "growing into interconnected systems that remember less by knowing information than by knowing where the information can be found."[13] John Lilly, the CEO of Mozilla Corporation, likens the current role of search engines to people trusting an all-knowing oracle, whose first, second or third link must be true. With just a little exaggeration, today, if somebody asks "why the sky is blue," the first thing anybody does is "google" it. A strong ability to synthesize is indeed needed in today's information-laden world, but this has also led to a tendency to skip creating new things and build on the work of others without much of source criticism. This type of mindset affects the ability to frame questions and to think about how to get the answers.

One of the biggest ongoing changes in our self-awareness is in the way people take care of their social networks, be they professional or private networks. For instance, many web services, such as Spotify, originally a Swedish service for streaming of music from record labels, allows their registered users' accounts to be integrated with their Facebook or Twitter accounts. By doing so, users are more easily able to share music with their friends as well as to access their friends' favorite music and or playlists. In other words, they make their musical taste explicit for others. This clearer awareness of the taste of one's own and of those in one's network has changed many people's listening preferences, and they have started to consciously cultivate their music profiles into one direction or another.

Part of Douglas Engelbart's definition for collective intelligence was that people change as the information systems that they use change. Whether it is accurate to say that through general usage of the web people actually change or not,[14] it can be stated that even though human nature would remain the same, societies that are built from people do change dramatically. Professor of Sociology at the University of California Berkeley AnnaLee Saxenian, acknowledges and emphasizes the difference between the younger generations' comfort with the web as opposed to older ones who are not capable of using this information vehicle naturally and who may react to it with resentment, suspicion and distrust. Prensky further described this difference between younger and older generations: "Digital Natives are used to receiving information really fast. They like to parallel process and multi-task. They prefer their graphics before their text rather than the opposite. They prefer random access (like hypertext). They function best when networked. They thrive on instant gratification and frequent rewards. They prefer games to 'serious' work."[15] Prensky even claims that there has been a measurable physical change to the brains of digital natives due to interaction with new information technologies.[16]

Web-savvy digital natives do have a clear upper hand in utilizing modern information and communication technologies, but this does not mean that digital immigrants couldn't still understand the web and its developments in a profound manner.[17] Digital immigrants may have to go through cycles of unlearning from their old habits, but at the same time digital natives may be missing the fact that the world has not always had the web, and they seem to assume that the web will always be there and they can rely on it. Innovation researcher Henry Chesbrough describes the difference between digital natives and digital immigrants via the example of traditional rotary phones and then push button phones versus touch screen dialing. Digital immigrants have seen these different modalities, but they had to unlearn each to start using the next. Their world was analog when growing up and then they immigrated into the digital world as digital technologies took over and became pervasive. For digital natives it has always been digital. There never was an analog world to unlearn as they were growing up and trying to function in this digital, interconnected environment. Chesbrough explains:

> So society really does change, but some of this change is truly demographic and generational and it's for older people. We have to almost unlearn what worked well before in order to pick up and make use of what's useful here, whereas for our children there's no question what they're gonna do. Of course they pick it up and go with it, why would you do anything else? Even things like a thank you note if somebody gives you a present. In my generation it was considered

> rude if you did not write by hand a thank you note. This is considered quaint at best in my children's generation, where an email, a text, a comment on a Facebook page are all perfectly acceptable ways to respond to gifts that you receive. The etiquette of the culture changes as these new technologies take hold and we in society differ in how we respond and incorporate these new possibilities into our ingrained habits that we were raised with. So this issue of unlearning for the digital immigrants is something that challenges us in a way it doesn't challenge the digital natives.

Regarding the social web's impact on cultures, Jimmy Wales relates an interesting story about a video he saw from a Latin American television program but in Spanish. It was Latin dancing except that they were performing a Bollywood song, they were singing in Hindi with a Spanish accent, and this was shared to him on Facebook by a friend who is a Saudi Arabian TV host. In a way that is a bizarre or at least peculiar culture mashup when someone from Saudi Arabia is referring to a video in Spanish of music from Bollywood. Wales explains the situation:

> What's interesting for those from the English-dominated cultural world is that the English-speaking guy was the very last guy in the chain here. That culture was communicated from Bollywood to South America and it was brought to me by someone in Saudi Arabia. So, that's really interesting, those kinds of cross-cultural impacts in a pure way that doesn't get filtered through Hollywood. It doesn't get filtered through *The New York Times*. Two cultures, Indian and Latin American, that know how to dance, they are impacting each other. These kinds of values are being transmitted around. That's going to accelerate the direct ability for some interesting music video from Tanzania to become a worldwide YouTube hit with no marketing budget.

All in all, the social web's effect on how we perceive people and cultures is unavoidable. A fascinating characteristic about the social web as a technology culture is its being a democratizing kind of technology. The WikiLeaks story shows how the social web's democratizing effect changes the status and authority of governments and what is possible for ordinary people – the social web has changed the relationship between governments and the people, the operational environment of governments, and it even seems to change governments themselves. AnnaLee Saxenian is still hesitant to lavish praise for the social web. Pointing out the opportunities for malfeasance on the web, she considers these kinds of optimistic scenarios ranging from the web "democratizing the world" to "we will all be one" being exaggerated. According to Douglas Engelbart, the big picture after all is that people start getting a much more complete feeling about who people are elsewhere, and they can follow up on anything whether related to an individual's behavior or a whole society. This may give a fuller feeling and understanding about the entire world and its events. An example of a societal change can also be noted from another personal story of Jimmy

Wales of Wikipedia, when he visited India and gave a lecture at one of the big IT university campuses there:

> Three thousand students came to hear me lecture. At the end of my speech they all rushed to the stage as if it was a rock concert. They wanted pictures and things like this. Like a visiting rock star or something. I'm running an encyclopedia! You're excited about this! That's a real change. The idea that young people are super-excited and huge fans and have a real passion and love for Wikipedia is contrary to the general social notion we've had since Elvis Presley that young people are getting dumber and dumber and dumber. In fact they're not. In fact they're getting to be really engaged in world of ideas and learning and knowledge.

Something that hasn't changed much is that people do incredible things, some good, some bad, in their everyday lives offline as well as online. Caterina Fake describes online behavior to be "Good behavior, bad behavior, generosity and altruism, side by side with slander or obnoxiousness." She explains that somebody online will make a suicide threat and someone else will get in the car and drive 300 miles to go see if they can rescue that person, and on the other hand someone will make up a cheat profile to get revenge on her daughter's rival in school and invent an online boyfriend only to dump her, evidently resulting in the rival's suicide. These kinds of incredible actions, both good and bad, take place offline, too, and most behaviors are not that different on the web from what they are offline. Yet, the nature of the web as a communication environment for conveying one's ideas, thoughts and emotions makes certain ways of acting easier and enables – perhaps to some extent even encourages – the extreme of action. Lack of judgment in these cases often causes trouble. For this reason, the social web is more flammable for questionable behaviors than in real life.

The negative sides of media have been debated for ages. Spoken words resulted in the death sentence of Athenian philosopher Socrates and he was executed by drinking a cup of poison hemlock according to Athenian law; the Church fought for centuries against written words it regarded as dangerous due to which numerous people were burned at the stake; many scholars considered novels and even newspapers to be harmful in the late nineteenth century and after that comics, film, radio, television, video games and the Internet have stood in the same line. Sir Edward Bulwer Lytton put the power of communication in a memorable way as the lines by Cardinal Richelieu in his play *Richelieu; Or the Conspiracy* in 1839: "The pen is mightier than the sword." Yet, neither content and media nor software functionality and features *per se* are either good or bad. The fast pace for generating and circulating information in the software influences us greatly, but there isn't any kind of intrinsic goodness or badness in the web in itself; the exceptional thing about it is that it can be used in so many different ways. Thus, the social web is much more than just a tool for humans use. It not only provides an opportunity for people carrying out their tasks, but the social web empowers people and their opinions.

It would be safe to say at the very least that the social web changes how we perceive people, countries and cultures, and that we are now exposed to more cultures than ever before. In a way, the web has made the world shrink. Indeed, there is no doubt that the social web has influenced people's lives.

How has the web changed business?

According to information systems professors Ritu Agarwal and Henry C. Lucas, information technology in general has the capability to change all work processes from manufacturing to service to office work, including the tasks that individuals perform, the nature of customer service and the way in which organizations are structured and supply chains operate; IT can fasten the emergence of new industries and the restructuring of old ones, individual national economies and the global economy as a whole, and most of education and research; finally, IT can change the way in which we all communicate.[18] The social web has essentially contributed to all of these organizational transformations to happen.

A big change in running businesses has been the adoption of the social web as a toolset for work rather than for private use only. This is interesting especially because originally there was no master plan in the web's early years to incorporate institutions, professions or learning into the social web, and yet this is exactly what happened. Social web has been integrated with intranets and extranets, enabling employees, customers and suppliers to collaborate in a new manner through corporate blogs, wikis and other internal and external platforms. Within the last few years web application platforms and software have also become more complex. The term Enterprise 2.0 was launched by Harvard Business School professor Andrew McAfee in 2006,[19] and ever since the development of social software and services has speeded up, producing numerous applications and platforms for it.[20] We call the organizational uses of the social web as *orgsome*, organizational social media,[21] and orgsome is becoming an enormous area for both research and business. Judy Estrin describes the shift to organizational social media:

> What started off as a mechanism to communicate likes and dislikes about music or kids finding their friends, that same power of connectivity is now moving into the enterprise as a mechanism to fuel communication and collaboration, and moving into academia and scientific research as a way to find experts, as a way to spark and fuel innovation. The same way the PC really started with the consumer and then came into enterprise. What people call social networking, it's almost a little bit of a misnomer by now where there's multiple applications of it, because there's the actual social part of it, which is about people and their social lives. But those same platforms are very powerful in enterprises and in other organizations in the public and private sectors in terms of finding experts, exchanging ideas, getting people to collaborate.

The social web has transformed the way how business is conducted also in more fundamental ways. According to sociologist Saxenian, its impact on business has been profound: "[Joseph] Schumpeter was right. There's lots of new creative business opportunities for many people, a whole new school. It's also destructive. It's destroying old business models, old companies." In practice, that is, a business model that works in a brick and mortar store can't simply move itself online without any thought of the particular characteristics of the web as a business environment. Intriguing new business models have already emerged and will continue to emerge to adapt to the specificities of the social web.

As the content and delivery of information for businesses change, the economics of business change too. Some companies will go out of business, but new companies will come forward with new business models and different capital structures and dependencies. For instance, the web has already revolutionized fields such as the music industry and banking. Podcasting, web-based broadcasting of music in which users can subscribe automatic detection of new files, became in the beginning of this century one of the hottest trends on the web. In October 2001, Apple's portable media player iPod with 5 GB hard drive for a suggested retail price of $399 was announced with the slogan "Ultra-Portable MP3 Music Player Puts 1,000 Songs in Your Pocket."[22] It quickly became a major business success, introducing a new word into common use. The term podcasting was launched by British journalist, Ben Hammersley, who wrote on 12 February 2004: "With the benefit of hindsight, it all seems quite obvious. MP3 players, like Apple's iPod, in many pockets, audio production software cheap or free, and weblogging an established part of the internet; all the ingredients are there for a new boom in amateur radio. But what to call it? Audioblogging? Podcasting? GuerillaMedia?"[23] Hammersley's short comment or rather one-word-question describes how podcasting was a crossbreed of Apple's brand name iPod and term broadcasting, even if podcasting is actually not related to any specific brand or device. Yet, it broke through becoming a widely used term. The editors of the *New Oxford American Dictionary* selected podcast as the Word of the Year for 2005 and added to the next online update of the *New Oxford American Dictionary* in 2006.

For another example, electronic publications have entered the market and introduced a major change in the core economic structure of publishing through the build-on-demand model, e-books and other means in this new type of publishing. The founder and owner of O'Reilly Media, Tim O'Reilly, explains: "If you look at the dynamics of how print books are sold, you pay a big advance to an author and then you have to really push that book into Barnes & Noble and Borders and the physical bookstores in order to pay back the author's advance. There's tight coupling between stuffing the channel and how much you can afford to pay as an advance. In e-books, there is no inventory. Whether it sells one or a million, you're just basically making one digital copy available. So there's no preorder." Of course, illegal uploading of copyrighted material into the web and people downloading it for their personal use threatens all kinds of publishing businesses, but thanks to the web there seems to be big opportunities also in the future for more small authors to be discovered and their creativity to flourish. Nevertheless, a well known book and music retailer Borders Group, Inc., which had nearly four hundred American brick-and-mortar stores,[24] became liquidated in 2011.[25] The field of banking, among many others, would provide similar examples of the change that is ongoing or that has already taken place.[26]

Some industries are withering as a result. Reid Hoffman thinks that newspapers are on a gradual decline and that they have a long slow slope to figure out a new model for themselves, but he warns, "There's a cliff coming. When you hit that cliff it'll be too late. So you need urgency now in order to figure out what to do. Here we are in economic turbulence and my belief is over the next years there will be massive closings of newspapers. We've seen a few, but there will be many, many more and it will be in any market." According to Terry Winograd the newspapers going out of business is largely due to the web. Newspapers used to provide a standard for reliable information, and they had a reputation to be guarded. *Financial Times, The New York Times,* and *The Wall Street Journal* have journalism rules. They double-check facts before printing them. Usually news disseminated by formal outlets are factual and defensible, whereas now when people hear something new, they blog it directly. The timescale required by the web for freshness drives the newspapers' decline. There are still people who want to read news on paper and prefer other inducements than rapidity, but press media conglomerates should be able to guard the high quality of their traditional papers and smoothness of their paper delivery services, if they wanted to keep their traditional paper alive and utilize its traditional high status as a springboard to the exploding web news market. It does indeed look like that many newspapers are dying down in an accelerating speed and to survive newspapers will have to find a new operational and business logic.

In a similar manner, the phone and telecommunication companies, which for a while almost literally owned communication, are having difficulty transforming themselves into new kind of companies. They have a long history of being huge players with only a few other players in their field of business. As a result, they traditionally aimed at setting the industry standards. It is a totally different world compared to the web, where standards and ways of working have become manifest not by committee decisions but by the facts of how people act. Tim O'Reilly anticipates that the crumble of telephone operators will continue, "One of the biggest disruptors that we're going to see in the next decade is going to be the death of phone companies." O'Reilly believes that something like the spinout of Skype by eBay has much more potential than traditional phone operators, either cell or landline, and continues: "You're going to have telephony as an Internet application independent of phone companies. It's already there for a lot of people. You're going to have other communication methods. The phone is just going to be one more Internet application." Telecommunication companies will, of course, still play a role for providing much of the infrastructure, but phone companies would face critical challenges in adapting themselves into this transformation period. Telephony as an Internet application is becoming a commodity which compels the phone companies to figure out how to get into the web operations. A representative strategic failure of phone companies is how little they utilized their call history databases for designing user services. They actually had multiple choices. They could have built a Facebook-like service, basically saying, "Ok, here's who your friends are, here are the people you call," they could have built a really interesting new address book application, they could have got into the speech recognition game, or they could have done a lot more with the locations data that they had. But they really didn't think that way. Of course, this is now hindsight, but as O'Reilly states, "the cat's sort [of] out of the bag, so all of the services that [future] applications are going to depend on don't belong to the phone company anymore."

Tim O'Reilly softens the blow a bit by predicting that there will be some innovation and new business models in the phone and telecommunication field that will perhaps enable some of the companies to survive. Nevertheless, the challenges for these companies will be huge. It is also important to understand that telephony is already a commodity in the sense that any product or service that major phone brands invent reappears as a knock-off within a couple months. In commodity markets, there is generally a primacy of brand and design. Once everything is so easy to imitate, companies have to really build a defensible brand. Other companies could make a phone that looked just like an iPhone, but it would not be an iPhone like the case of cheat iPhones in China have demonstrated, when there is an actual difference in the user experience between the real and the phony product.

Some big changes can take place also in traditional areas such as manufacturing when alternative business models begin to be applied to hard goods. Production-on-demand is one much debated example. For another instance, even if information services in a car are important they are not considered even close to the worth of the car yet, but at some point a dealer might be able to sell the information services and give the car away for "free" or subsidize it the way phones are already subsidized in many markets today. The economics of many industries indeed is re-shaping, and similarly the public sector is likely to follow. In some cases, companies could come up from a huge number of niches and turn into economically attractive mainstream articles shaking the status quo of the markets.

Beyond the withering industries, yet another type of change in business that has taken place is the emergence of *hybrid companies* that combine the non-profit and profit sides of business and operations. These build upon the idea of companies that are non-profit or fundamentally for public benefit, such as Mozilla Foundation promoting open Internet, but which are funded through competition in the market.[27] In December 2004, Mozilla launched a campaign in *The New York Times* advertising the free, open source web browser, Firefox, as an alternative to market leader browsers. Within a year since the release, Firefox surpassed 100 million downloads. This was a result from its intensive marketing campaign as well as publishing its major contributors and top referrers and organizing appealing festivities for the Firefox community. Mozilla Foundation also drew attention because it sponsored charities, for instance, after Firefox reached the target of 500 million downloads in February 2008, it visibly supported the UN World Food Program, receiving wide publicity from doing so.[28]

The hybrid approach is gaining momentum for two reasons. First, it is quite inexpensive to form virtual organizations, and the cost of collaboration with other people who have a similar social mission is very low. It is easy to start a web server, a wiki, and start to collect other people who share the same views, no matter where in the globe they live. The challenge of hybrid companies in this respect is that more important than the location of its participants is that organization fulfills its original intentions – otherwise there will be no community. The second benefit to hybrid companies is that the web's successful distribution mechanism quickly reaches masses, perhaps millions, of people who can boost its work. This provides an opportunity to create significantly more revenue than charities or public benefit organizations have historically been able to generate. Even with a few cents per user but with a million users, there can be enough money to kick-start new types of enterprises. Once a revenue stream is established, of course, it is still necessary to invest in talented and passionate people in all levels, and in doing so hybrid companies must compete about expertise with companies whose goals are strictly business and which may have significantly greater resources. The hybrid business model seems to have multiple benefits, but many of the ethical concerns with hybrid companies in the social web have not played out yet.

The overall economic transitions have been, according to Paul Saffo, technology forecaster and futurist, "from the industrial economy dominated by producers to the consumer economy dominated by consumers, to a new economy now where the new economic actor is someone who both creates and consumes in the act." With regards to the overall changes in business, the web has also extensively changed our institutions and professions. Sociologist AnnaLee Saxenian explains that the web is transforming, for example, the professions of librarians and journalists, and she expects to see more and more fields, industries and institutions to dramatically change. One of the occupations that have been in transition is that of software engineers and designers.

How has the web changed software design?

The way that software is being developed has already changed remarkably within the last two decades; it has become possible for users to participate in the actual development process, and even more so now with the social web. Broadly, participation may take one of two forms. Participatory design as developed in Scandinavia emphasized that end-users would have a significant say in the design process; the early participatory process was typically implemented for designing work-oriented systems, and it was especially union workers who were involved in it to be able to influence the design and use of computer applications at the workplace.[29] With regards to the social web, participatory design approach could be utilized, for instance, when citizens and administrators have a shared web space and social web technologies for cooperation and communication are utilized to enable personalized services for the citizens.[30] This, of course, should not be a mere formality or just a trick to try to get users more committed into using the system. In spite of some similarity in ideas behind both this type of participatory design and the social web, they have a fundamental difference. Even if participatory design enables the participation of more people, it does not really lead to distribution of power, but the primary designer still is the one who drives the process. In the social web, users are not only subjects who provide data, but they are actually helping to drive content development and thus implicitly also systems development.

The form of participatory design that has become more prevalent is to invite user representatives to participate in design workshops during the various stages in the software development process. This is related with user-centered, or human-centered, design, in which the focus of the designer is on the experience of the user rather than the technical construct *per se*. For years, Terry Winograd has advocated for software design to start truly from the human-centered viewpoint and use iteration as a way to match the software to the people as opposed to starting from requirements specifications viewpoint and then engineering the solution. With traditional software, one could test it on a few representative users and then put it out into the world. Changing it required a new release, which in most cases was long after the original one. Today, the web makes iteration extremely effective for many kinds of software and the full user base may participate instead of just user representatives. A web service such as Google may be different from one day to the next without the user noticing anything about it. With web-based applications, as soon as one changes it, the world is using the newest version. There is no separate distribution process. The other advantage is the data immediately being available after iteration. Practically any web-based service can log what people are actually doing, producing tremendous quantities of information as opposed to what one would see in a small test. Quick responsiveness to user desires has become vital in modern web development. The University of Auckland researchers, Shahper Vodanovich, David Sundaram and Michael Myers, expect that the underlying assumption that users always resist technology, and resist a change, is disappearing with the generation of digital natives. The potential impact of this, of course, on the paradigms of computer science is huge.[31]

The web also dominates current software development to the extent that a majority of traditional information systems are being "webized" so that they can be used via web interfaces, and this holds true even with many legacy systems.[32] Web-based services have become much easier to use over time and people are now much more familiar with how the web-based services work. The web has in itself become a user interface metaphor. The web has also radically changed the revenue streams and business models of software companies. A big change has been moving away from the user pay model. A few years ago, the way these companies made money was by selling software, but Google and Facebook do not sell software nor do many other software companies. Advertising has become an essential part of many viable new business models. Revenue models that are very different from the shrinkwrap package sales in the business realm have made a big difference in the way how business is conducted.

A less visible part of the changing scenery in how software is being developed is the slowly raising awareness by software designers to the issue of social responsibility. Researchers and software designers should indeed consider more deeply about the potential range of uses for technologies and applications they are developing. This is particularly important for web developers due to the vast reach and influence their designs may have. In the future, the need to pay attention to social responsibility is likely to be even greater. Social responsibility entails also the opportunities of computing for doing good, such as environmental awareness, persuading for adopting healthier lifestyles, and promoting employment in developing countries. For instance, the low-cost employment aspect is present in MobileWorks.com, a service which distributes assisting global business tasks to be completed exclusively by workers on mobile devices in India, Pakistan and other similar less developed countries.[33] But as with most inventions, web products can be used also for malicious purposes. Terry Winograd provides an example of careful consideration of social responsibility:

> It's very easy to say "oh, I would never do anything bad. I'm building a system which could have negative effects, but I would never let it." And to realize that's not your ability. Once I've built it, if I don't own it, I cannot control who's going to use it for what. So, then I have to take a step back and say "Well, are the uses of it so much biased towards the negative that it's better not to be built." Or as it is with most things, does it have some good and some bad uses. Then it's not a clear answer is it better to be built or not. The question here is really to get people thinking, to get the computer scientists thinking in an aware way.

A similar transition occurred in the early 1980s. Technical understanding of computers in society at large was very poor. The small number of people who actually had an understanding of what computers could do resided in the universities, research labs and similar settings. Winograd and his colleagues felt that they had a responsibility as people knowledgeable in the field to make sure that the public debate included realistic understanding of the limitations of computers. In 1981, a discussion group was founded on a computer message system at the Xerox Palo Alto Research Center, and two years later, in 1983, a non-profit organization called Computer Professionals for Social Responsibility (CPSR) was registered.[34] It focused on the dangers created by increasing utilization of computing technology in military applications and warfare, opposing, for instance, the Strategic Defense Initiative targeted on space-based defense systems planned against strategic nuclear ballistic missiles. President Ronald Reagan had announced the initiative in March 1983, and it was widely called in the world as the "Star Wars." At the time, there was a huge oversell by the military of newly developed computer information systems. Winograd and his colleagues recognized early that privacy was a major ethical issue also for individual users, and they saw their role in that organization as providing the kind of technical knowledge to the public that would let them make better decisions on social issues such as the privacy concerns. They felt a responsibility as people who were building computer systems to worry about the ultimate uses of what they were developing.

What then does social responsibility in software design mean? Rather than being a straightforward formula determining what could or couldn't be researched or developed social responsibility is a frame of mind, which seeks detailed attention to questions that need to be asked and answered. Even if people may well come up with different answers, it is imperative that the developers of the future web carefully consider the ramifications of their designs.

As can be noticed, the social web already has caused tremendous changes in people's lives. Thanks to these changes, the emphasis on the web is now on issues that are user and socially driven and stem from society rather than technologies.

6
Six Paradoxes

Bebo White:
The web is prone to hype.

Even though there seems to be no great technical roadblocks to advancing the social web, there are still many issues that need to be recognized and resolved. Paradoxically, many of the good and worthy factors in the social web have their flip side that bring challenges or is even serious and negative. These mainly result from shifting from a virtual space into something that connects people in real life, the social web, and they relate either to what constitutes the real-world "me" or the relationship between me and "my friends" in the virtual world and vice versa. The former comprises *privacy, identity and credibility* paradoxes, and the latter is composed of *friend, filter and value* paradoxes.

Privacy paradox

Henry Chesbrough:
We need to develop a much richer understanding of privacy in this world.

The social web is about sharing, but people on the web have at the same time both the need to keep their privacy and to share information about themselves and they seem to be unsure what should and what should not be shared. This is the privacy paradox. Admittedly, challenges with security and privacy have existed ever since people started using computers, but with the social web these challenges have multiplied. Many of the modern web-based services require one to register and/or reveal different types of personal information, and the information systems also record data about user's online behavior including purchasing patterns. Moreover, because of tightly connected networks bad things may happen to a multitude of people at a glance.[1] People also rarely seem to be aware of how powerful and how pervasive the information on the web is. They may rather think paradoxically that since the information at the web is electronic, it is not going to last, whereas in reality because of web crawlers, search engines and other modern information technologies, a piece of information uploaded into the web in most cases also stays there (at least some copies of it, even if it isn't readily available for all other users all the time). Because information today is much more accessible, much more searchable, and much easier to retrieve by a vastly greater number of people than ever before, we must consider anew what is private and what is public. In doing so, the professional side has been somewhat better defined, but the personal side has still remained quite unclear.

A complicated issue related to the privacy paradox is who should be able to know about a user's behavioral patterns. Google's then-CEO Eric Schmidt stated in December 2009 that "if you have something that you don't want anyone to know, maybe you shouldn't be doing it in the first place." There emerged an intense discussion on the web with many furious commentaries on Schmidt's opinion.[2] Many were shocked, saying that there are things people want to keep private, which still does not mean that they are doing something bad. Indeed, for different reasons people might not want to express, for instance, details of their health even to their close relatives, not to mention employers or insurance companies, which might use the information in some cases against their interests. At the same time, companies in different fields spend lots of resources to analyze any user data they have access to, such as data about a user's purchases and their web navigation. There is prevalent tension between the true interests of users and companies.[3] And yet, users yearn for tailored services, which can't be provided without users revealing to service providers any information about their preferences, interests or behavioral patterns. Something with even greater concern is, however, when someone integrates data from multiple different sources and profiles a user based on that. Of course, this is nothing new in the sense that for a variety of business, political and other reasons companies and governments have been spending massive amounts of time and money to track what groups of people or even individuals think and do, but now with the available information systems, computing power and social sharing the opportunities and likelihood for getting profiled grow almost exponentially.

Location-based services have been jubileed widely, but the fact that users' location might be mapped and suddenly available to other people raises concerns. The real implications of that to ordinary people haven't really played out, but the vision could be pretty scary. People haven't quite thought through what might happen with these new types of social web services; just think of what could happen if one tweeted with geotagging and people with bad intent knew where one actually is and what they are doing. Generally, there is still immaturity in understanding how to really utilize the social web and which of its features mean for better or for worse and why. The use of many methods of inquiry such as surveillance and control has divided people, even states and countries in the past, and it keeps doing so in the social web. As human history has shown, new technologies are often misused, and thus it is worth proactively looking sensitive issues such as the privacy paradox. Ideally, of course, if designers were a little bit more thoughtful about how the technology could be misused and thus exercised more social responsibility, they might notice features to put in or other features to avoid, which are much harder to add or delete after the fact.

Some of the new operational and business models may also bring with them privacy concerns. In the early days of the web, mainstream computer scientists commonly thought that the web didn't really matter because it was not on one's own computer where one could have access to the source code. This type of thinking has changed dramatically, in particular with the issue of the cloud. Cloud computing is an important contemporary trend in computer science, which builds upon a similar idea about user-generated content and treating software as a service similarly to as the social web does. Cloud services build upon the model in which end-users do not need to use their cognitive resources to manage and configure the computing power and data storage services they are using. An increasing amount of individuals' own data and services are now located on somebody else's servers as opposed to being on their own machines. This also means that they do not know the geographical location of data or the configuration of the system that delivers the services. The increasingly interactive web has already moved towards cloud computing as a key software infrastructure, which puts additional importance and urgency for resolving the privacy and security concerns. As more web content is migrating into the cloud, challenging situations are arising. The field of software engineering should bear responsibility for resolving the technical problems related to the cloud, but the more general rules for how individual users, user organizations and service and infrastructure providers handle difficult situations should also be worked out. Sometimes documents have been revealed accidentally. In other cases, problems with data storage location or connections can cut people off from information they need. Consider Gmail, when it goes down millions of people are immediately affected and cannot get their work or other activities done. In contrast, when using a standalone email system, if one's system goes down, the user is the only one affected. Terry Winograd explains that in cloud computing there is *tighter coupling,* and whenever there is tighter coupling there is also more mess. The global financial system is an example of tight coupling where there is also more danger of a large-scale breakdown.

Many privacy issues, however, exist also with regards to the communication between regular users. Most of the time when one publishes information, he or she is choosing what will be published. It is published on the Internet, and yes it may go more broadly. Yet, one only has to worry about certain kinds of lack of judgment. Should one publish a picture of oneself goofing around, a prospective employer or client may find it, so not such a good idea at least considering future career. But what is even more important is what other people publish about you. Perhaps someone else took a picture of you fooling around and published it. Reid Hoffman explains that if somebody says on the Internet that your "company sucks," a company can deal with it. A bigger deal is the complicated notion of human relationships, because between individuals it is much harder to sort that kind of thing out. Thus, even if the free flow of information is a powerful tool to provide access to a diversity of viewpoints, to communicate ideas, and to create innovations, it may also cause many unintended consequences as its by-product.

Parents are particularly anxious about how their children could use the web and still maintain their privacy. It is important to realize that children's view of privacy in many cases differs from that of parents'. The things that they put up in their Facebook accounts may be things that parents would keep to a close circle of friends. Children may sometimes also recklessly post ill-considered comments without realizing that everything they put on the web stays there. Some might regret it later. Even with a different concept of privacy from their parents, children should be thinking about what to post and where to post. The differences between generations in treating privacy should be discussed between children and their parents, cultivating a sense of privacy. The implications of privacy settings in social networking systems such as Facebook are relatively difficult for laymen to understand. For instance, a party planned on Facebook ballooned to an unmanageable size and ran out of control in Germany when 1,500 guests showed up to a teenage girl's birthday party simply because she forgot to mark her invitation to her friends as private on Facebook. One hundred police officers, some on horseback, were needed to try to keep the herd under control. The result was that 11 people were arrested, one police officer got injured, dozens of people hurt their feet on broken glass; firemen had to extinguish two small fires; and the girl had to flee her own party.[4]

Privacy is to a great extent a matter of opinion, and it is also treated differently in different communities and countries. Yet, there is a general erosion of personal privacy in cultures all over the world. Laws and best practices for dealing with many of the questions regarding privacy of information as well as intellectual property ownership are still to a great extent unresolved.[5] Many questions remain open: How long does a picture on Facebook stay there? What if someone takes a picture of you without you knowing about it or compiles a falsified collage and places it up on the web with a caption that is untrue? How much power do you have to change a reputation acquired that way? Or, what is slander anymore? Some people seem to be obsessed with privacy issues, and to some extent that is a chimera. However, while they may be overly worried, most of the concerns about privacy and security are still real. There are plenty of examples of abuses of the web and lack of judgment coming back to haunt people, and there is anxiety about all of the opportunities for malfeasance on the web, whether they are fraudulent interactions or cyberattacks. Even though there are some technologies even within the social networking communities to deal with some of the privacy issues, the privacy paradox seems to be unavoidable and "pervasive in this world of the interconnected, always on, going forward, location-based networking and computing capabilities."[6]

Identity paradox

John Lilly:
The real weakness of the web is that identity is not very strong in it.

The social web is fundamentally about one's real identity on the web. Paradoxically one of the most severe weaknesses of the social web is that even if a person's identity is acknowledged it is not strongly represented. Users will "know" partially the person behind a web account, but in most cases they would not still really know the person in any depth. A meaningful foundation for the discourse of an individual's real life may not be apparent. In a way, this encourages indiscriminate anonymity, which all too often results in a general degradation in the quality of discourse. Of course, there are some noteworthy exceptions of this general rule. For instance, authors in the *Economist* are anonymous with few exceptions of authors of special reports, debaters and guest contributors,[7] and it still is one of the most respected magazines in the world. Yet, the identity paradox concerns social web users all over the world. The influence of the social web in our lives has gone as far as that if one does not have a profile in a particular popular social networking system, others may start to ask do they have something to hide for, which may become an issue, for instance, when others check someone's social network profile before making a decision to hire the person.

One of the key aspects of identity is anonymity, which, further, may both protect privacy and incite to violate one's privacy at the same time. Thus, the identity paradox is intertwined with privacy paradox. Because of anonymity, people are emboldened to express thoughts they would never say in direct social situations. Professor of Sociology Erving Goffman wrote about virtual and actual identity already in 1963, when he said that a discrepancy between them spoils one's social identity. He stated: "[Hence, *omission ours*] our increased willingness to chance improper behavior when wearing a mask, or when away from home; hence the willingness of some to publish revelatory material anonymously, or to make a public appearance before a small private audience, the assumption being that the disclosure will not be connected to them personally by the public at large."[8] Many such comments can be directed at individuals, and this type of "flaming" happens easily on the web, for instance, through anonymous comments on blogs. In some cases, a profile on the web may represent a person who does not even exist. Of course, this is not uncommon in traditional media either. Book authors sometimes will write under a pseudonym, and a reader may not know who the author really is. For instance, there was a mathematical series of books by someone named "Bourbaki" who did not actually exist, but rather "he" was a committee of mathematicians in France, and yet people considered him as one of the greatest mathematicians of all time.[9] Mathematician Paul Richard Halmos described the story of *Nicolas Bourbaki* in *Scientific American* in 1957:[10]

> His name is Greek, his nationality is French and his history is curious. He is one of the most influential mathematicians of the 20th century. The legends about him are many, and they are growing every day. Almost every mathematician knows a few stories about him and is likely to have made up a couple more. His works are read and extensively quoted all over the world. There are young men in Rio de Janeiro almost all of whose mathematical education was obtained from his works, and there are famous mathematicians in Berkeley and in Göttingen who think that his influence is pernicious. He has emotional partisans and vociferous detractors wherever groups of mathematicians congregate. The strangest fact about him, however, is that he doesn't exist.

But what happened with Bourbaki can go much further on the web. You can have bots, for example chat bots, which are responding to you and you may think you are talking to a real person. A eurodance musician, Basshunter, also known as Jonas Erik Altberg, made a song "Boten Anna" ("Anna the Bot," in Swedish) in 2006, which became a hit in the Nordic countries, Poland and the Netherlands. In the lyrics, a man falls in love with Anna, whom he does not recognize as a bot. What had happened in real life was that there was a bot called Anna in Altberg's IRC channel in Basshunter.se. One of his friends helped him to start the channel and told Basshunter that he would insert a bot to aid an administrator in controlling and guarding the channel against unwanted attacks. Just as he was explaining the operation, someone known as Anna showed up in the channel. Basshunter automatically assumed that it was "Anna the bot," which his friend was talking about. Two months later, he realized that this Anna actually had not been Anna the bot, but rather his friend's girlfriend. This was a humiliating experience and no doubt a good spark for creating the hit song.[11]

An area regarding the identity paradox in which extreme concerns often arise is massively multiplayer online role-playing games, ranging from playing 48-hour sessions of online games and skipping going to school or work to getting addicted to games or the Internet. Violence in such games causes special alarm, and in some cases it seems to have been a factor leading to the fine line between reality and virtual reality becoming blurred with some users, leading into tremendous trouble in their personal lives.

One of the grave attacks on one's identity is identity theft, or, for that matter, theft of reputation, and social networking sites now have become a prime target of phishing. The Anti-Phishing Working Group, founded in 2003, has adopted the task to inform public about dangers of spoofing and identity frauds. The group organizes Annual Counter-eCrime Operations Summits, and it receives strong support from web-linked industry and business, including banking and other financial institutions as well as e-commerce companies.[12] Its representatives declare that worldwide cybercrime, including identity theft, totals upwards of $1 trillion a year.[13] This huge pile of money, $1,000,000,000,000, can be understood better when compared to expenses to fight hunger and extreme poverty in the globe. The United Nations has estimated the cost of ending world hunger at about $195 billion a year.[14] Thus, in theory hunger and extreme poverty could be ended five times with the annual cost of cybercrime.

It is evident that the challenges related to identity in the social web are tricky and the identity paradox is likely to stay.

Credibility paradox

> *Judy Estrin:*
> *Anything can be made to look wonderful on the web.*

In the original web most of the information that anyone could get was either from people he or she knew personally or from people who were part of the academic, media or publishing institutions. In the social web, people communicate heavily with others who fall into neither group. They do not know them personally. They have no idea with whom they are associated, what background those people have or what they are doing in their real lives. Judy Estrin describes the ease to manufacture content that is highly misleading: "Little companies can be made to look big. Fake companies can be made to look real. Suddenly a politically motivated organization looks like a vanilla nonprofit without an agenda. People put up opinions as facts. We have to understand that maybe you can't believe everything you read." This is the credibility paradox. Thinking about credibility all too often is forgotten in everyday life, and it is easy to become misled on the web. Some user groups are especially vulnerable such as children whose judgment to estimate people's hidden motives is not yet fully developed. When users are facing a smorgasbord of information, indeed they need, in addition to understanding one's own needs and motivations, to have the ability to determine what constitutes a reliable source of information and to be prepared to look for more than one source. Criticism and value judgment must be carried each time by the user. According to source credibility theory,[15] expertise and trustworthiness of the source are the key elements contributing to someone's credibility.

Wikipedia is an example of the persuasive powers of the social web. In the early days of Wikipedia, many were doubtful that anyone would ever look at it, and some considered the idea that anybody would be able to edit entries and make material available just as "a plain stupid idea." It was generally believed that nobody would ever trust Wikipedia. Ten years later, the same people are using Wikipedia and the quality of information in many cases is very high, in particular regarding search for non-sensitive details. With regards to the credibility paradox, Wikipedia becomes inflammatory when more sensitive issues are concerned. Caution is needed even when handling top web search results. There is a general tendency to believe that the first things that come up with web searches are the most believable, which is not necessarily true at all. Even if PageRank points to a certain document, it does not necessarily mean that the link target is any more accurate than some other document. It might just mean that it is more inflammatory, being related to the link source in some emotional way and exciting users. It has a connection, but the semantics of the connection may be something totally different from what the searcher had in mind.

Generally speaking the web has managed to earn users' trust, and in many cases consumers tend to trust the web even too much. Some people simply regard statements as authoritative because they have read them on the web. It has become common that people will look up something on Wikipedia, and they think that it must be true because it's a curated social site, or the web is regarded as true simply because it is considered to be fully open and available for everybody who is able to read. Yet, almost anybody can say practically anything in the web or add whatever they like to Wikipedia, and it appears just as authoritative as real facts.[16] The notion of trusting a web site just because it looks professional is debatable. This is an old media issue in new form – being subjected to information, opinions and misinformation – and it looks like the old problem of media's authority has not changed much after all. However, the web and some of its well-known applications still have some of their technological cloak of expertise, which older technologies like clay tablet, parchment, paper, telegraph or radio lost a long time ago. Neal Sample, Vice President for Social Platforms at Yahoo!,[17] puts forward the claim that the web is actually not any worse than traditional media regarding the credibility paradox, but because of this relative newness with it "people have higher expectation[s], and those expectations aren't always met."

Maintaining credibility is equally important for companies. The information presented for users must be trustworthy, but at the same time system development and content expertise must also be conveyed for the users for them to deem the obtained information credible. One of the greatest challenges for any organization on the web is that people may at times be too suspicious – when people judge that they are not credible when they actually are – and changing this perception is extremely difficult. In many cases, small firms with smaller resources to develop and maintain their websites and services suffer from this. Also, one of the biggest business threats social networking systems face is that after gaining credibility they would lose it and they would not be able to recover from it. For instance, for Facebook being the rockstar company of the social web means that anything they do the media will acknowledge, it will get published, and there will always be somebody who complains about it. Their type of business concept is highly vulnerable since it could break down with a single but critical enough mistake. Moreover, the media, including the social web, maintains enormous power over companies no matter whether the information they reported is credible or not.

It is important to recognize two credibility related *myths*. First of these relates with the common idea that the content in the social web would be a result from everybody participating in producing it. For example, Jimmy Wales claims that "The biggest misconception most people have is this idea of Wikipedia being ten million people writing one sentence each." A glance at Wikipedia articles may show that an article has been curated or edited a thousand times, but actually two or three individuals did 500 of those edits. Jimmy Wales explains about Wikis and in particular about Wikipedia that people seem to be thinking in terms of very atomistic interactions, very small changes, somehow emerging into an encyclopedia, whereas "in fact a deeper understanding is that there is a community at Wikipedia. People know each other, doing a much more traditional dialogue than people realize, or they talk about things like reliable sources and the quality of information. They are discussing and debating the details of articles, what should be in there, which is much more of small group collaboration than a mass wisdom of crowds type phenomenon." Indeed, there aren't always many who produce the content and everyone is not an equal contributor, and in some cases it is also a few people who make it their hobby to write into Wikipedia.[18] Some of the larger ordered items that have come out of these communities are the product of micro-collaborations rather than masses of people coming together in communities. In many cases, this leads into better overall information quality and quicker processes than with all open collaborations. However, it also opens up the possibility of providing obscure or biased information via tools such as Wikipedia, which are generally peceived as open and collaborative.

The second myth is that people might think that the web is inherently open, just because that has been their experience. The reality is very far from that. Some countries limit the use of the web, and technologically this is relatively easy to do. Terry Winograd explains that "People tend to think of the web as inherently open because that's the way we've been using it, but in fact in China it's not open in the same way and it's perfectly technically feasible for them to do that." Popular services such as Facebook are not fully open, either. Mainly due to business reasons, one can't take all of their data out of Facebook and put it somewhere else in a simple and effective way. One could very laboriously reproduce it elsewhere, but one's data doesn't have any support for this kind of transferability. So due to political, business and other reasons the web by no means is inherently open. Yet, the fact that the web was and remains free and based on open standards was not a forgone conclusion. Tim Berners-Lee, the originator of the web, deserves credit for this, because he was insistent that the web should not be owned by anybody, and later the World Wide Web Consortium continued with the same ideology. Nevertheless, Terry Winograd expects that due to the low level of true authoritativeness in the web in general, new kinds of social institutions will have to emerge so that people know what they could trust and how.

Friend paradox

> *BJ Fogg:*
> *Weak ties do not make you happy. It's the quality of your strong ties that correlates with happiness. We are not necessarily on a great path from a happiness perspective.*

In the social web, there are certainly people that one knows slightly, but in point of fact one doesn't know them really. Moreover, people seem to become easily fixated on the number of "friends" they have in their social networks to the extent that the number becomes regarded as an indicator of the strength of their network, as if the number of connections is the crucial matter instead of the nature or quality of those connections. This is the friend paradox. Judy Estrin finds this as a very dangerous situation that may fool people: "Whether it's in the professional or personal world, you have a circle of friends who are really your friends. Then you have a set, next set, and then you have a set of acquaintances. But if you suddenly look to those acquaintances and you flatten it out and consider them all equal, you lose the real benefit of those connections that are really deep connections. This has both profound social implications in terms of how we grow up and how we socialize."

In reality, the number of deep connections is very limited. University College London Professor of Anthropology Robin Dunbar proposed a theoretical cognitive limit to the number of people with whom one can maintain stable social relationships in *Behavioral and Brain Sciences* in 1993, explaining that the volume of the neocortex imposes the limit on the number of deep relationships. The Dunbar number suggests that there are roughly 150 people that one can keep in his or her head.[19] The number was popularized by Malcolm Gladwell's *The Tipping Point – How Little Things Make a Big Difference*, published in 2000.[20] Following the Dunbar number, many think that people may have some 150 close acquaintances, and that number doesn't change when they go on the web. They may have 10,000 Facebook friends, but there's still a certain number that just mentally people can relate to in a more solid way. However, there are other views to this issue as well. Reid Hoffman claims that even if the web does not change the fundamental facts of how human psychology works, a kind of "prosthetic computer" such as a friends' network may allow you to stay in touch with a larger set than previously thought possible. Which of these views holds true remains to be seen in the future.

In the past, one had a good sense of the people one knew and other than that there were few people with whom one communicated. Today, people whom one never met are asking to be one's friends on Facebook, and yet even if they become someone's "Facebook friends," they rarely become one's real friends. At the time of the web service known as Friendster, it became kind of a joke that people were not really friends but rather they were "friendsters." Thus, some kind of *semi-anonymous interaction* reflects the era. People are interacting with others whom they would only know indirectly through their online personas. This also means that the social web which embraces a large number of connections may in fact be *dilutive* of real relationships. There can be friends "de jure" on social or practical grounds, but there are also friends "de facto" real friends, who have proved their position in one's life by sharing experiences to the extent that both parties trust, are fond of and wish the best for each other. What, then, makes people friends with each other? According to Tim O'Reilly, it really is the joint history that makes people friends: "If we've met twice briefly we are not friends. But when we meet a third time, a fourth time, and a fifth time, every time we get to know each other better. We might become friends. We don't say one day, 'will you be my friend?'" Furthermore, just because one can connect to someone does not mean there is a real benefit in doing so. Social web users seem to easily adopt a habit of declaring social connections on loose grounds. The entire issue of social rules online seems to be revolutionizing people's social life, and we as a society are going to have to go through a learning process with these new idioms and paradigms. The interesting question from social and psychological perspectives is whether it is good, bad, or just an interesting new fact of life. This also remains to be seen.

The dilution of real relationships may result in *lightweight keeping in touch* with one's true friends, the strong ties. Stanford-based psychologist B.J. Fogg articulates this concern regarding the social web: "It's actually hurting our strong ties. Our closest relationships are becoming weaker. Individual humans only have so much bandwidth to manage relationships. If I'm managing 800 friends on Facebook, I'm not gonna be able to manage my close relationships as well. So we're trading off, bringing weak ties closer at the expense of our strongest ties. Some of them slipping from us." The tradeoff that ends up cutting out strong ties is a cause for serious concern. What seems to loom here is a lonesome person in a multitude having many but shallow connections. This ambiguity in narrower and surface-level communication also concerns Reid Hoffman: "On the minus side, there's always a worry about do I spend a lot more time looking at my mobile phone or my computer screen when I would've made more of an effort to sit with people in real life." However, he continues stating that "but people still like this kind of interaction. We get [an] enormous endorphin and neurological rush from it."

AnnaLee Saxenian, sociology professor at the University of California Berkeley, is suspicious of the nature of the social relationships on the web, suggesting that "just like email conversations are a narrower band than a face-to-face conversation where you have the facial interaction, conversations and interaction on the web are also very narrow." Indeed, Twitter encourages one to take what they have to say and fit it into 140 characters, and in many cases compressing what one needs to say makes their message much clearer. However, one can not always express a deep comment that simply because most of the important things to deal with are much more complicated than that. Even if one would consider a discussion thread as an entity rather than a single message only, narrow forms of media still have a tendency to handle things at a surface level.

The large number of social connections, declaration of these social connections on loose grounds and compression of messages may lead to keeping in touch with people in a very superficial way, and yet even this still requires time and effort. Tim O'Reilly forecasts that the social web will keep influencing us greatly via whom we befriend and spend time with: "We have to make choices in our life about how we're gonna spend our time and who we're gonna spend it with. Some people make bad choices, some people make good choices. Technology changes us, no question, but this is not a new story."

Filter paradox

Paul Saffo:

Wikipedia is an interesting form of social media because many watch and few produce. It's sort of a throwback to the innocent early days of the World Wide Web.

The amount of information on the web has exploded. The good news about this explosion is that there are tons and tons of information. The bad news is: tons and tons of information. It doesn't necessarily mean that there is too much information available at the web about all possible imaginable issues, but rather there is too little filtering and in particular too little ability to distinguish meaningful information. This is a flipside of the fact that everybody can put material on the web. This results into tremendous fluidity of connection.

As shown by Jeff Conklin in his seminal article at *IEEE Computer* in 1987,[21] the fact that the users of hypertextual information have to pay a lot of attention to follow the many branches of information leads into struggling under cognitive overload and a great need for tools to ease their situation in this. As a result, funneling and filtering information and verifying and securing its relevancy have become a space for new business. Thus, the challenge is how one can aptly and effectively filter out irrelevant information. Paradoxically, one of the promises of the social web is that it can ease a user's information bloat and cognitive overload through social filtering, that is filtering out irrelevant information via social connections, while the social web at the same time directly adds to the information explosion.

What has recently happened is that many people rarely go to sites offered by news companies anymore, but they rather go to Google news and other similar services which act as their filter. There has also been a major shift in time spent from watching television to being online (of course, much of TV is available online, too).[22] Many people would rather go to their mobile phones or computers and make use of applications which help them interact with others. That is part of the social web's effect. Most importantly, people look at their accounts in social media systems and say, "Oh, so-and-so links to this, let me do it, too," or they follow someone whom they consider to be an expert over a specific topic. Thus, their "friends," "tweeters," or others in their social network are the ones who are bringing them the information via newsfeeds, tweets or other means, act as their personal and trusted sources of information. Thus, people use their own networks as a trust filtration device.[23] More generally, the emergence of social filtering has changed the way news is perceived. Each link or recommendation received carries additional meaning through the person recommending it and through his or her relationship to the receiver. Because of these social meanings one may end up reading stories that they otherwise would not read. Whether good or bad, but one may even start wondering why a close friend is sharing a particular piece of information; did they perhaps encounter it personally in some way? Thus, in the social web, really interesting information to an increasing extent is coming through one's own social filters.

In best cases, the filtering of information based on one's own social graph may help find suitable information, and it may be a very effective tool to manage the burden of information overload. However, in spite of its promise, social filtering may add cognitive overhead when one starts following many more acquaintances than one really can. It may be very difficult to get rid of meaningless connections in social networking systems. In real life one doesn't normally "unfriend" with people, but in Facebook one may have to do so. Further, accepting too many Facebook friends, for instance, may lead to filtering out some of the true friends, either because some of the "Facebook friends" overwhelm with lots of low-quality web content, or because some of the true friends are not active on the web. Of course, those who rely on social filtering only may limit themselves into certain types of information only.

One of the positive sides of the social web is that everybody can find or create one's own habitat. However, there's also the bad side of it like we see with extreme occasions such as the school shootings when those youngsters who have a distorted psyche find similar others and they reinforce each other. This happens surreptitiously when having these similars as one's gatekeepers; the information they end up getting is strongly biased and in reality restricted (even if they may think it is not). Then one "gets filtered" through one's own gatekeepers and social search. It may happen easily that the social web becomes one's key information channel, a gate to the world. However, this also means that one gives power and influence over one's own life to his or her friends and in this manner limits one's view to the world.

The networks can indeed reinforce tendencies, whether in good or bad, and sometimes even stunning observations can be made of what people are not aware of. Let's think, for example, about "anime otaku," or extreme fans of anime, animation originating in Japan, the popularity of which exploded on a global scale in the 1990s.[24] The parallel interest expressed by otakus in their chats and the social web further strengthens their commitment to anime and manga. But otakus do not bridge to other communities much other than with j(apan)-rockers or cosplayers, some of whom would like to keep their specialized community apart from the greater community. This is an example of the issue of *echo*, which means that there are likeminded people in the network only, or at least that there are very few others and people circulate the same information over and over again. This can also lead to modern tribalism – *eTribalism*. Whereas the general expansion of the social web incorporates many voices and the potential for discovering new information, pitfalls include the possibility that everyone will find a community of exclusively likeminded people and will not bridge.[25]

Echoing may even become a springboard for the formation of *web mobs*. Historically, groups have sometimes turned into mobs when they have lacked diversity and independence; when individual people did not feel being responsible for their behavior when they were part of group acting in the same way; some ideas have even ended up with total madness as in the case of massacres in wars. According to Mark Granovetter, a "mob" is a product of a complicated process, in which there are instigators for a certain action; most people are in the middle of the group, and even if most people will join the mob, there are principled people who will never riot.[26] Similar phenomena, web mobs, could happen in the social web too, with people accepting ideas from instigators and acting similarly to their peers, without feeling responsibility of their own behavior as part of a group. In this era of extraordinary opportunities for people to collaborate with each other, a challenge is the issue of cloistered communities in collision. According to Paul Saffo, an example of such a situation is when extremist or fundamentalist groups that have more or less happily lived in their own closed communities in their own bubble suddenly bump against each other on the web with conflicting values. Indeed, there are many issues related to the filter paradox that still need to be worked out.

Value paradox

Paul Saffo:
The biggest risk is that we amuse ourselves to death.

Users always want to obtain value (of some type) from using any information system.[27] The promise of the social web is big: For companies, the social web is fertile for innovation; individuals may get support for maintaining one's social connections, access to diversity of viewpoints and increase capacity to communicate ideas. Yet, one often gets very little true personal value from using the social web, at least when the time used in it is considered as a part of the equation. There is a strong demographic stratification to services like Twitter so that the younger one is, the more likely they are to spend their day tweeting. Sociologist Mark Granovetter speculates that for people to find the time for so much activity, they are at least partly multitasking or they must be filling in pieces of time during which they would have been daydreaming. Many consider digital natives to be more affluent with multitasking than digital immigrants, which may bring them extra value. However, the danger in multitasking is that it can lead people to distract themselves and run around with unimportant things instead of holding close to the permanent things, which are vitally important in this age of vast change.

Another issue related to the value paradox is what we call *web pollution*, man-made, even if perhaps automated, "waste," which contaminates the web environment. Having tons of information available does not mean that all or even most of that information would be really valuable. To an ever-growing extent, there is much material on the web that makes no sense and that is really not useful for anything good. In some cases, waste may have some kind of instrumental value for the polluter, but it does not render value but rather causes instability, disorder, harm or discomfort to the person whose web environment becomes polluted. Software support to filter out web pollution and to associate meaningful pieces of information with one's true values becomes more important day by day.

One may also end up becoming a web polluter oneself. Social web applications can be used to publicize inane and inconsequential information that produce frustrating information overflow for others, such as "Hi, I just finished eating a bowl of brans" or, "Oh, I'm cutting my fingernails." We may be, or at least think we are, learning things from people or sharing things with people we normally would never have communicated before, but we should also ponder whether this part of the phenomenon means that we are actually talking to ourselves rather than to other people or for social reasons. This kind of talking aloud pollutes the social web by obscuring the information people actually want to get from it.

Unessential information flow is not the only problem. Oftentimes blusters of the day are found in the web to storm and rage, but ranting is not limited to some extremist web pages. The tone of many blogs, even well-respected ones, can be dubious if posts have not been carefully thought through before they are presented to the public. There are some really good blogs out there, but there is also a lot of garbage, and yet even some of the best bloggers are ranting in some ways. This flatness poses a challenge, because it can be difficult to recognize the really meaningful blogs from the rubbish.

One more issue related with value paradox is that of web skills. Once people have deliberate access to the social web, they may start reaping the benefits from it, but getting value out of the social web requires skills. Evaluating source credibility, paying bills, doing homework, and applying for a job all require web skills. In practice, web skills are being required of everyone, even from the elderly, the golden aged digital immigrants, and yet people rarely are in a position to master all those web skills that they would need, but they are lacking behind in skill level. This also implies that we as a society are becoming more dependent on the web. The excessive supply from which people can appease their curiosity and easily find things in which they are interested at the web, to which many are already accustomed, reveals the society's strong dependence on the web, and this dependence can become a weakness in an interference or fault situation as demonstrated in the case of Hurricane Katrina. Once the network or power is down, some people say that they easily start to feel completely useless when they do not have their computer and network available. In worst scenario this may lead into Internet addiction disorder,[28] which has received a growing amount of attention since the latter part of 1990s. Even though researchers do not agree about a formal diagnosis or treatments, subjective "withdrawal symptoms" are very real to those people who suffer from it. Regarding value paradox and web skills, it should also be noted that technology may close gaps for those who use it but create gaps between those people who use the technologies and those who do not. For people that have initiative or motivation, the world is opening up in ways that it could not have before; their views and expertise can be made to complement or perhaps even to augment each other. Passive users perhaps may be consuming more information but in reality end up considering less option than before.[29]

The value paradox is also related with the filtering and identity paradoxes. The social web's tendency to encourage focusing on surface-level activities and connections rather than those that have a high priority in one's life, and it becoming a tool for boosting one's identity or it even starting to be the defining factor for one's identity, may end up twisting one's true identity.[30] Paradoxically, people may live in an *illusion of individualism*, being busy expressing themselves in the social web and thinking that they have a listening audience, while in reality they are just part of a profiled group in a massive web service based on social filtering with little or no true audience.

Finally, regarding the value paradox, even though many experts consider the overwhelming supply of entertainment as a strength of the present web, futurologist Paul Saffo is concerned about the ever-increasing role of entertainment in our society, and he caricatures that the biggest risk is that we amuse ourselves to death.[31] Amusements do not contribute much to work or resolving global challenges after all.

Part III

Social Web as an Innovation Accelerator

7
The Quest for Zero-to-One Innovation

Paul Saffo:
The biggest opportunity [for the social web] is to create new vehicles for invention and innovation.... The web accelerates the velocity of innovation.

Caterina Fake:
There are many uses [for the web] that nobody's thought of yet. There are still infinite possibilities for innovation as well. I don't know as if you can use the Internet in a wrong way or have a wrong idea of what is it.

Innovations are conglomerates of individual innovators' personal creativity, collaborative brainstorming, business sense and technological opportunities. They may come from people being in the right positions at the right time or from a prolonged passion for technological development or business activity. Thus, innovation creation could be achieved through different ways. Furthermore, innovation is more than invention in that it also requires the right timing to be successful, causing a desired change in target audience, and it often takes many great inventions to get to a good innovation. Innovations are often thought of as being the same as technologies, but innovations do not necessarily have to have a technology component within them. For example, one can innovate in business, delivery, organizational, or marketing models, or in terms of ease of use or usefulness. Many also equate innovation with business or entrepreneurship, but actually one can be an innovator also without achieving any business success by oneself.

Two main types of innovations exist: incremental innovations and Zero-to-One innovations. Incremental innovations provide gradual betterment or next generation of products or services, whereas Zero-to-One innovations have the capability to create something new, breakthroughs, that can disrupt the existing markets. Companies may naturally target a variety of innovations in different contexts, and for this reason they need to consider an innovation portfolio and to define how much they want to invest in different timeframes. Planning horizons for different kinds of innovations vary. Incremental innovation keeps current products competitive or aims at leapfrogging competitors, whereas future growth aims at new markets and it usually doesn't have anything to do with current products.

Judy Estrin, a serial entrepreneur and CTO of Cisco Systems, emphasizes that if a business is looking for incremental innovation, there is a narrower form of questioning, collaboration, risk and time horizon of patience, whereas when one is looking for a Zero-to-One innovation, there are broader questions, more open fields, more patience, and more risk.

In all innovation, a genuine need or a genuine problem always has to be recognized and staying close to customers may help doing so. The social web helps incremental innovation in that by being close to their customers companies can better understand customer behavior, needs and wants. Judy Estrin suggests that the ideas for gradual betterment and next-generation planning can come almost from anywhere, most often from the customers: "You want to be very tightly connected with your customer and those requirements and the people working in the mainstream businesses. Like factory farms, where you're trying to mass produce, no defects, just keep making it better and better." For future growth, however, the primary focus is the capability to generate Zero-to-One innovations.

Large and small companies, entrepreneurs of all kinds and others spend a lot of time to think about how to create Zero-to-One innovations, and there is great interest at the research funding agencies around the world as well. For instance, the National Science Foundation in the United States has the Science of Science and Innovation Policy program trying to make a scientific approach for studying how innovation happens.[1] The biggest business opportunity for social web innovation is when a company, whether big or small, is able to develop a novel product or service that can shake the existing markets, however, these novelties are also hardest to develop.

Disrupting existing markets

> *Reid Hoffman:*
> *Once you've got a version 3.0 product, you'll listen to your customers a lot. That's much easier, but the big ones like the one to two and the zero to one innovations are very hard.*

There are many successful businesses that are not particularly innovative. Companies in different business domains may well be successful just as long as they are able to find a good team and execute their business plan. Serial entrepreneurs often repeat what they did in their first company; if it succeeded the first time, they repeat the same business model or the same kind of a product in the second company. There can also be "me-too products," which are just copies of existing ones and which still are very successful. But if one wants to make something new, figure things out that don't exist, that's the fun part. And many people want to innovate; that is the reason why they get up in the morning. A special aspect of innovation relating to the social web is that it is possible to start revolutionizing and disrupting technologies that are relatively young. In most industries, this cycle is much longer. The car industry may be revolutionized, say, on a 50 year scale, but the Internet industry on a 10 year scale or even shorter.

According to Ben Shneiderman, also Zero-to-One innovations can come from working closely with customers: "The good companies have a close connection with their customers and they will get many requests from their customers. It's quite appropriate that a company should invest the majority of its resources on the requests from their customers, because it's a direct benefit, it's short-term, the payoff is high. But every so often a customer comes up with a problem that's a little different or a researcher has a new solution to an old problem. That may produce some very interesting breakthroughs that lead to other places." Yet, Judy Estrin warns that "if all you do was listen to your customer, you will only get incremental innovation. Breakthrough comes from understanding [customer input], but then deviating from [it]."

Some companies have decided to let customers "vote" over their product planning. However, this approach does not directly help to generate Zero-to-One innovations. Voting, of course, is fine in terms of obtaining information from customers to understand the general opinion, but for the most part people only can respond based on their needs at a specific moment and they don't have an idea what might happen in the future or which are the directions where new technology could go. For this reason, companies should not be making strategic or policy decisions in a vacuum only based on customer opinions. If a company wants Zero-to-One innovation, it has to be able to come up with ideas that will become possible in the near future and then get people to spark their imaginations. Most innovations come when people think out of standardized path. Zero-to-One innovations often originate either from scientific breakthroughs or technologically driven developments, which are independent of the company's daily operations. These kinds of breakthroughs typically result from a company's long-term basic research or from some larger endeavor by a related research community, and they require sufficient and broad investment in research and development activities.

Admittedly, it looks like some companies have the rare capability to produce Zero-to-One innovations through their operative business processes, R&D activity, and the social reach they have via their customers. However, Reid Hoffman explains why operative businesses in reality rarely are able to produce Zero-to-One innovations: "Most companies suck in innovation. Negative, not zero, terrible. The problem that they have is, once you have customers and a deployed product, a lot of the times the people in charge of that are really incented to do asset management. Grow this thing that you have, make it a little better, make some more money of it, get some more customers to use it. They're not incented to take big risks with it. So only if it went to zero that's a serious problem." This way of thinking about innovation still dominates businesses, reflecting also the training the managers have received. They think about innovation as if it were stock portfolio management rather than thinking of themselves as entrepreneurs. A person investing in the stock market may invest relatively safely in hundreds of different companies, but an entrepreneur is like a person investing in one company and investing when it's unproven whether the idea will work or not. Thus, being able to produce Zero-to-One innovation requires much more than smooth regular business operations.

Designing a product or service from its very beginning with the aim at a breakthrough means a very high risk for failure, and many companies choose not to pursue these. The pattern of some big companies is that they don't do the Zero-to-One innovation but rather let others do it and they simply buy it; when the developers of these start becoming a more mature, interesting company, big companies buy them and integrate them in. Of course, when it becomes evident that the new approach really is viable, there will be many large companies competing about it. Nevertheless, this risk-avoiding behavior in larger companies leaves much space for small nimble companies to develop products that can be plugged into larger companies.

Traditionally, innovations have been mostly considered as a technological issue and for the most part to originate from technical experts. Real techies may indeed understand well the opportunities that technology enables, but at the same time their thinking is often severely constrained. The starting point for social web innovation is short if technological opportunities rule one's thinking to the extent that one is not really able to think without considering technology first. According to Bebo White, the real innovations do not come from technologists, but rather from people who have a vision of how the technology can be used to make their lives better. According to Judy Estrin, the most thrilling type of innovation is "orthogonal" innovation, which is disruptive as well, but not a breakthrough from a technology perspective; rather it means using existing technologies in new ways.[2]

Another pitfall is to think that simply bringing together people from different backgrounds would be enough to foster social web innovations. Yet, sociologist Mark Granovetter states that multidisciplinary research rarely works out due to the simple fact that these people do not have a common vocabulary. That being said, there must be something extraordinary in those research laboratories, such as Bell Labs and PARC, which have been capable of producing breakthroughs via assembling teams of people from different disciplinary backgrounds. Somehow they have mastered getting people with very different ways of thinking to work together on a problem rather than discuss about the problem only. Indeed, the key to making these groups not waste their time has been to focus on multidisciplinary problem-solving rather than trying to create multidisciplinary research projects, workforces, or discussion groups. To be able to do this, actual work environments need to be structured so that they create significant interactions between people who have vastly different disciplines. This cross-fertilization is a major factor for innovation, and the social web can be a major player in it.

The challenge for the social web in this regard is that much of organizational knowledge is in peoples' minds. A lot of the communication that allows people to talk across paradigms involves tacit knowledge rather than explicit knowledge, which in most cases is much harder to communicate through the social web than convey for example in face-to-face situations.[3] But technological tools for knowledge sharing are making innovation processes more efficient than it has been in the past, and the social web's potential to ultimately support both problem-solving and idea generation has become essential for innovation. For instance, through an internal wiki someone who is working in a large company could ideally find another employee in a different division of the company who has a similar task, researching similar things and working on similar concepts. When they find each other and start collaborating, they may become more effective, whereas before they were duplicating each other's efforts. In practice, these kinds of things happen all the time in organizations, when workmates find each other in new ways in a professional sense through the social web.

Even if a company could come up with something really new, they still have many barriers to overcome before making it into a successful business. Intriguingly, large companies often face with special challenges in their search for social web innovation, because their previously successful businesses may inhibit innovation.

Challenge of large companies

> *Reid Hoffman:*
> *The "how do companies manage innovation processes?" [is] very much of a problem. It's unknown.*
>
> *Terry Winograd:*
> *Big companies are not doing a bad job. It's just very hard within the structure of a big company to have the kind of initiative that you get with independent companies.*

It would be tempting to think that innovations still would take place, as Schumpeter suggested, mostly in large companies thanks to their vast resources. Yes, large companies do have their own undeniable strengths such as a multitude of users readily available. For instance, think about launching a product at a company, which may immediately have 10 million, 100 million, or 500 million users. What these kinds of companies can do is to send a prototype or a new version of a product to a small percentage of customers and that product will probably be adopted into use just because those people already are their customers.[4] The flip side of the coin is that no one would know if their product succeeded on its own merits or if it succeeded because the company had pointed millions of users to it. As a result, the company would not know whether the product would fail eventually because it actually isn't satisfying any user needs. Thus, a huge user base makes testing of ideas and iteration much easier, but in order not to get quasi-innovations, innovations should at least ideally rise and fall on their own merits.

Innovations can happen within large companies, small startups or even outside of any business context. Large companies do face special challenges, however. The web has changed the way how companies both large and small should innovate, and yet many companies have been in denial. B.J. Fogg explains that old name brands are actually having a really hard time with the social web: "They don't know how to do it. From the early days of Facebook applications, looking at the top 50 applications, not a single one was from a major brand. Knowing how to innovate in the social web is really different than what brands used to do." True, it may be easier to still think about how to do old broadcast, say, a TV advertising campaign, since they know it well, however, in the social web the same approach is not going to work anymore, because there friends are inspired by friends and social filtering dominates sense-making efforts. This kind of a new operational environment may even appear unpleasant and risky to traditionally established companies. Jimmy Wales comments along the same lines with some critique on the capabilities of big companies, including large web-focused companies, to understand social web innovation: "Google is all about algorithms. In fact, as a brilliant company not everything but almost that they've attempted to do that has a social component has failed – because it's just not in their DNA. They have really smart people there, but they just don't do social very well. Then we have Flickr, Wikia, and Wikipedia, which is really all about the social. There is very little algorithm involved in it. So for Wikipedia it's this huge enormous thing, and there's almost no algorithmic stuff going on at all." Ideally, to understand social web innovation, the size of the company doesn't matter, but in reality should it matter, the smaller and nimbler is better, because large organizations have a lot of organizational inertia in them.

In all big companies, including those that have been successful on the web, it is hard to get things from drawing board into production and then into the real world. When Yahoo! had bought Flickr, Yahoo! still was just a ten-year-old company and more importantly it was a web company, but it already had difficulties getting products shipped out the door.[5] Traditionally, one of the greatest barriers for Zero-to-One innovation in large companies has been between what designers think up and what the company is actually putting out as in real products. Yet, quite likely there are plenty of people with brilliant ideas in any given large company, but it is the processes inside the organizations that are blocking people from refining their ideas. Something like YouTube was probably ideated internally in many companies several times before YouTube launched. The breakthroughs are not missed because nobody thought of them, but rather they are missed because the structure of the company was not set up in such a way that those ideas had a change to emerge. The obstacle is related with the organizational structure more than anything, and the businesses often end up *preventing innovation* when in their daily operations they want to assure uniformity and quality. All too often the managers and other executives do not feel comfortable with new ideas, because these may threaten the company's daily operations. If a company wanted to develop innovations internally, it would have to invest remarkably in R&D and give the R&D employees full or relatively high independence of regular business operations. All large companies, no matter of the age or business field, face this challenge.

The innovator's dilemma, defined and made well-known by Clayton Christensen, Professor of Business Administration at Harvard University, suggests that a company may be busy in feeding the cash cow to the extent that it can't grow any cash calves.[6] New products and services can't be shipped out the door, because they are competing for resources with the older, established products or services that are taking up all the oxygen in the room. Allocation committees determine who gets funded, and one has to compete with someone else's proposal to get funded. Rational decision-making becomes embedded in social structure. Too often companies are locked in their core businesses in such a way that they can't really come up with any Zero-to-One innovation. The innovator's dilemma is likely to remain as a key challenge for managing the innovation portfolios in large companies also in the future.

A challenge in large companies, however, is still that all too often managers and other responsible people are not personally really interested in doing something truly new. In the case of the social web, this implies that those who are most interested in applying the social web for organizational uses often are web designers, software programmers or researchers, who have realized that there is a problem in their company when markets are moving in one direction and their company is going in another direction. They understand that the company needs to change its direction to get on the train, but they do not have the organizational status and responsibility to drive efforts in their organization. In some cases, employees in a company know well what they should be doing, but they still have to bring an outside consultant with a brand name and a little more influence to make things happen. They have to get "an excuse" for allowing people to innovate.

Another risk the large, established companies, such as Coca Cola or Honda, have in addition to innovator's dilemma is a brand risk. They always have to consider the possible effect on the brand of how they act; if they make a new type of trendy application and it totally fails, that would mean they would look foolish. This is a legitimate concern, because brand is most valuable for these companies and they do not want to damage it. Companies that do not have so great brands can accept greater risk and failure in this regard and most social web companies thus can take much more risk. There are of course many ways to guard the brand as such, but what the companies can do in the social web innovation sphere is they can invest in a partnership with small companies, they can sponsor and inspire workshops or they can encourage innovation that is not necessarily attached to their brand. By doing so, they may have a joint interest or ownership stake when the innovation takes off. They can also buy a company that is already succeeding and plug it into their company. By doing so, they are buying a process, team, an installed user base or perhaps just removing a competitor.

Quite surprisingly, all too often many big companies don't take the long view into innovations. According to Caterina Fake, they don't have the stamina to see a product through its whole life cycle and whether or not it succeeds; instead, they pull the plug on things after a year. No start-up would act similarly. A start-up might run out of money, but they wouldn't call it quits and say they failed very hastily. They would think that maybe the ideas just haven't found its audience yet, or they would try new things. For instance, Twitter languished for three years, and only after that experienced a boom. Mozilla Firefox was floundering for years, too, before it broke out. An opposite instance is Jaiku, which was released in July 2006 and sold to Google in October 2007. *MacLife* praised it in its October 2007 issue, saying that Jaiku was a microblogging service that went beyond Twitter.[7] Jaiku was a forerunner at the time, and it would have needed more time like Twitter did to make it as huge a success, but for one reason or another Google focused on other things and didn't let it flourish. In venture funding a major risk, whether related to startups or big companies, is that venture capitalists are often the most impatient of all stakeholders – but luckily not always. An example from the pre-Flickr era is Game Never Ending; should the Game Never Ending have been shut down, there would be no Flickr as such. It is the same story with Blogger; its developers actually were building Pyra, collaborative project management software, whereas Blogger was a side project for them to communicate with each other on their project management software.[8] The company ran out of money, and if the venture funding hadn't continued or had they kept working only on their project management software, then there would be no Blogger as we know it.

False negative error

Henry Chesbrough:
One of the biggest challenges in innovation today is the technologies that don't fit the businesses, but might have tremendous value in some other area.

Mårten Mickos:
You never know who will be able to innovate and make use of innovations.

A key question in the new innovation economy is what kind of company is able to adopt new technologies quickly for their business advantage, and what kind of company is able to develop these technologies and how. According to Mårten Mickos, CEO of MySQL, betting on who will be the winner is one of the great mysteries of business and nobody will be able to know this in advance: "You never know who will be able to innovate and make use of innovations. It would be boring if we knew. But there are no obvious answers. It's good news for all entrepreneurs. It means no matter how powerful and mighty your competitors are, if they are managing that process properly you can run faster and you can win. It's a very healthy thing." Just consider Amazon and their successful cloud offering. Before they started doing this very few would have guessed that Amazon would be able to produce a cloud service of the type they are. People knew them as booksellers, yet they managed to create a new thing like that. At the same time there were other vendors, who should have been the obvious producers of clouds and yet they weren't able to do it.

Innovation researcher Henry Chesbrough warns companies about mistakes in evaluating the business potential of a new information technology, in particular false positive and false negative errors. If a new innovation fits with the existing business, it is probably going to be well executed by the company that created it. A false positive error takes place when the company thinks that it will fit in their business model and it is successful when screening and evaluating it at the checkpoints, but when they take it into the marketplace it fails; it is false positive because it looked positive, and it still turned out to be negative. In general, companies spend a lot of resources and they have many processes and approaches to minimize the consequences from false positive errors. The more challenging situation, however, is with innovations that don't fit with the existing business – the false negative error. Evaluation may provide a falsely reassuring message to innovators that there is no business opportunity, when there actually is. Henry Chesbrough explains the nature of this false negative error:

> What most companies don't have is processes to manage false negative evaluation errors; projects that don't fit the existing businesses and therefore don't look very promising. If you had a way to explore alternative business models for these technologies, some of them might actually turn out to be quite valuable. The Xerox technologies are sort of exhibit A of this. Ethernet, Adobe and PostScript technologies, Documentum and others, these are all projects that started in the internal laboratories of Xerox, all got evaluated internally, all had the internal funding stopped, went outside, were able to find external financing to continue, but the business model no longer was constrained by the copier and printer business. Now the business model was free to evolve in ways that might really maximize the value of the technology.

In his interesting article, Tim Wu analyzed the centralized innovation practices of the Bell Labs.[9] The employees in the early Bell Labs were left with a lot of freedom to pursue what interested them, and this lead to winning several Nobel prizes by the employees of the company. But the lab was still different than research universities; when the interests of its mother company, AT&T, were at odds with the work carried out at the laboratory, the mother company dictated. The flip side of this was that some great inventions remained unutilized. For instance, the first telephone answering machine based on magnetic recording tapes was invented by Clarence Hickman as early as in 1935, but it would not appear in mass markets in the United States before the 1980s, and even then it was not because of Hickman's invention, but because of another invention made later in Germany. This exemplifies false negative error. AT&T believed that magnetic tape and the telephone did not have much to do with each other, or perhaps even worse that they were simply incompatible with each other. In their evaluation, there was no enough interesting business opportunity there. What they saw was only that magnetic recording would change the nature of telephone conversations, restricting the telephone usage. Of course, this does not diminish the great value of work carried out over the years at Bell Labs, but it shows how false negative errors work. Bell Labs couldn't disrupt the markets, when its mother company, the giant AT&T, almost in a monopoly business situation, could not see the business opportunity.

Another example of false negative error is the world-class industrial research laboratory of Xerox PARC, which in its day in its chosen areas with some of the very best researchers in the world was doing wonderful technological breakthroughs in man-machine interfaces and designing new architectures for how people could interact with and master the capabilities of computing without having to learn arcane computer languages. And yet this tremendous wellspring of technological potential was housed in a company that made copiers and printers. Xerox was good at finding technologies in its laboratories that helped them sell more copiers and more printers, and it did not have a problem in recognizing innovations that fit their existing business. Xerox's problem was the technologies that don't fit the businesses but which might have tremendous value in some other area. These things in Xerox that ultimately found a different path into the market had to leave Xerox in order to become valuable.[10]

Of course, evaluating technologies is not black-and-white, but rather a technology that can look attractive to one company may look unattractive to the other. Let's consider the cloud, for an example. Businesses that have been making a lot of money for Microsoft include the best-seller operating system Windows, the Office package, as well as the video game console Xbox 360.[11] Microsoft Research is one of the largest software research laboratories in the world with a multitude of talented researchers and lots of resources, and it seems to be doing a great job of looking through its deep technical laboratory for projects that fits in existing businesses. But the false negative error, the innovations that they come up with that don't help existing businesses, is a great challenge and cloud computing is a prime example of this. Microsoft's money-making businesses don't map very well to the cloud; Xbox does as regards multiplayer online gaming, but the other ones have the legacy infrastructure and installed base to bring along which remarkably slows them down. Many of the things that Microsoft is doing will not help their money-making machine, since they have no path to the market within the company. On the contrary, Google does not need to worry about an installed base of files from years ago; they can much more simply provide a new offering. This means that Google can deploy technologies in the cloud with a clean sheet of paper, whereas Microsoft has to develop and exploit technologies in reference to their existing installed base of activities.

Insight into and expertise in the web

Terry Winograd:
They [Google] were just very good at building systems, putting them together.

John Lilly:
Once you do find a revenue stream, you really need to invest in good people in all levels.

Hector Garcia-Molina:
You need to have flexibility, freedom, and good people. That's secret sauce.

Much of expertise into information systems development and software design is about understanding design patterns, paradigms, standards and best practices, and even though some of this experience stems from practice and experience much of it can be obtained through education. Solutions for issues such as how to build a profile page and what kind of information should be in it are well known. While seeking to create Zero-to-One innovations, one can then rely on these foundational design principles and build their own contribution on top of them without reinventing something that already exists. But much of the innovation is about special insight. Google's success teaches an important lesson about that companies should *combine expertise in information systems development with the insight into user behavior.* Many of the technical tradeoffs Google's founders made when designing the company were driven by a deep understanding of web user behaviors. Terry Winograd explains how Google in an early stage understood that a fluent web service must be very fast and reliable: "You treat something very differently if it comes back before you lose attention. That turns out to be sub-second, more or less. They were the first ones to really emphasize that. They had the page rank, which meant that in general the pages were more relevant to what you wanted to find than the algorithms that the other web search engines used."

Winograd explains how his own thinking about computer science previously had started to change from technologically oriented aspects to softer user related issues: "My work with Fernando Flores [in the 1980s][12] really got me thinking in a different direction about what it meant to use technology and what it meant to build models of the mind. That was a tremendous shift in my orientation away from a kind of mechanistic way of thinking and design to a more experientially or phenomenologically oriented view. That led to the way I think about human-computer interaction, which is very different from the artificial intelligence." Shifting away from technology's dominance changed Winograd's thinking about the design process, and it became not only user-sensitive but user-centered.[13] A similar thinking has become crucial to succeed in today's social web.

Another pioneer in putting user-centered thinking into practice is David Kelley,[14] one of the founders of IDEO Product Development, a worldwide leader in the user-centered design of products and services, the whole company of which is build around a human-centered design-based approach. IDEO is a technology broker whose design solutions are used in tens of different industries, and it is often regarded as one of the most successful design firms in the world recently. David Kelley's core motto states essentially that enlightened trial and error is better than exhaustive planning by a brilliant mind. In practice, this simply means that designers don't figure it all out first, but they actually create it by learning and trying; this also implies that design as a process is actually more about articulation than engineering.[15]

An important component for companies to obtain insight into and expertise in the social web is *hiring the right people.* Ted Nelson tells a story of Datapoint Corporation,[16] which designed what we today would consider as a computer. The vision of the company and the product came from the founder, but the specifics of the computer on a chip came from a high school student who later became their engineer. The mastermind behind this technological design was Harry Pyle, who was later hired to participate in creating the ARCnet internal network,[17] as well as several other technologies. According to Ted Nelson, people who are able to repeat great innovation processes should be the ones to hire, and they should be given a job they want to do, because "if you give them [tasks that] they don't want to do, then they'll turn it into a mediocre job just like everybody else." Hiring the right people is central in the social web, because the business in it is after all about brainpower and insight, not about man-months or knob number. Even most innovative companies often have reasons to acquire expertise from outside of the company. For instance, Facebook was known to be very fast innovating by itself, but in August 2009, they still bought a company called Friendfeed. They may have done so to take competitor off the table, but they seemingly also bought a good team.

Interestingly, when somebody gets hired to a company, the organizational culture will be introduced to that person, but rarely is the expertise of that new employee made known to his or her fellow colleagues in the company. This may, in fact, remarkably slow down the new employee becoming an effective employee, often taking months before he or she is actually supposed to become productive. The social web can change this. It can provide a means of telling others in the organization about the newcomer's knowledge and expertise and at the same time sharpen also the newcomer's understanding of the meanings of the organization, and in this manner accelerate the newcomer becoming capable of contributing to the company.[18] This may remarkably quicken the innovation processes.

One practical, simple way to gain more insight is to learn from other companies. Reid Hoffman explains that he learned a number of lessons about building a successful business model and getting a product effectively distributed in this way: "I was very influenced by looking at SixDegrees.com back when I was starting SocialNet. I hadn't realized financial strategy and distribution strategy was so key. I saw SixDegrees and on Hotmail, spreading your product through the actions of millions of individuals doing things, interacting with each other was extremely interesting."

Making it over the threshold

Vint Cerf:
Innovation without adoption isn't useful.

Henry Chesbrough:
Business models are too important to be left to the business people.

Even if a company were capable of building a Zero-to-One innovation, there is still a long way to go and many barriers to break through, to get the innovation adopted into actual use by any larger audience. In fact, many companies in a new industry fail to commercialize their invention, and they may either simply vanish or be taken over and merged with other businesses. The history of the automobile is an example of this. Most big automakers are rollups of hundreds or thousands of little ones. In the early days, there were literal garage shops and people who just put together a new car. This is not very different from how the

PC industry evolved. There were people making PCs, in many cases, literally in their garages; Michael Dell and others started selling the PCs out of their dorm rooms in college. Some companies survived whereas many went out of business. The same thing happened also with software. There were thousands of small software companies; most of them got gobbled up or were put out of business. Tim O'Reilly predicts that this will happen in the social web as well: "Out of [the] PC era, we have a few giant companies. Why should web be any different? Most of the companies are going to die or be acquired. The innovation will move somewhere else. A lot of people end up with this idea that somehow there's something wrong with the model if a bunch of companies fail. That's actually how it works." The fact that many companies fail in a new innovative industry does not mean that the industry has failed. Innovation doesn't stop, even if where it takes place may change.

One of the issues to resolve is *cost-benefit tradeoff.* This includes money if users are paying for it, time and cognitive tradeoffs. It takes real effort to learn to use technologies and applications, remember them, and continue to use them, and many viable technologies never quite make it over that threshold. People easily start using a new application or service and realize a month later that they have stopped just because it was too troublesome or that it wasn't worth it for what they were getting out of it. Terry Winograd pinpoints the key design challenge: "The barrier which we as designers have to worry about is how [to] not just make it useful in principle, but make the usefulness sufficient to overcome those inertias in that sort of sense of 'what is it really worth to me?' There's a high cost to doing something new."

Another facet of the cost-benefit tradeoff is the *time to payoff.* Very often, there is an effort at the time users put the information in, but they don't get an immediate payoff for it. For one example, if software designers are asked to document their code they still don't do it, because documentation doesn't pay off while they are writing it. It pays off only later if somebody is reading it, and the benefit later may not even be to the designer but to somebody else such as another designer, or a manager in the company. In practice, most software designers will only document the rationale behind their designs if it is mandatory,[19] which shows how hard it is get users to do things when it requires real effort from them with no visible short-term payoff.

In any business, developing a viable *business model* that really works is the key to make it over the threshold. In fact, succeeding to create a new business model that works in practice may be the hardest part of all innovation. Even Google has been criticized for not being able to monetize YouTube sufficiently.[20] In such situations, the practical message for start-ups, which are creating social web applications and trying to find and define new business models, is to build services that people *really* want to use. Indeed, in today's hyperactive world, we may see a whirlwind of activity and new packages, but the question is how different these packages are and what's new about them. The key is in looking at a problem differently. One should focus on the concerns that really matter and keep doing things without letup, always asking what really is the point behind the planned product or service. If the value creation in this sense is evident, one possible scenario is that the start-up may be sold even without a tested business model and plugged into another enterprise as a part of their preexisting system or business model. For instance, over the years Microsoft incorporated into their operating system many features that were once the basis of a different company. There have been all kinds that they bought, absorbed, and made part of their products and enormous profit machine, but if these were taken apart the bought companies would not be very successful. The same phenomenon likely will happen with many of the technologies, platforms, and applications of the social web as well. Nevertheless, early thinking about a viable business model will help most social web companies to bring their offering forward.

In large companies, one of the most difficult challenges related to success in getting an innovation over the threshold is not related with the competition at all, but there is the frustration from people on the technical side of the organization about it that "the business side don't see the value of what we're doing, and they never even tell us why," or that "we've worked on this project for years, it's never been shipped, we have no idea why." They may have been working on a project years earlier, but they couldn't get anybody to pay attention. Then they see something in another company that looks a lot like what they have been working at, and it's a success. This is a story that has been told dozens and dozens of times in many different versions. However, a medicine for this problem suggested by Henry Chesbrough is "to have some sense in your mind about what a business model might be for the idea that you're working on." Like any hypothesis, innovators' having an idea about a *potential business model* is something that helps focus the inquiry and gives something to anchor into and learn from. It doesn't mean that developers would lock in that suggeted model throughout the activity, but that they would be thinking about that as part of their project or more generally as part of their work. Chesbrough explains that the most fundamental reason for scientists and technologists to do that is that "it's the business model that really determines what will happen to a technology. If you leave that to the business people, then you've abdicated any control over the direction of your project." Thus, if developers, in addition to the things they always do, include an idea about how the business model might play out, ask a proper set of questions from this angle and engage with a right set of resources to test it, they will have a much better sense of how the project will play out.

Businesses have a hunger for Zero-to-One innovations because via its potential to disrupt the markets it lays a basis for success. Large companies face special challenges, however, a key challenge being the false negative error. Companies need to maintain and upgrade their insight into and expertise in the social web to expect to be successful in this unique operational environment, and yet there are still many issues related to their organizational processes to take care to get an innovation over the threshold. The Big Question that still remains for us is how to do it in the social web.

8
Social Web as an Innovation Ecosystem

Paul Saffo:
The important thing about [the] social web is that innovation doesn't occur in a vacuum.

Henry Chesbrough:
The innovation has moved from being an activity inside a single company's own four walls to more of an activity that takes place in a network of participants.

The social web is fertile for innovation, and the power of the social web lies in its networks of users and in the larger whole that the service offerings and users jointly make. Companies and organizations can use many software technologies to help shape and influence these networks, but much more than only providing those technologies is needed. This is especially so because individuals can choose which networks to participate in and how actively to participate when they do. Thus, for users to stay in a network and to contribute, they need a software environment which satisfies their needs, interests and requests. The highest payoff for a company comes if it is vital enough to create a vigorous ecosystem through which others can deploy their services to develop applications, which provides a powerful user experience and which encourages and cultivates the spirit of innovation around a software platform they provide. If a company is able to sustain such a platform, continuously provide positive user experiences and nurture a business ecosystem on top of it, it will have a very powerful position in business.

Social web as a software platform

Vint Cerf:
In the Internet, you do not need permission from others to explore.

One might easily think that web development simply equals building software applications that resolve given problems. Practical applications, of course, are always needed. Yet, the biggest business opportunity doesn't exist in developing single applications, but developing environments that enable the development of applications. To understand this, let's consider how the Internet beneath the web came about. Originally, there were a handful of people who all were working to develop algorithms for this type of communication to happen and who tried many different approaches; TCP/IP was the major step from point zero, but in reality the progress happened piece by piece. This well-known protocol received its current highly esteemed position only long after its creation, which is what often happens with innovation, namely something is understood to be an innovation only afterwards, following several stages of progress. First, someone gets an idea, then another one changes it, and the change works. One doesn't hear about all the other changes that didn't work. When this type of gradualism worked with the development of the Internet, it was because the people working on it focused on a general picture rather than a specific objective, like in a space research program, and they were able to *make individual contributions to the overall program*. The same structure was also in place at Xerox PARC in the 1970s.[1] In their case, the researchers were originally given a relatively high level of freedom to explore, to go deep into and to find where they could contribute within the overall framework in the research center.

Much of the social web innovation should similarly focus on treating the social web as a platform which makes it easy for users to innovate against what has been developed. Tim O'Reilly explains this by using the web mapping space as an example:

> If you look at Google Maps, they were not the first to have an API for developers. The Google-driven innovation was that they had an Ajax kind of interface to web mapping so that you could move it around and you had a more tactile experience with it. Hidden in that was also the fact that some hacker said, "Oh, wow we can decode this data, and we effectively have an API." And they created the first mash-ups, which was housingmaps.com. Second was chicagocrime.org, which was mapping up government crime databases onto the Chicago map. So a couple of hackers figured out that there was something you could do because of the data that Google had exposed. What Google did was brilliant. Instead of trying to shut them down, they said, "Oh, fantastic idea," and then they opened up an API, enabled it. So Google really became to the platform play in the mapping space.

The key with this kind of platform thinking is that through generating content and bending the technology, users are able to contribute to the overall innovation framework. In the case of a web platform, they are offered a means to put their ideas into practice through it rather than just use it as a communication vehicle. Internet pioneer Vint Cerf emphasizes that what is needed is "platforms that allow others to experiment in benefit." Another social web example is Google Earth, a virtual globe, map and geographical information service, on top of which people can put their own information. The central element in it is to create an infrastructure that allows people to try out new ideas and applications without having to go to the trouble of assembling complex information such as a spherical map of the Earth that are already there for them under the Google Earth rubric. And yet this was not the result of an inborn master plan; Google Earth was originally a web application, but it became a platform.

It is critical to understand that developing a platform differs from developing applications. Neal Sample, Vice President for Social Platforms at Yahoo!, describes that the key in platform development is to find the essence of user experiences, build that out as a software feature, and make that available to application developers. This process creates the building blocks, which the application developers can then assemble in their unique way. All can have the same platform features but in a different order or in a different domain. For an instance, the only big difference between various local review sites for restaurants, hotels and movies is the domain, because people are doing the same thing, commenting and rating. The platform developers will need to abstract the domain and potential applications, and try to get to building of those core functions that are needed by the application developers. Neal Sample describes the existing situation:

> Connecting to users, whether following like a one-way pointer on Twitter, two-way reciprocal connection on Facebook, or friends in Yahoo! Messenger communications, that's a social platform. That's the kind of thing that you find in all of the vertical applications as you find users connecting to other users. Sometimes it's reciprocal, sometimes it's acknowledged, sometimes it's mutual. The core platform challenge is to find what those essential core experiences are and then make those available to application developers. We find them in connections, identity, updates, vitality, or event streams, things that people are doing. We find them in several different places. As platform developer[s], what we do is we say, "Look, we're gonna build out these capabilities," such that the vertical or the application developer can come along and say "ahaa, you're providing service A, B and C that I need for my vertical experience."

A smaller profile photo or a slightly different connection graph is not a major issue at all in platform development. First and foremost it is about conceptual modeling in which the capability to see things from different viewpoints and abstraction levels becomes essential. The vision that all of the features are down in their core functionalities is required. What is also needed is disciplined software design and development, because the platform has to be robust and it has to pertain to very high usability. Whether using traditional software engineering or newer agile development approaches, the software solutions need to be carefully designed and documented. This is important because whenever a change in the software is introduced, it immediately affects the lives of a multitude of people via all the applications that utilize the platform. The users in the social web will quickly abandon a platform or an application which fails to deliver what it promises.

Application developers in the social web often face deadlines for delivering new features "within two weeks," "over this weekend" or even "later today," and the content has to keep updating and upgrading without breaks. This environment is very different from traditional hardware development, in which 18 months, in many cases, is the fastest that an idea can become anything on the shelf. The speed of development may sound like total madness also to many traditional software developers, but these super fast cycles are a hard reality in social web development efforts.[2] Moreover, with information technologies converging and the social web blending in all software and hardware, software and even hardware professionals suddenly have to learn to act in this new operational environment. This is a major challenge for many companies and individuals, and it creates opportunities but also destroys old businesses. Acting quickly is hard for any large company, because speed is not in their corporate DNA, and yet, one of the essentials for being innovative in the social web is to act and react quickly without losing accuracy. Fastness, *wiki*, is the key. Once again, providing a development platform plays a key role for being capable of achieving this rapidity. If a company is able to develop such a platform, it can innovate with rapid cycles and its customers can do the same. In some cases, their business partners or end-users can even do a significant part of the innovation for their benefit.

Practical guidelines for social web application and platform developers

1. Do not overthink
Jimmy Wales: "Avoid excessive a priori thinking. One of the things that happens to people is they try to overthink it from the beginning instead [of] just getting their hands dirty trying. You could never anticipate all the potential human problems. Sure enough, some of it happened, some of it didn't. But let's get started and we'll figure it out."

2. Deliver something small soon
Ben Shneiderman: "You may have great ideas and all kinds of visions and hopes to change the world, but to make progress you need to do something small soon. Not a great vision which never gets accomplished, but what are you going to show me in the next two weeks. That's a way of getting things done. It's a way about moving forward in life also. Don't get stuck in grand ideas but reduce to something that you can do tomorrow, somebody that you can help, some person you can help tomorrow."

3. Make it simpler
B.J. Fogg: "Make it simpler, and get it out there faster. Almost always web innovators are trying too much too soon on it. I say: Cut this, cut that, cut it down to the kernel. If the heart's not working, the arms aren't going to work anyway. You can add stuff later."

4. Revise, revise and revise
Caterina Fake: "The great thing about the web is that you can build stuff, put it online, send it out to twenty of your friends, and you get them all to use it and see if it works or not. If it fails, you take [it] down or you rewrite it. Then you do it again, and then you do it again, and then you do it again. And then day after day, you spend all of your time iterating and figuring things out as you go on."

Technologically, to develop the social web as a platform, companies will need to provide an *Application Programming Interface* for others to be able to bend what they have created. There is nothing radically new in providing APIs *per se*. Traditionally, well-established and dominating software companies have provided programming interfaces for their systems, but, in reality, their attitude often has been, "If you'd like to use our API, leave your contact information and a sales person will call you." Huge sums of money would be charged to build any ports into the system for others, which kills the spirit of openness and chokes any deeper collaboration. The partnership could have been there, but the software company didn't think that its collaborators actually could increase its cashflow or – even more importantly – help make its product better. They did not consider their software product as a platform.

Closed APIs, APIs that are open to a very limited set of participants only, do not seem to fit well with the rapid development cycles in the social web. Rather than building and providing an API for business partners only (though there may be certain situations that legitimate this), with open APIs anyone can build applications on top of it. Naturally, this means that much independence is lost since platform changes now affect so many stakeholders many of whom are unknown to the platform providers, but the opportunities for doing business multiply a thousandfold. An example of the power of open APIs is Flickr. As soon as it opened its API and started to charge for access, its business model took off. It was the opening of the API that really made Flickr what it is rather than Flickr's ideas or the implementation of photosharing.[3] In a similar manner, Facebook earned its clarified position as a leader of social networking by opening its API so that anyone could develop their own applications into the platform and by using it.

Also Yahoo! has opened up many of its APIs. Its set of technologies allows users to obtain information from Yahoo! and other data sources and mix it together on the web. Yahoo's developer platform is opened up to such an extent that a standard-based open social web application could be installed on the Yahoo! homepage. The benefit of this is that there is instantly a potential critical mass or even a huge audience, when potentially hundreds of millions of users suddenly can start using the application. In some ways, the platform is an undifferentiated canvas that says, "Look, bring your application directly to the audience."[4] Yahoo! has also opened vertical applications like email, letting people build features into it. For example, a company called Xoopit built an application that lets users see all the photos and videos attached in the email and organized them into folders so that one could browse everything that happened to be in the mailbox. Yahoo! eventually bought Xoopit.

Providing APIs outside of a company, whether fully open or just for a limited number of business partners, normally also means providing some kind of *software development kits* to promote and ease the building of applications by using the platform. Typically, such a kit is a set of development tools obtained via the web itself. These development kits may range from simple files to sophisticated hardware and software environments, containing, for example, debugging tools, technical notes, and reference designs. In some cases they may be licensed, but for an open API they should be free for all. In any case, the point behind these software development kits is always to encourage and help developers benefit from the platform.

The whole idea of the web as a platform can be taken one step further. Tim O'Reilly depicts the current era of the web as an operating system. In his view, "the systems that we're building are increasingly information subsystems of this next-generation operation system that's going to allow us to build a whole new generation of smart applications." Indeed, a platform is at least conceptually a kind of an operating system. According to O'Reilly, software engineers in general have not fully come to grips with this idea of the web as an operating system and the system services that are needed to build applications today. O'Reilly, who organized a conference already in 2001 about "Building the Internet Operating System," continues: "If one wants to build a location-based app, whose service will he call to figure out one's location? That's an operating system service. Whose speech recognition am I gonna use? That's an operating system subsystem. The competition over this is going to be to figure out who owns those subsystems, and does somebody pull them together. It's not about who writes the low-level code to a particular phone."

People generally tend to think that operating systems are something to be taken as given and that they are somehow frozen to be where they are, but in fact operating systems also change over time, and they do so in a much more profound way than providing new software releases only. Tim O'Reilly explains this change:

> When you look at the, say, IBM 360 operating system or even earlier, the kinds of things that they were dealing with are very different than the kinds of things you deal with, say, in a PC operating system. All of these things that we take for granted as part of the "operating system" were applications. For example, the X Window System was sort of an application layer thing, you didn't really think it was part of the OS. If you look at the way that Linux grew, the Kernel is the OS proper. But when people think about [how] it's the kernel [it] is kind of like the sun at the heart of the solar system and there's all these orbiting planets, planetoids, and there's this huge sort of gravitational system that includes a lot of things.

Some central applications within an innovation ecosystem may actually become a part of the "operating system."[5] In other words, many things which start as applications, such as Google Earth, but which to an extraordinary extent empower their users, end up as platforms or parts of them. Sometimes even a very basic technology can become a platform for innovation and collaboration or a key part of it. For example, the Wikipedia community still uses IRC heavily, which, even though it is quite old fashioned, is robust and the users like it.[6] Since often we may realize only much later that something actually was a success, it becomes vital to create the platform to be tolerant of giving people time to question the status quo, think about issues differently and try out things. Ideally, the web as a platform should be a software environment in which crazy ideas can be tried and have permission to fail.

In spite of all nice features a platform may support, in the social web the audience is the critical mass. In a way, the audience is also the platform. A company that succeeds to give a plausible promise of some data-driven platform gets more people using it, and at least ideally the more people use it the better it gets. Indeed, what makes the idea of the social web as a platform so tempting is its potential driven by network effects in data with a multitude of users. Platform development in the social web holds tremendous business potential and this holds true also in individual software professional level in such a way that if web application developers can turn themselves into web platform developers they can remarkably raise their market value.

Social web as a business ecosystem

> *Henry Chesbrough:*
> *The boundary of the firm is becoming more porous. More things can come in from outside than before and more things from inside are visible to the outside than before. [This] even changes our model of what we mean by a firm or an organization.*

The term ecosystem was coined by Arthur Roy Clapham, who went to Oxford University to study with the encouragement of Sir Arthur George Tansley in 1930. It was in the early 1930s when Clapham suggested the term ecosystem to Tansley, who was the first one to use it in print, championed the term and defined the ecosystem concept. He described the concept strikingly in his article "The Use and Abuse of Vegetational Concepts and Terms" in the July 1935 issue of *Ecology*. "These ecosystems, as we may call them, are of the most various kinds and sizes," he wrote, "They form one category of the multitudinous physical systems of the universe, which range from the universe as a whole down to the atom."[7] In the context of the social web, an ecosystem is a trendy word denoting a number of different stakeholders with different goals, motivations and ways of working, which together make a whole. In nature an ecosystem works in a perfect way, when even the waste produced by some will be needed by others. Of course in this sense, the social web, or any other technology for that matter, will never be a perfect ecosystem. Yet, even with this much lower level of ambition it may be used as a phrase to direct attention to taking the various diverse aspects that make the whole into account. What constitutes an innovation ecosystem in the social web is a matter of viewpoint. Different stakeholders may consider different entities in the social web as ecosystems; a social web platform may be considered as an ecosystem; the whole web can be considered as an ecosystem; in some sense, geographical areas are like ecosystems. Yet, no absolute definition is needed, just as Tansley left his definition open.

Let us still characterize the innovation ecosystem and their business sub-ecosystems in the social web. A business ecosystem consists of the users and other stakeholders that participate in it and the information systems included in the environment with which the stakeholders interact with each other and through which they communicate and influence each other. Higher-order patterns of these ecosystems cannot really be predicted or understood by a simple summation of the parts but rather by interaction between the stakeholders and systems. The feedback loops between stakeholders and systems regulate and sustain local and global user communities in the environment, while ecosystems are sustained by the diversity within them. Reid Hoffman emphasizes that it is important to understand how these ecosystems in the social web pull together, how innovation is incented, how long-term investment is done, and "how constituencies between investors, entrepreneurs, customers, employees and everything else is all baked into a healthy system." Setting up a platform that enables relatively independent groups to try new things is a combination of network infrastructure and a social infrastructure. To be able to do this, both the software offering and a large user base must come together in such a manner that the social web operates in a given platform. However, something more than that will be needed to make successful business. The creation of a full innovation ecosystem needs as an elementary part of it a business sub-ecosystem which would open up various business opportunities and keep one's product and service offering vigorous, and the social web is critically important in creating, maintaining and sustaining this network-based ecosystem.

Sometimes a specific software solution may, as a technology, be much better than the leading solution in a certain field, domain, or business area, but the industry leader, however, is almost always the one who is centrally located in the big picture and often the one who is in the position to coordinate between information systems. For instance, after the first web crawlers started to produce a lot of raw data, Google came out with tools to make sense out of that, and it started to coordinate that information. Later it also developed different subsystems, such as for speech recognition, which were good enough for it once again to coordinate businesses in conjunction with its search database. Microsoft's path to success is another example of successful ecosystem thinking. With DOS and later with Windows, Microsoft was able to create an operational environment where many different startups could try to make innovative software and where they had enough platform support and enough social system support. The company then allowed these relatively small visionary-led groups to experiment with their new software. Often these successful applications ended up being bought by the platform owner. For example, most of the things Adobe sells, except the original PostScript, was started by another company within their overall ecosystem and then adopted, and Google has YouTube, Google Earth, Google Voice, and others. For this reason, it is one feasible business strategy for small companies to purposefully develop software products for ecosystems in which they can be plugged in various contexts.

The eyeballs by definition are valuable for business in the social web and in the ecosystem thinking the number of users accounts even more. There are several social web types, like blogging and many of the social networks, which never spend a dime on marketing, but rather rely on the number of users and the word-of-mouth effect. They bet on the power of viral marketing, which started out as a socially driven phenomenon, but for them it has become a business-driven one, because they are using it to help propagate their products and brand. Reid Hoffman describes the power of viral marketing to reach customers: "For somewhere between 5 and 30 million dollars of capital all-in, you can create a product that reaches ten million plus people and has a healthy growth curve. That's all of the capital you put in, because the marketing essentially, and the sales essentially, take through natural viral distributions on the website."

One way to build an ecosystem is through offering technical standards which would be valuable for the other players in the ecosystem when building their applications upon them. In this way, the standard becomes a platform in itself upon which others could build. When other companies then build upon these, an ecosystem formulates, consisting of several companies building and supporting on top of the original standard. Henry Chesbrough uses the telecommunication as an example of this:

> The mobile telephone and handset business isn't a matter anymore of how long your battery will last, how big your screen is, how clear your signal is, even whether you use GSM, CDMA or these kinds of standards. We now are looking at things like how many apps are available for this handset, how many contributors are active in the community developing these applications. What about your carriers in these areas, what kind of support are you getting from them? All of these external parties are really part of how you compete in the mobile communications marketplace. A company that does an excellent job in its own activities on the handset can still get crushed in the market if they haven't got the surrounding ecosystem of third-party participants, those people that you don't control, that aren't on your payroll, but nonetheless may be the key to your success or failure in the marketplace. This is something where we see the web in its full glory and we see some of the challenges that the web poses, because for companies who have been successful in the earlier era now have to master new skills. They have to engage with new people and new organizations that previously were unimportant to them.

Over the past few years, many of the borders between different businesses have become blurred, and this has provided an opportunity for companies and people from outside an industry to come in. If those outsiders understand how do it, they can enter an industry and have surprising success even though they don't have a long history in that business. Apple's iPhone and Google's Android are good examples from the success in mobile phone business. Both Apple iOS and Google Android operating systems have attracted hundreds of thousands of applications with billions of downloads, and the figures only seem to keep growing. But the most remarkable thing with Apple and Google is that they only entered the mobile phone business at a very late stage, for instance, compared to Nokia, the leading mobile manufacturer for many previous years. Nokia was at first fighting against iPhones and Androids with the Symbian operating system, trying to compete as an open source operating system. Later it formed a partnership with Microsoft for using Windows Phone operating system as the platform for its phones.[8] Henry Chesbrough notes that "in some sense, Nokia is a digital immigrant itself in the sense that they had tremendous success with GSM a decade and more ago, and they've really executed very well." They have been able to build low-cost manufacturing globally and to become the volume leader in the world in the number of handsets built, which are tremendous achievements by a company that used to make rubber boots and forestry products. However, Chesbrough explains the challenge that Nokia faces: "We have to give tremendous credit to what they've done in their achievements. All these wonderful achievements in the past will go away quite quickly if they aren't able to translate them into this web world, where it is these networks, communities, ecosystems, all of which are outside the boundaries of your own organization."

Indeed, the determining success factor is what kind of applications and services a platform makes accessible within its ecosystem versus other platforms and ecosystems. In Nokia's situation, it became a game between Nokia versus Google Android phones versus Apple iPhone. Nokia as a telecommunications company hasn't historically focused on software or web, to say nothing of the applications, platforms or ecosystems for the social web. They had the Ovi service in their offering, which means that they were aware of and working on these challenges, but they fully engaged with this kind of thinking late. Further, most research labs have a very carefully constructed set of metrics to manage and measure their success, and by looking at the metrics it can be predicted what will come out from these labs. According to Henry Chesbrough, one aspect of Nokia's struggle was that it was gearing its research labs to engineering-focused tasks such as how many patents and invention disclosures they were going to get. While these had been historically of great importance for them as a telecommunications company, relatively few in research and development operations seemed to be worrying about the change the social web was bringing about – the new ecosystems, third-party partners, end-user communities, creating applications, reference designs and software development kits that are published to the world and get others to build on top of and to contribute for. In the research and development operations at Nokia, this was not something that was being measured, and thus in achieving their metrics, they fell well short of what they needed to do to respond to the competition with Apple and Google. Companies like Nokia and many others which face these kinds of challenges by no means are in a unique situation. In fact, it happens relatively often that a company which is a leader in a business can't stay competitive because there are too many things to protect, the innovator's dilemma. The company loses its capability to innovate – and it has to work very hard to regain it. Companies facing this situation must renew and often also redefine their strategy in this new type of an innovation and business environment.

A surprising example of ecosystem thinking is suggested by Neal Sample, who spent time as a post-doctoral research fellow at the Office of Research and Development of the Central Intelligence Agency, working on cloud-based software solutions for the CIA.[9] Sample describes that the CIA essentially funded his ongoing research and supported it as an innovation program and that he was surprised by the openness of the CIA, which anticipated something from his dissertation work on bridge scheduling. According to Sample, "[They said,] 'We're going to go ahead and fund what you're doing because we think it's interesting and let you work on it in ways that you want to work on it because we want to get good ideas. We don't necessarily want to direct your research and direct your study and say, "you have to work on this particular problem, you have to work on it in this particular way, you have to get this particular outcome for us."'" Sample continues: "What was great about it was the funding agency that you would've thought would've been the most closed were saying, 'What we're going to do is we're going to fund an open research program, we're going to let top innovators think about the things they want to think about, work on the programs that they're working on, and we're going to let them take it to the next level.'"

For innovation ecosystems the CIA's research approach bears a powerful message. Sometimes it may not be directly obvious how the social web could help a company with some specific question. Open developer programs or other social web mechanisms do not necessarily bring anything new for the companies right away, but they provide an opportunity and a way to learn something new from the environment early enough and to position the company centrally in the emerging ecosystem. If openness is a central resource, the social web can create a business ecosystem that encourages innovation and curbs stagnation. Ideally, when people spend more time with convergent technologies and more time on the web itself, the platform has a chance to get better and there will be more innovative opportunities. What is needed are ways to nurture these innovation ecosystems. By helping user communities and by fostering a culture of innovation, the company may end up improving its own innovation record as well, because innovations are created to an increasing extent as a result of operations in these ecosystems.

Yet, it would be a false idea to think that companies developing innovation ecosystems would be doing it just for fun or as philanthropy. Even though through their openness the platforms to some extent contribute to the democratizing effect of the social web, they at the very same time lead into inevitable consolidation of power by some set of players who are in the position to aggregate the user-generated content. This is particularly so because it is not easy to jump over to another platform and move all of one's social network related information into it. In a way, users get locked in these applications and platforms that they already have started to use. Therefore, in spite of innovation ecosystems' openness, it also becomes harder for competitors to get into the play. In sum, every long tail has a dog that is attached to it – the question is who owns the dog. In innovation ecosystems it is normally the platform provider.

Terry Winograd notes realistically that most often what drives technological development ultimately is money:

> It's funny, these detachments right now from very popular web things that actually don't make money. But the view is they will, because they've got enough eyeballs. So it's the ability to attract people. What attracts people? Is it usefulness, is it emotion, is it fads? The answer is some of all those things, and you'll see different products which pick different ones. Nobody likes Microsoft Word very much, but it's very useful so everybody uses it. There are other things where people just have fun. Most of the stuff on YouTube isn't very

> useful, if you take entertainment out of the equation for use. On the other hand, people spend a lot of time. They do it. Games traditionally have been a case where you have a tremendous market. Tremendous potential for getting users involved.

Understandably, in the companies' eyes the value paradox particularly relates to monetary value. The business models of the web, however, still are somewhat elusive even today, and many companies struggle with the lack of a precise definition for their earning logic. They may have great success in attracting viewership to their sites and eliciting participation, but they have much less success in turning this into money. Indeed, in most cases, exchanging eyeballs into euros or dollars is not a simple and straightforward process. When News Corporation acquired MySpace, it did cost $580 million. The company has subsequently written down that investment quite a bit, because there has been great difficulty getting money out of MySpace. When Google acquired YouTube, it paid $1.65 billion, and it publicly predicted that YouTube would become profitable for it very soon.[10] It has been pervasive; it has been tremendously successful in terms of getting viewership and it has a whole community around it, but it has not been a big moneymaker for Google.

Bona fide reciprocity requires that companies which make a foray into social web activities must understand that the principles which were applied when they brought end-users into the user community should remain in tact. For instance, Facebook was able to attract hundreds of millions of users with one set of rules, which, however, were not very tempting for the company to build business around it. When Facebook has been trying to change these terms of use, it has received a furious reaction from its users. This exemplifies the need for establishing a solid business model upfront; changing the terms of use afterwards implies very high risk that users will flee. Although Facebook has been able to avoid this situation, it is hard to know whether it, or any of the other currently popular social web applications or platforms for that matter, will still be around in five or ten years. The social web will keep changing. Henry Chesbrough explains this through *tension* between value creation and value capture:

> The things that Facebook does to attract people to join its site, upload your information and then engage in posting what's going on with you, reading about what others are doing, that creates value. But for Facebook to monetize the value, they've tried a number of times to slightly alter the terms of service, or slightly alter the control over the information that the users have put onto the site, and the users feel like, "Wait a minute, we were doing business with you on one approach, and under one set of terms of service." It happens that those are not the best ones for Facebook to monetize, so Facebook is trying to alter the terms of service so it can now do more targeted, directed marketing, value capture kinds of activities. And the community is rejecting it, saying, "No, we've been with you for a number of years on this basis." That's that tension between value creation and value capture.

Sustainability being the key, Chesbrough further elaborates on the continuous struggle between these two poles related to the value paradox, value creation and value capture, by noting that the dimension that is the most important would be to be able to define the inflection point where a technology really becomes widespread or pervasive and sustainable. For instance, one of the reasons why the dotcom era did not sustain itself very well was that there were lots of people coming to the sites, but there was actually very little profitable economic activity occurring. Chesbrough explains that "initially, it was doing quite well and these companies would have an initial public offering at quite high valuations on the promise that this is going to convert into profits at a later stage. When that promise was broken and it became clear that there was no prospect of profits anytime soon, that's when it all collapsed. This issue of how do we convert viewership, participation, engagement into money, remains a viable challenge even today."

Social web as a user experience

> *Henry Chesbrough:*
> *You can't own the community.*

Even though the social web has become a key part of many information-intensive products and services, simply developing a technically feasible software platform for the social web and innovation ecosystem on top of it is not enough for its users to stay and operate in the network. The platform has to equip its users with strong support for deep comprehension of information, capabilities to refine and conceptualize by building upon that understanding, to communicate and share the conceptualizations with others, and to collaborate with them to enable the growth of collective intelligence and to foster innovation.[11] Furthermore, it has to provide an engaging user experience to motivate and encourage application developers and end-users to start contributing into it and to keep doing so.

Hasso Plattner, the founder of the German enterprise resource planning software company SAP, has been pushing for a number of years for the company to change its design thinking to be more user-centered, but Plattner, even though being the founder, major owner and chairman of the board of the company, yet has not had the power to enforce such a change.[12] The reason for this is that organizations have a tremendous weight of culture and tradition based on the way their systems are produced, and changing them is not as simple as waving a flag and telling people to think differently. Plattner's experience shows that *innovation cannot be led from the top only*, but the whole organization needs to adopt similar thinking, and proper core competences and business values need to be brought in if they don't already exist in the organization. Despite being able to develop and deliver a robust and technically feasible software platform, its business success is far from self-evident. It is vital to continuously nurture the innovation ecosystem on top of it by providing engaging user experiences for both the application developers and the end-users, whether consumers or organizational users, so that they keep contributing into it. Hypertext visionary Ted Nelson describes the importance of being able to provide positive user experiences by a striking remark that "software [to me] is a branch of movie making. It's not 'like' movie making."

The provision of positive user experience becomes ever more important with user communities which go across organizational boundaries. Henry Chesbrough explains that "For many companies today, much of their innovation success depends on people that are not on their payroll, that they cannot directly manage and control. Instead, these are people that have autonomy and independence. They are people you can influence, you can motivate, you can encourage, but you can't dictate to these people." Thus, one of the most central goals in developing social web applications, and even more so in developing social web platforms is to be able to provide motivating and persuasive experiences for users. Henry Chesbrough further explains the reason for this:

> Not only do these web-based technologies change the innovation process, not only do they change organizations, they also change the way we understand people and their motivations. If you pay them to do something, they'll do it. It's not that that's wrong, because in many cases it does work that way. But there are other currencies as well. Money is one currency, but reputation is a second currency. If we think about these ideas of gift-giving and reciprocity, you could think of that as almost a third currency. So we have a more rich sense of what motivates people to engage, to participate, to contribute, to innovate. It isn't simply about paying them money anymore. You have to motivate them, you have to lead them, you have to engage with them.

Chesbrough uses the SAP as successful example. It has a very complex, vertically integrated set of code and technologies, but even so, they have come to understand user communities in a very deep and thoughtful way. One of the main principles SAP started to build upon was that its user communities are not owned by it. Thus, the issue is how to lead user communities without owning them. SAP gives its time, contributes resources, makes suggestions, and tries to lead new initiatives, but it's really on a gift-giving basis. Mårten Mickos confirms that the same happened with his web database company: "At MySQL, I instilled a lot of rigor and hierarchical organization of the company, but at the same time I was very excited to live in an ecosystem with so [many] voluntary actions where you couldn't force people to do certain things. You had to attract them and let them make the decision. If you had a good enough value proposition, they would join. And if you didn't, they would abandon."

More generally, Chesbrough explains that norms of reciprocity become part of how we exchange gifts between each other, as opposed to command and control; where there's no gift-giving involved, there's no reciprocity involved. Chesbrough continues:

> You can't own the community. You can encourage it, you can help organize it, facilitate it, and lead it, but you don't own it. Everybody in the community at

> any time can opt out and go somewhere else, and just refuse to participate any further. Once you understand that you don't own the community, it changes the way you relate to the community. It's much more of a gift exchange set of relationships, where you give your time as a member of the community to the community. This idea of influence versus control is a very far-reaching aspect of this new world that we're in, where we are learning from each other, we are influencing each other.

Yet, if developers are going to ask more from the users, it also demands more from them, namely to get users to participate, share their views, generate content and bend the technology, they will have to maintain a certain amount of trust both between users and about the system. For providing powerful user experiences, the capability to motivate, encourage, and persuade participants, both developers and end-users, has become a core competence for modern innovation ecosystems.

The social web has dramatically accelerated the transformation of the business environment by connecting pockets of innovation and core businesses from different parts of the world. A key approach to social web innovation is to create and maintain software platforms, which are capable of continuously providing positive user experiences, to nurture business ecosystems on top of them and to bake it all into a tasty cake – the innovation ecosystem. Organizational thinking and strategies still needs to be shaped to foster future growth and support processes related to this type of social web innovation.

9
Social Web Innovation Strategies

Caterina Fake:
There's no innovation deficit.

Neal Sample:
Innovation can come from any corner.

Search for innovative ideas is an essential activity for successful companies in any field. After all, incremental innovations by definition take place gradually and also Zero-to-One innovations almost always happen in stages. A potential misunderstanding about seeking for innovations is that one could start to think that let's simply go look at how Google, or any other really successful company for that matter, innovates and let's just copy that. But a search engine only copying Google could never beat its rivalries, and moreover a pharmaceutical company couldn't take the same risks that a web company could. One might also think that innovations are always born differently without any formula or accidentally without a roadmap. Still, attempts have been made to define a pattern. Joseph Schumpeter argued during his American period in the 1930s that those who would produce innovations would be the big companies, because only they had the resources to do it. He drew upon early twentieth-century capitalism, and regarded large established corporations and government agencies as key entrepreneurial entities.[1] History has shown that this idea of the remarkable role of large companies has been partially true, and yet this is not what is happening now. Social web innovations do not happen typically within company research laboratories, and even if they could, companies would have to keep open communication with outsiders. After all, incremental innovations by definition take place gradually and also Zero-to-One innovations almost always happen in stages. B.J. Fogg explains that "You can't just bet on one horse. You have to have a bunch of horses in the race and you see which one wins. Just try stuff and don't get too committed to any one solution. Just keep putting it out there." Mårten Mickos suggests that there are many successful formulas in any given situation: "Wherever we are, there are always many paths to success. So companies need to choose. Some companies choose to do only internal innovations. Some companies choose to do ecosystem-based ones. Some acquire them, some license them. You can't do all of them, so you have to limit yourself to some."

As the only way for innovation to happen is not only internally and organically, but it can be driven from the outside as well, new outbound means for searching and finding innovations are urgently needed. In their search for social web innovation, companies need to adopt a particular strategy. Four families of outbound methods for seeking social web innovation proposed here are:

- Userwatching
- Crowdsourcing
- Open innovation
- Nics

Userwatching includes observing the user behaviors of both regular users and the nerds. Crowdsourcing asks users to suggest ideas, whereas open innovation opens organizational problems for users to suggest ways to resolve them. "Nics," or networked improvement communities, connect similar types of users from different organizations to communicate over their similar interests. After introducing these innovation search strategies, we will raise issues related to cultivating within-organization methods of innovation as well as the more general issue of the premium on youth in the creation of social web innovation.

Userwatching

> *Jimmy Wales:*
> *Users are building things – we're making it fun and interesting and we're seeing what they wanna do.*
>
> *Ben Shneiderman:*
> *The most reliable payoff comes when you work with real users, real companies, and listen to them about what problems they have, solve their problem, and then you generalize and evaluate and come through with a new idea.*
>
> *Wagner of Charleston:*
> *Come and see Esau / Sittin' on a see-saw / Eatin' 'em raw!*

Userwatching means observing the user behaviors of Average Janes and Joes as well as watching how the Alpha Geeks bend the boundaries of technologies. The latter is technically oriented approach, whereas the former is human-oriented.

Observing average users in their everyday life was an important developmental step for movies in the 1930s,[2] and similarly it is important also for advancing the social web innovation. But who then is the average user? Dave Feldman, Director of User Experience for Yahoo! Messenger, wrote in his blog "The Myth of the Average User: Your Mom Knows How to Click and Drag": "We try to get them in the lab but they end up being smarter and more interesting than we wanted. In fact, we've never met an Average User."[3] Admittedly, there is no point in trying to define someone as an "average" user, but nevertheless users whose use behaviors reflect that of the majority segment of the population is worth observing.

Traditionally users have been approached by gallups, surveys and structured or semi-structured interviews in order for companies to reach an understanding about user opinions, habits and ways of working, but another way to watch regular users is to give them tools for them to resolve their own challenges and problems in the context of their everyday lives and see how they use those tools. Observing the Average Joe, how regular users behave, is by definition monitoring activities close to human life, and it is one way to come up with better understanding of people's actual problems. After Hunch.com launched questions-and-answers based social web service with five hundred topics, it rapidly grew to have 55,000 topics and 28 million questions answered.[4] In this manner people actually did reveal fine-grained information about themselves into the social web service, which acts as data that can be used in order to give people better answers. Very importantly, the social web can serve not only as a track record of past activities, but it can also support real-time communication and encourage people to interact through it.

Observing the Average Joe is in fact a very important practice to help ensure that social web developers are not designing solutions only for themselves or people like them. Ben Shneiderman describes the challenge:

> Many developers instinctively design for themselves. Really, their job is to design for a wide range of people, not only the professional expert users, but the novices and the beginners and those with low literacy, poor language skills or poor vision, hearing, or motor skills, people who are older, people who are younger, people with small screens, with laptops, with large displays. Small, wall and mall size displays; understanding that there's the flexibility. Any good design has to be plastic enough to fit different people, different situations, slow Internet, fast Internet, all those things need to be accommodated.

In addition to observing regular users, innovations may stem from scouting how technologically exceptionally savvy users behave. Over hundred years ago West Virginian geek, Wagner of Charleston, became famous of his touring alive snake-eating act. But he was not the only geek around at his time; otherwise, the Kansas state senate would not had passed in 1903 legislation to forbid exhibition of "Glomming Geeks," who were mentioned among other things to eat live snakes. In fact biting of heads off snakes was a common geek stunt in the early twentieth-century sideshows.[5] Even though the original meaning of geek was not related to science, the similarity is that geeks of today are also carefully watched, when others want to see how geeks do their "stunts," perhaps wishing to extend their own limits by following or even surpassing what the geeks are doing.

In the social web, one of the key things that companies can do is pay attention to the ways in which individual users want to push the bounds of their product. Those who really bend technology are the extreme users who have extreme cases, the Alpha Geeks. Watching the Alpha Geeks outside of the company means basically giving them tools, following them, and seeing what they come up with using those tools. Tim O'Reilly explains: "Much of my thinking about the future comes from watching individuals who were just playing with things that are not commercial. Companies often don't pay attention to innovation, because they're looking for the commercial innovation, and yet it's often non-commercial innovation that eventually becomes commercial." For instance, long before it became recognized by any wider audience, a web development trend related to sensors was recognizable with Alpha Geeks who were practically just playing with sensors to see what they could do.[6] A handful of companies were following them, and they were able to figure out new products via this maneuver. By watching the Alpha Geeks, whose approaches and applications often are very far from being truly business oriented, one may recognize development trends earlier than their competitors do. In fact, much of their activity is something that used to be a very central task by paid staff in a company's R&D lab.

According to Mark Granovetter, Alpha Geeks are not mainly trying to make much money, but rather they are just a little bit eccentric and typically out of the usual commercial and business networks, and Alpha Geeking appears to be typically a male kind of activity in which eccentrics are often in networks of people who have similar interests as themselves. Stereotypes related to Alpha Geeks are that they are itinerant, constantly comparing notes with other technical people, yet too awkward to communicate in traditional ways, nevertheless always thinking about what could be done in a new way. A central part of the phenomenon is that by actually showing others what they have made they are able to see the others getting excited in a way that they could never do just by talking to them. Thus, input from the Alpha Geeks would normally also demonstrate their ideas rather than ideate only. The challenge with Alpha Geeks is how to create contexts for inspiration, recognize an inspiration and keep the environment sticky enough so that they keep coming back to the operational environment provided.

Regarding Zero-to-One innovations, the major drawback in observing the Average Joes despite having relatively high likelihood for success is that it often leads to incremental innovations only, whereas watching the Alpha Geeks who can bend technology can be a very powerful tool for creating technically-oriented Zero-to-One innovations, but it is strongly biased towards technology and engineering *per se* rather than user behaviors and needs. Caution is needed in applying the Alpha Geeks approach since their work, even if social by nature, may be highly inductive and not necessarily rooted on actual use or usefulness. Nevertheless, both userwatching approaches can be very useful strategies for social web innovation.

Crowdsourcing

Mårten Mickos:
If you don't listen to the world around you, you're just missing out of 90 percent of the innovation discussions.

The term "crowdsourcing" resembles and in fact originates from "outsourcing," which is essentially about finding cheaper labor sources outside of a company.[7] Software companies outsource their programming, for instance, to India because it's cheaper than programmers in California. Jimmy Wales criticizes using the term crowdsourcing:

> That term really disrespects the communities who are involved and what they're doing. In fact, if somebody thinks of their work as crowdsourcing, they

> approach [it] in the wrong way. So we have, "This work that needs to be done, how can we get the public to do it?" rather than saying, "Gosh, we have all these interested people who are very smart, what is it that they wanna do, and how can we help them do something that they'll find interesting and exciting?" Although in practice maybe those end up being the same thing, the difference in attitude can really impact the design process in a negative way.

Thus, the connotation of the crowdsourcing term is somewhat misleading, and yet it is an extremely powerful term. In our definition, crowdsourcing is much more than just providing a platform and waiting to see what happens, or expecting that customers will innovate for you: A common false idea about crowdsourcing means that if you're really smart, companies would be just throwing things into the world and letting the users do the job. In other words, they would trick the public into doing the work for them. Crowdsourcing doesn't mean to find out "what everybody knows" or "what they all think" either, pursuing of which would only provide already out-of-date information, which is useless for innovation creation. Rather, crowdsourcing means compiling a new interpretation based on what the masses of people think or "what people think as a whole." This emphasizes the capability to aggregate and generalize knowledge more than only collecting opinions or ideas from users. The ability to understand what the masses think, to generalize from it and then potentially to deviate from it to make a difference to competitors provides a great opportunity and channel for creating Zero-to-One innovations. Yet, even if the capability of the Renaissance Man of the social web, to be able to generalize, is (and it should be) appreciated in the modern information society, it is all too often neglected in practice. For instance, when companies hire people, they still have the tendency to emphasize very narrowly defined expertise over generalization capabilities. It might well be that none of today's organizations would hire Leonardo da Vinci, the great generalist, who was able to contribute into multiple different sciences. Thus, when the issue of the desired skill set for the future – being a T-shaped person – is considered at the context of business and society, it becomes much more complicated than what it looks at the first sight. Companies and organizations need to re-think what skills they should expect their employees to have, and governments similarly have to re-think their forms of education. What needs to be re-thought concerns not only technological skills, but also cognitive abilities for abstraction and conceptual modeling.

In his book, James Surowiecki provides an insightful discussion about crowdsourcing or as he calls it, "the wisdom of crowds," and how to derive information from end-user communities and aggregate it to something new.[8] According to Surowiecki, the challenges that can be addressed through this approach are problems for which some answers are better than others, problems that require group members to coordinate their behavior with each other and problems that relate to challenges of getting self-interested, distrustful people to work together.

The crowdsourcing approach[9] suggests that there is no need to rely solely on experts and in some cases it could even be considered harmful and costly. Rather the approach suggests that through different kinds of information aggregation functionalities it would be possible to figure out how people in a group think as a whole, and that in some cases groups are actually smarter than the smartest people in them. Surowiecki admits that a group as such does not get smarter over time, nonetheless, this approach emphasizes that groups do not need to be dominated by exceptional people, but only that the group has to be large enough. For a group to operate in an expected manner, diversity is necessary, and the best way for a group to be smart is for each person in it to think and act independently. Decentralization also encourages independence and specialization. All information is not equally important, and more is not always better. A critical element of the crowdsourcing approach that relates to most of the conjectures above is that end-users should not be working closely together on resolving the problem at hand, because too much or too detailed communication may kill the diversity, making group members too much alike. Debates with disagreement and contest must be allowed to enable the best decisions, whereas striving for consensus may eliminate independent individual thinking.

Crowdsourcing has never before been possible to the extent it is today. Consider Wikipedia for an instance. To enable hundreds of thousands of contributors to participate in creating content for Wikipedia is a remarkable showcase of this and an opportunity for regular users to play a central role in the development of the social web. While there are issues around Wikipedia, the number of errors per paragraph was regarded as actually comparable with the Encyclopaedia Britannica in *Nature* in 2005.[10] There are also group filtering and group collaboration techniques that contribute to higher quality, and much of the rationale behind the information presented at Wikipedia in fact locates at its discussion pages. Some specific crowdsourcing applications, such as the MobileWorks or Amazon Mechanical Turk,[11] help to seek human intelligence to perform tasks that computers are unable to accomplish. For instance, the Mechanical Turk enables requesters to post cognitive tasks, such as choosing "the best" among many photographs, whereas users can choose the tasks which they want to accomplish in order to get monetary payment; those who request a task to be done for them can ask for or test the qualifications of a user before letting them engage in a task, and the results can also be accepted or rejected by the requester. Even areas such as manufacturing are being transformed because of crowdsourcing. For instance, threadless.com is a company that sells T-shirts, but the novelty is that it has crowdsourced its design process in order to shorten its manufacturing process. Tim O'Reilly expects that we will soon get into situations in which a design for a physical object will be crowdsourced and it will be sold before it's ever made, which is basically build-to-demand.

Crowdsourcing is particularly important for modern software design, according to Mårten Mickos:

> There's just a mathematical reason for it. If you take all the software engineers that we have needed to develop the society to this level, how many people did it take to develop where we are, all the banking systems, ERP systems, and web systems? [Most] of them are white men between the age of 40 and 60. So a small, small part of the world. But today on the internet you have a

hundred times more people who deal with software and are knowledgeable about software. No matter how smart people you have in your company – and of course you should hire many smart people – if you don't listen to the world around you, you're just missing out of 90 percent of the innovation discussions. That's why I believe in crowdsourcing. Not that I would do everything with the crowd, not that I would let the crowd decide. But ignoring it is just plain stupid. It has to do with these just mathematical proportions. There are just so many people out there. Even if half of them were stupid, even if 90 percent of them were stupid, the remaining 10 percent out there is still more than you can ever hire into your company.

Indeed, through the social web crowdsourcing has become a powerful method for understanding what the masses of people think and how to invite them to help in creating innovations. Yet, crowdsourcing also has severe restrictions. There are times when users want expertise rather than opinion, and of course not all the information in Wikipedia should be treated with equal value. For instance, one probably would not bet their child's life on a particular sentence found on Wikipedia. Another concern is, when, how, and to what extent this approach would prove to be useful in organizational settings. Furthermore, a group does not have a personality or a focus. Thus, even though individual users may show emotions towards a group they belong to, a group does not have the ability to show any kinds of emotions towards individuals nor does it bear social responsibility (even if individuals in it perhaps may do so). The major philosophical concern of the crowdsourcing approach is why we should think that the masses of people would be right after all. Groups are oftentimes good at choosing from options, but not necessarily at inventing something new. John Lilly shakes his finger and views crowdsourcing as a pejorative approach: "[You put] a lot of amateurs together and see where their gut is." Indeed, following the crowd is not always healthy, nonetheless, crowdsourcing is a major approach for social web innovation.

Open innovation

Judy Estrin:
The framing of the question becomes almost the hardest part of open innovation.

Henry Chesbrough:
To really do open innovation well, you have to make systemic changes in many parts of your innovation process and your organization.

Open innovation is a specific instance of the crowdsourcing approach. Like all crowdsourcing, open innovation makes the assumption that companies can and should use external ideas on par with internal ideas to advance their technology and to create Zero-to-One innovations.[12] While crowdsourcing focuses on taking contributions from many individuals, aggregating them into a reasonable whole and putting them to work, open innovation means opening the problems of companies to others, too. The others may be similar companies, experts or single persons, depending on how the open innovation process in organized and managed. Open innovation provides a great opportunity to directly learn something that can help resolve problems in the organization, but the solutions still need to be implemented by the company.

Open innovation lends itself very well to many businesses. Naturally, there are many different flavors of open innovation, from which different versions work in different projects, and there are areas where a company would not do it or use the approach only in a setting which has been defined with extra caution. Some companies feel that they can't talk anything about their innovation until it is on the markets, which means they can't utilize the open innovation approach. In other business areas companies can do open innovation because they then move faster on the technology side and they protect themselves against competitors by being fast and by also enabling sales channels via open innovation. Moreover, it is easily forgotten that innovation is not only about technology, innovation can be done also on time to markets, positioning the products, nurturing the ecosystems, and ways for using the distribution channels.

Yahoo! is an example of a company that uses open innovation as a key organizational process. It has gone all the way to an open strategy by opening up much of their data as well as their user experiences for software developers. Yahoo! launched their Hack Days originally in its headquarters in Sunnyvale, California, and ever since these have gone global, more recently similar events have spread to many other organizations. Hack days particularly help develop, utilize and mix and match APIs. These software development events for ideation represent proactive openness in which a company is able to identify experts and leverage their capabilities and give individuals a chance to excel by ensuring that companies, students, and single hackers working in their own garages can show up and showcase what they are doing. Neal Sample, Vice President for Social Platforms at Yahoo!, explains that these events and Yahoo! University Hack Day Program[13] work well for ideation:

> We run an event that we basically invite hackers to come to and build new and interesting things on Yahoo! and other open APIs, so they can come in and build on our TV API, so we have a widget API for IP enabled and connected televisions and so we had folks come in to New York City a couple of months ago. They came in for 24 hours, built what they could and then demoed it to their peers. What we found is that this is a fantastic outlet for grassroots folks in a very low-cost way to show up, showcase their talents, and potentially build something great for themselves, sometimes for Yahoo! but in any case they're getting out there and they're [active participants] in the innovation cycle. So one of the things we've been doing is that from a non-technical side we said, "Look, let's hold events that will foster innovation, that will help Yahoo!, will help the tech community, will help the web," and we've been very successful in that space as well, so we have a pretty good innovation story. Other people are catching on as well, we've had one of the longest-running open hack programs that's been truly open. A lot of companies have had sort

> of developer events, where you come, you listen to the company talk, you maybe get pitched on buying a few tools or whatever, but there wasn't any development going on at the developer events. It was really an outbound kind of marketing program. Yahoo! said, "We're gonna say forget all of that and this will be exclusively a development event and we'll work on ideation and we'll work on innovation."

In a similar manner, eBay's brand is molded and guided by its community empowered by chat rooms, eBay University and eBay Live! annual events. These enable members to meet one another as well as the employees. However, to reach this stage has been a long process that began in the mid-1990s.[14] In addition to companies, also many government organizations and universities are using open innovation tools that take suggestions, for instance, to figure out how to become more efficient, and then people vote online on the suggestions provided.

According to John Lilly, however, open innovation is an excellent idea in principle but in practice it is quite difficult to implement. One of the most important things with both the crowdsourcing and open innovation approaches is how do you frame the question. Judy Estrin explains that "if you don't frame the initial questions correctly, you'll get garbage. So the framing of the question becomes almost the hardest part of open innovation." The second question is how to encourage people to contribute. Thus, it is by no means self-evident that a company is able even to collect relevant ideas. The third challenge is how to find the most suitable suggestions. The pitfall is that the only thing one may get out of open innovation is a seething broth of ideas, which are with us everywhere, and to make a product or a company from those ideas takes a great deal more work. In most cases, the granularity of a product idea that one needs in order to get from an idea into the market is something totally different from what one can expect to get from the open ideation. According to Judy Estrin, open innovation can be "good for idea collection, but then you need some filtering to think through as to whether they are viable ideas for future growth of the organization." In many ways, the ideas are the easy part, whereas making these ideas real, where one has to go through all the social, structural and distribution barriers is difficult. Yes, getting an idea from a dream to reality is the hard part.

One of the mistakes organizations easily make with the open innovation approach is that they think of open innovation as just bringing in more external technologies, but not changing their business model and internal processes. However, if a company has a bottleneck in the system and it puts something at the wrong side of the bottleneck, the bottleneck is just as constrained as it was before, and nothing more will get through. Open innovation expert Henry Chesbrough explains:

> To really do open innovation well, you have to make systemic changes in many parts of your innovation process and your organization. Many companies are looking at open innovation as a tactic that they can just do a little bit to bring stuff in and that then they're done. "No more, we've adapted open innovation,

> and now great things are going to come." That's not how it's going to work. If you don't make these other changes, you will put more in at the beginning, but you won't get more out at the end. In a sense, you haven't really been any more innovative if we define innovation as getting ideas into the market. All you've done is [create] a more busy, congested beginning stage of your process.

No matter what the chosen strategy and approach in a company is, when companies become locked in their core businesses, their mainstream business can't really innovate any more. Open innovation may help but it has to be very carefully implemented. In any case, because there is a high likelihood that some competitors will utilize the open innovation approach in one way or another as part of their business strategy, the minimum that a company should do is to educate themselves about the strengths and weaknesses of open innovation.

Nics

> *Mårten Mickos:*
> *People do want to share.*

Douglas Engelbart suggests *networked improvement communities*, nics, which break organizational boundaries either within a company or outside of it, as a way to help a company's collective intelligence grow and to foster innovation creation.[15] According to Engelbart, the "improvement of improvement capabilities" through nics is a high-payoff opportunity to create high-performance organizations. The nics may be based on those social networks that exist within the company or bridge outside of it, and in some cases they may even provide a way for competitors to collaborate. The challenge of nics is, of course, that sharing business-related information with others is always a matter of serious concern. An immediate thought might be that it would be impossible to share anything with competitors, because so many ideas and processes are classified, but there could be useful things in some business domains for a company to share and of course to learn from others. Some business activities are very competitive, whereas some other activities tend to be less so, and some even seem to focus on very basic and generic matters. For this reason, even competitors could consider cooperating at some levels. Also business activities in different business areas may prove to be surprisingly alike, and there may be some pragmatic reasons for competitors to collaborate such as high-cost, high technology acquisitions.

An example of nic is *open source community*. Open source software enables the use and modification of open source software code and the distribution of the original or the modified code without having to pay royalties. Such software is typically created within open source projects, which are initiated by individuals or groups that want to develop a software solution to meet their own needs. Open source is big in software today, and in fact, companies all around the world are already using at least some open source software in many of their business operations. Those who participate in these open source based nics not only participate into resolving organizational problems but in practice participate into building software solutions for it. These stakeholders, whether organizations or individuals, want to improve their capabilities through these nics. O'Reilly started advocating open source in the latter part of the 1990s with the idea that the open source community isn't thinking enough about the implications of the Internet, and he started to build a mental model about what happens when combining open source software and the web approaches.[16] O'Reilly explains what had previously happened to IBM: "IBM effectively broke the dominance of the proprietary hardware paradigm when they released the specs for the IBM PC and anybody could build one. They didn't realize that they were changing the structure of the industry more profoundly in another way. As hardware became a commodity, software became much more valuable. Because they didn't understand this, they signed away their future to Microsoft." The important lesson was to recognize that both open source software and the Internet were commoditizing software in the same way that hardware had become commoditized in the era of the IBM PC. The free and open source advocates were missing the other half of the story, namely that always when something becomes commoditized something else becomes valuable. What happened was that services and data through the web became valuable, and the social web took over.

One of the most notable examples from an open source community in which people are working on in a nic-like style to jointly develop the software code is Mozilla Foundation and its web browser, Firefox. A hybrid company Mozilla has collected a group of experts around the world who contribute meaningfully to the technology development and who aim at openness and try to help others to develop a skill set. It has various ways of filtering and prioritizing their design aspects, and Firefox is shared in about 80 languages. Volunteers of localization teams are skilled and technical, and they are able to make, for instance, decisions about keywords shown in the browser in a local language. Thus, these volunteers are actually also designing the product at the same time when they are users of it. What Mozilla does through these nics is not a free-for-all approach, rather it is something that we call "curated crowdsourcing," more structured and more directed than regular crowdsourcing. Firefox's success probably can't be replicated very easily by others, but it does set a certain standard, and the way in which it has been able to harness collective intelligence is inspirational for all who wish to use the open source based nics approach. More generally, the idea of encouraging users to participate in software design and enabling them to co-create products that they want to use are important modern design principles.

The story of MySQL, an open source relational database management system, is inspirational as well and demonstrates that in addition to crowdscourcing and open innovation also nics can have very high business potential. In spite of being open source software, and even though it did not have much commercial activity initially, MySQL had an inherently commercial design, and it eventually was sold for $1 billion to Sun Microsystems. In Mårten Mickos's, CEO of MySQL and after the acquisition Senior Vice President of the database group at Sun Microsystems, personal view, he did not transport MySQL from a non-profit side to a commercial one, but just built up on the commercial side. Mickos explains what happened:

> We learned over time that there were two types of users or customers. There are those who are ready to spend a lot of time to save money, and others who are ready to spend money to save time. With that distinction, we learned how to reconcile the two worlds, how we could have both a product that is completely free of charge and then we still charge money. To us, it was like rocket science and developing something new, but this has actually existed in business before. Newspapers, many times, operate like that. They give away their newspaper free of charge to the readers, but they sell ads to the advertisers.

Computer scientist Hector Garcia-Molina thinks that it is actually a mystery how open source software in general can be so good as a product of a community of people just working with no real official management. However, according to Mårten Mickos, "Open source is not driven by charitable thoughts. Open source is driven by big egos, by pragmatist thinking." Mickos explains that open source programmers "share because they want their ego to grow, they want their career to improve, [or] they want to fix a problem for themselves." According to Mickos, because of these motivations the technology world would never run out of open source contributions. Nevertheless, in his view the open source model is universal and happened to software only because software people were the first ones to fully embrace the Internet, and any trade group that fully embraces the Internet would see similar nics. Thus, we may well start to see open source-like networked improvements communities in journalism, research, art and other fields.

Internal innovation

> *Judy Estrin:*
> *A lot of the new tools in innovation are terrific, but they're not replacements for investment in research and investment in small groups who are innovating around a problem.*

In terms of organizational structures, managers have been traditionally trained to think that innovation happens in the research and development labs of big companies, the approach of which could be called as the Division of Innovation approach. However, according to Reid Hoffman, the only cases that can be pointed to large companies being innovative are when they have generated such huge profits that they have been able to spend it all over the place: "For example, most of the really big research labs are financed by businesses which could be called monopolies. Microsoft, large R&D lab; Google, people are making that claim; Xerox back in the day had patents on photocopying. Photocopying was essential to all business and made huge amounts of money from it. So to do that requires the fact that you just print cash." Of course, all companies would like to be able to simply create innovations internally in a highly controlled environment, but even the most successful company research labs have not been able to produce very many Zero-to-One innovations. John Lilly uses Apple labs before the iPhone as an example of this more general phenomenon: "Apple's labs are full of smart people. But they only really ever productized two innovations. One was QuickTime and the other was the color Macintosh, the Macintosh II. It's actually quite a low track record. It's a hard thing going from inspiration to idea, and it takes a combination of being open to kind of crazy things, being willing to invest without knowing whether it [is] going to pan out or not, and being so undisciplined once you have the critical mass of an idea that it could be useful, if you will."

Even if there have been some examples of very fruitful R&D departments, such as Bell Labs and Xerox PARC,[17] this Division of Innovation approach is costly and does not seem to be a effective for social web innovation. Rather than creating big Divisions of Innovation, something more is needed to be able to do internal innovations. Of course, large companies have already tried many variations of organizational structures and incentives in order to innovate: workforces within a company collecting employees from different departments; inter-organizational collaborations and information systems to promote fluent information exchange between companies; business networks connecting with strategic partners such that they are able to contribute to solving problems in a company. In Yahoo! Caterina Fake was involved in starting a rapid product development environment, which was a separate entity inside of the company where they could create a new product, build it and launch it on the web without much extra burden on the company. Similarly, Judy Estrin, CTO of Cisco Systems and Board Member of Walt Disney Company and FedEx Corporation, suggests *small independent groups* to be created instead of very large R&D departments:

> You have to have small groups, little gardens or greenhouses that are loosely connected to the mainstream business. They can either be within your business, or they might be a connection with a university or a startup, or all of the above. You might have some groups [be] internal. But those gardens you manage completely different. You have different metrics, different people, different goals. If you try to mush it together, you won't end up with the type of environment that you need for that future growth, innovation.

A related idea for large companies is to have what we call *rapid reaction teams*, which are available to be invoked and then "sent" wherever they are needed at a given time. For many companies, these kinds of rapid reaction teams for product development would not be the only concept development or prototyping teams that exist in an organization, but they would be a new type of asset that could move more quickly inside of the company wherever it is needed the most for a relatively short period of time ranging from a few days to a few months. These teams could be small with relatively little funding and changing personnel. An important thing with these rapid reaction teams is that in the spirit of the social web they are always ready and willing to demonstrate what they can do. Just like athletes and sportsmen in team sports, they have to play well in each and every game, and they have to be fit always to show they can contribute. This approach hasn't yet been widely utilized in companies.

A strategy beyond molding organizational structures is *very fast experimenting*, very quickly – wiki – trying things out, which also goes hand in hand with the idea of rapid reaction teams. Many businesses already do a lot of experiments on the social web and they do them very quickly. Much of this is possible because experiments can be run in real-time or almost real-time in the contemporary web. In fact, fastness with which companies move in the social web has gone largely unnoticed from computer scientists. The dilemma academics have is that a solid scientific, academic experiment may take months just to learn that it's not through a review board, whereas in many cases a practical experiment will take only 24 hours. B.J. Fogg explains that startup companies are learning much more quickly than academics because they don't have slow processes: "[Academics] really ought to be watching these nimble companies doing field experiments and working with them because that's a fast way to learn. It's much easier to create new experiences and get them out to the world faster and cheaper."

In this era of social web, academics and other experts should, indeed, listen more than ever to users and companies. Henry Chesbrough, an academic himself, explains, "Managers are smart. Businesses are running experiments all the time. Academics don't pay enough attention to what businesses are actually doing. There's a lot we can learn from businesses, from their experiments, and in turn, if we take the time to really understand what they're doing, with the research training that we have and with some additional research and reflection, we really can make a contribution to these businesses and help them improve. But it takes a lot of listening, a lot of learning by us as part of helping them learn and improve as well." Naturally, to adopt this kind of a mutual approach for maintaining their relationships to companies requires from academics a different skill set than traditional master–apprentice thinking.[18] A balanced partnership means a high level of trust and mutual respect.

Yet another strategic direction following the spirit of the social web that has been adopted by some companies is known as *innovation timeoff*. An example of this is Google in its policy to encourage its engineers to spend 20 percent of their working time on projects that personally interest them and to give their employees freedom to do things on their own. For example, Internet pioneer Vint Cerf, who works for Google, uses some of that time to work at the Jet Propulsion Laboratory in Pasadena for working on the interplanetary extension of the Internet. Other efforts may be more down to earth but still close to the hearts of the employees. From the managerial point of view, one might think that this time is wasted, but it actually seems to be just the opposite. According to Google Vice President Marissa Meyer, 50 percent of what Google launched in the second half of 2005 was built out of this 20 percent time.[19]

Google seems to have inherited the idea and developed its recipe for it based on its own history. Hector Garcia-Molina describes how Google spun off from a research project run by Garcia-Molina and Winograd:

> When Terry and I wrote that proposal [for the National Science Foundation for funding for the project from which Google later spun off], I don't think the word "web" appeared once in the proposal, because as we wrote it the web was just beginning. The sort of funding we got was not to do web research, it didn't talk about search engines, it talked about heterogeneity of information and services, interesting research agenda. But the National Science Foundation is flexible and they were not that interested in us doing exactly what we sent in the proposal. Their key goal is to do good research. So as the project evolved [and] the web became popular, Larry Page came up with the idea of ranking pages in this ingenious way. Both Terry and I said, "That's great, sounds interesting, go ahead," and we gave there the resources, the time, and he went off. We had the resources and the freedom to say "yes." I'd done the same thing with other students: "Hey, that seems interesting, go off, and spend six months playing with it." Some cases it fails, they don't come up with anything good, but we just move on. The Google case it did work out, but you need to have flexibility, freedom, and good people. That's secret sauce.

Professor Garcia-Molina considers the innovation time off similar to baking a cake and eating it, in which you of course first have to bake the cake before eating it. If we want more innovations we must give people resources to do it, whereas if we constrain people too much they're just not going to be that creative. Moreover, innovation can not be driven from the top. Most social web sites, including Facebook and YouTube, were initially developed by a small group of young experts without a very clear view of where their sites would grow. In a similar vein, most designers and researchers are eager to innovate and what should be done is to unleash them, give flexibility and freedom to innovate. If there are some spare resources, a designer or researcher should not immediately have somebody on his back pressuring him to do things in the fashion that has usually been followed. What is needed is structuring work days and the work environments so that there is some time which is totally unscheduled and totally unpredictable – if innovations are truly encouraged. The goal of innovation timeoff is to give time and opportunity to explore new ideas in order to get into Zero-to-One innovations.

Premium on youth

> *Mark Granovetter:*
> *Breakthrough innovation almost always comes from people who are under 40.*

In addition to the specific audiences from which to seek innovations and ideas and ways to improve an organization's internal workings, a more general issue needs to be raised, namely the premium on youth in the social web. And yet, although the benefit of this is at least partially true, it seems to have been raised to a myth-like level.

Young people can often think differently about the future when compared to the older generation. Mark Granovetter claims that Zero-to-One type of innovations almost always come from people who are less than 40. He illustrates this with an example of Ronald Coase, born 1910 and a Nobel Prize winner from economics in 1991. The most famous publication of Coase, *The Nature of the Firm,* which is the beginning of all transaction cost economics, was published in 1937. Granovetter explains that when Coase was interviewed and asked how he came to write that paper in the way that he did, Coase said that it was because he was 26, and he was not well-trained in economics yet. If he had been well-trained in economics, he would not have said all those "ridiculous things," which turned out to be very important and interesting. Coase himself said in his 2003 lecture about "The Present and Future of Law and Economics" that he got support from his young contemporaries, not from his "betters." He thought that the general significance of his tale is that new ideas are most likely to come from the young, who are as a group most likely to recognize the significance of a new idea.[20]

Naturally, there are differences between business areas and application domains in regarding age. If there is going to be an innovation, say, in hydroelectric power, that innovation will most probably come from a major utility company working in partnership with scientific research in a traditional way. In most cases, you would not expect a 14-year-old kid to have an innovation in that kind of area, because it's a very mature field, and the innovation is going be a very detailed, technical innovation. In contrast, the social web still is a very young industry. None of us would be shocked at all if in five years from now we have a 24-year-old digital native who, when he was 19, started something that has now become a top social web innovation.

In a way, youth has taken over the world of innovation, and older people have in many cases lost their advantage. In the web space, there is a premium on youth, the digital natives, and as such it is a part of youth culture. Jimmy Wales emphasizes the importance of young people innovating in the social web partly because it's a young enough industry but also partly because of what it essentially is, a social industry, which implies that it's about people and how they interact and now particularly through the new means of interaction such as the social web. When there is a premium on youth and at the same time many company employees mostly represent digital immigrants, there is a special social order for seeking innovations via other approaches than internal innovating only. There is a "subscription" for userwatching, crowdsourcing, open innovation and nics.

Yet, digital natives are often given credit for understanding much more about technology than they actually do. B.J. Fogg explains: "The received wisdom in the U.S. is that teenagers know everything about technology and the web, but the fact is that they don't. They know well what they use all the time: Facebook, online games, YouTube. Kids are generally more adventurous than the adults, but kids do not have everything mastered." It is globally true that kids are used to clicking and trying things, whereas older people have a different mental model.

When objects were mechanical, you could actually break them. Kids don't have so much of that fear. They are used to the rhetoric conventions of trying things. But this thinking also has its flipside. Fogg continues: "Young people may apply their concept of undo to the other aspects of their life that are [not] undoable, like: 'I'm gonna get a tattoo...Oh, undo!' Guess what? It's really hard to undo." Moreover, in spite of the current premium on youth in the social web, the situation may be upside down in the future, namely when the digital natives become the majority, it may suddenly be that digital immigrants are the ones who can think outside the box and bring ideas from one field to another.

All in all, companies should understand the premium on youth, they should allow people timeoff for innovation and they should be capable of carrying out rapid experimentations through small independent groups, rapid reaction teams and other similar means. Yet, even these newish business management styles can only do so much. Newer outbound methods for searching and finding social web innovations will be needed. The outbound means to search for innovations include userwatching, crowdsourcing and open innovation approaches as well as participation and encouragement of nics. The greatest business opportunity comes when one is able to create an innovation ecosystem, which combines a set of these innovative strategies with an experience rich web platform for others to innovate against and to nurture a business ecosystem on top of it.

Part IV

Social Web as a Humanizer

10
The Next Generation of the Web: The Humanized Web

An American computer scientist and a pioneer of object-oriented programming and window-based graphical user interface design Alan Curtis Kay remarked about technological developments in 1971 that "the best way to predict the future is to invent it."[1] In this endeavor, understanding that the web will keep evolving is important, though trying to predict when certain developments might occur is usually only guesswork. This is especially so because things that are perceived as good are expected to happen right away, like a child who wants promised sweets immediately rather than after a meal. Still, even though it is difficult to forecast future developments, and in particular their timing, it is important to prepare for the future web.

It would be tempting to think that since the web has already been around for quite some time and since there has been a lot of activity around it, it has already reached its peak. Yet, it is much more likely that we have seen only the beginning of the web's development. What is it that the future of the web holds for us? Professor of Computer Science at Stanford University Terry Winograd says of it that "the most important orientation that will happen is not a property of technology, it's how people use it. Whenever you're thinking about the development of technology, you always have to return to the question of the human needs, human uses, human concerns." To conceive this, let's first consider the meaning of the term technology, however, not according to the discourse of German engineers in the late nineteenth century about *Technologie* and *Technik* linked to engineering profession, as more often would be done, but rather the Classical Greek word *technología* (*τεχνολογία*) which meant the study of art, skill and craft. Admittedly, there seems to be no continuous history of usage linking the classical Greek *technología* to its currently generally accepted meaning, but when the term reappeared in Latin in the sixteenth century its connotations were close to the classical roots, and later in the seventeenth and eighteenth centuries it was several Protestant theologians, who adopted the term. *Technología* applied arts as a whole, but in practice it focused on liberal arts and specifically in the higher education. It had little to do with mechanical arts.[2] By noticing the aforesaid, it is easier to go back to the question of human needs, uses and concerns, regarding the development of any technology.

Today, information technology is already embedded in everyday things. For instance, when one enters a car, it can recognize their telephone through a Bluetooth connection; one could type the address of their destination in the navigation system, speak it aloud or email it to the car, and it will display the directions through the navigation screen; the navigation screen may have real-time communication and intelligence guidance, possibly re-routing around construction work; if one gets a short text message, the car could read it when driving along, and so on. Many people are already living most of their life online, but in the near future we will most probably see even greater movement of offline interactions in the real world to online. Through recent developments, such as cloud computing, people can increasingly access most of their work, content and entertainment on a variety of devices from almost any location in the world. They can connect to their online social networks when they are out jogging, sitting in a park or enjoying the sun, communicating with far-away people in the middle of other activities. This is not only in private computing, but also in work-related matters. Technologies that enable this are already available, even though commercial feasibility of a currently available technology is a whole another question. In any case, maintaining full communication is the key. When people have the "connectedness" everywhere, they cannot help thinking about the world differently. The dominance of technology is gone, and the sociality of the web keeps bringing people together.

Generally speaking, humans have a tendency to treat differently people they know. Some of this effect takes place in subtle psychological ways. For instance, with photos – which is a way of sharing lives – one may get a quick emotional connection with a bunch of other people around oneself. When social interaction takes place through a webpage that has an individual's picture, certain emotions are triggered because of facial recognition, and when an individual recognizes a face, their response pattern may change.[3] If a picture conveys a thousand words, it probably is a lot more with the context embedded in a photograph. The implications of this facet of humanizing effect are fundamental. Consider flaming in email. Since people were not forming a deep social connection in traditional email, they easily ended up writing something emotionally harsh. In 2010, more than 3 billion photos were uploaded every month into Facebook. The role of photos in the social web is just an example, but according to Reid Hoffman, the founder of LinkedIn, the social web not only has lead "to more connections with people but it also has led to more emotional connections. Indeed, it has humanized the Internet. There is much more dialog between people as opposed to, for example, between a media outlet and a person" (but not users of other social networking systems). Interestingly, Pew Internet study on American users of popular social networking systems found out that active Facebook users felt more likely than other web users that "most people can be trusted."[4] Thus, this study, at least implicitly, suggests that tools like Facebook have the capability to increase general trust perceived by its users. Another example of the humanized web is using the social web to follow what is going on in a country in turmoil.

Reid Hoffman explains that the United States and its allies "listened to voices" on both sides through blogs during their invasion of Iraq in 2003. According to Hoffman, "that kind of connection around a field of battle [helped] humanize both sides." In a similar manner, the social web is becoming a "watchdog" for abuses of corporations and governments and it has also influenced areas such as running elections and transparency between governments and its citizens.

These societal changes have produced unexpected implications of significant magnitude and consequence. It is safe to say, at the very least, that the social web is humanizing the web, and the major expectation on the horizon is the web becoming more and more humanized. In the epicenter of this future web are new sense-making and collective intelligence technologies, and enabling of a new level of user experience through increased interactivity and persuasive user experiences. The nomadic social web is already an ongoing web development thread, eventually leading into the social web becoming a giant sensor network. All of these will keep changing how people think and communicate and how innovations will be created in the future.

New sense-making technologies: trailblazers

Vannevar Bush, in "As We May Think," The Atlantic Monthly, July 1945:
There is a new profession of trail blazers, those who find delight in the task of establishing useful trails through the enormous mass of the common record.

In his article "As We May Think," published in the July 1945 issue of *Atlantic Monthly,* Vannevar Bush described interesting concepts that much later, in today's social web and future humanized web, are getting realized.[5] Bush's dream was to "give man access and command the inherited knowledge of the ages." A mechanized machine which he called *Memex* would be a human's "enlarged intimate supplement to his memory." It would be a personalized aid to memory to recall associative "trails." These trails could be personal based on one's own experience, but they could also be the experience of authorities or one's friends.[6] Bush described the Memex owner's trail in this search for an explanation for a problem or challenge at hand:

> He has dozens of possibly pertinent books and articles in his memex. First he runs through an encyclopedia, finds an interesting but sketchy article, leaves it projected. Next, in a history, he finds another pertinent item, and ties the two together. Thus he goes, building a trail of many items. Occasionally he inserts a comment of his own, either linking it into the main trail or joining it by a side trail to a particular item. When it becomes evident that the elastic properties of available materials had a great deal to do with the bow, he branches off on a side trail which takes him through textbooks on elasticity and tables of physical constants. He inserts a page of longhand analysis of his own. Thus he builds a trail of his interest through the maze of materials available to him.[7]

Even several years after its creation, this Memex owner's trail would not have faded. Instead, he could talk with a friend and apply information from the trail as an example to solve another problem and pass the whole trail to the friend. Bush explained:

> The historian, with a vast chronological account of a people, parallels it with a skip trail which stops only on the salient items, and can follow at any time contemporary trails which lead him all over civilization at a particular epoch. There is a new profession of trail blazers, those who find delight in the task of establishing useful trails through the enormous mass of the common record. The inheritance from the master becomes, not only his additions to the world's record, but for his disciples the entire scaffolding by which they were erected.[8]

Bush thus recognized an emerging profession of trailblazers. The model for this new craft was an imaginary historian, the main reason being that historians produced intellectual material for others to digest. Bush carefully retained this same idea in his later article, "Memex Revisited," published in 1967.[9]

Trailblazers are desperately needed in the social web. Having a multitude of information everywhere around us on the social web causes a cognitive burden for us as individuals, and very easily this leads to information bloat in us. Researchers have suggested different kinds of solutions for trying to manage this type of anxiety. For instance, graphical maps over the overall information content and its subsets, landmarked spots in the information space, personalized bookmarks, and guided tours through the content help users recognize important information and stay on a steady path through the information.[10] Trailblazers are also needed, because even though people do often find interest in many diverse topics they still do not want to personally spend time to do research about them. Most often, they just want to follow what others recommend them. More recently, the emergence of social networks with more powerful tools to share links and tools to control what to receive has made social navigation possible. This type of social navigation happens, for instance, when people share links on Facebook or Twitter and then others go see what their friends and business acquaintances recommended them.[11] Indeed, it is the users who typically create these trails and share them with others. Of course, some similar activity has happened before in email, IRC and other communication channels, but via the social web it has become much easier and much more common. There are many services today that get more traffic from social network sites than they do from search engines, which till recently was by far the most modern method of referral. Many people follow tweeters or Facebook friends, who share, say, three or four interesting comments or links a day, which even may be essentially all of this person's social web activity. This may be in the form of a one-sentence comment on history, science, or other interesting topic. It is a mode of discovery to see it from those persons, because it is often something that one probably would not have had time to find oneself. Jimmy Wales explains of such a Facebook friend of his: "I don't know what he does all day long, but he's out there finding these things, setting them along. It's wonderful. It's always surprising. Sometimes it's funny things, sometimes it's science, sometimes it's a silly video on YouTube or whatever. But his judgment is good. There are [also] other people like that." Note the words "his judgment is good." The content has to be of very high quality and the timing has to be right. Wales's friend is akin to the trailblazers that Vannevar Bush described years earlier.

Not all people in a community can be trailblazers, of course. In reality, in most communities many more people only observe than produce information. People who belong to an online community, but rarely or never produce information, are sometimes derogatively called "lurkers."[12] To get an idea of how common this type of user behavior is, Blar Nonnecke and Jennifer Preece studied health-focused email-based discussion lists and found out that more than nine of ten people stayed only as lurkers.[13] More recently, Michael Muller, N. Sadat Shami, David R. Millen, and Jonathan Feinberg reported that in their quantitative comparison regarding an enterprise file-sharing service called Cattail seven of ten users (72 percent) were regarded as lurkers. Whatever the actual percentage of lurkers is it is a common behavior.[14] The point actually is that lurkers are modal users and it could be so that "we are all lurkers, at least some of the time, in most of the social systems that we use."[15] For this reason, we suggest here a more positive term, *tracer*, to describe this type of user behavior in the social web. As tracers join online communities for different reasons than those who create content actively, their relationship with trailblazing is different, and yet tracers still need trailblazers because they start losing their interest in the community without the trails and other content created by trailblazers. The sense of community of tracers perhaps is not as strongly established as it is with the active ones, in particular trailblazers, or they may just be satisfied with reading and browsing. Nevertheless, the user behavior of tracers rarely is hostile towards the active users, and they are an important part of a community even if they contribute very little or perhaps nothing explicitly. Moreover, also trailblazers need tracers. Without tracers, trailblazers would not have anybody to pave the way for. Thus, tracers bring tacit knowledge into the social web communities, when trailblazers polish their ideas to match with the interests of tracers. There is a great need for both trailblazers and tracers in every community. Managers of an online community who are considering their position on how the content will eventually be created should note this important synergy that exists between key players in the future humanized web, the tracers and trailblazers.

New collective intelligence technologies: context accumulation

Tim O'Reilly:
Context accumulation is really how our brains work, and yet our systems are not yet designed to do context accumulation very effectively.

Google's representatives famously said that their mission is to organize the world's information, and that they are doing it through search.[16] Search is here to stay, and it will continue to be a dominant way of making sense of information in the web. However, there is a lot of cognitive overhead involved in doing knowledge searches that users often don't even realize, in particular so because to a great extent users still must try to think like a computer. For this reason we are little by little moving away from keyword or text string search, and new sense-making technologies are emerging on par with search. In particular, the social web is inherently tied with the idea of collective intelligence, which emerges from the collaboration between users that form a group or a community.

Collective intelligence was emphasized by one of the famous innovators in modern computing, Douglas Engelbart, in the 1960s.[17] Engelbart describes the importance of integrating pieces of knowledge to each other in order to make the full knowledge space more meaningful, commenting:

> It seems to be so critical to all humanity, if we could really, really, really learn how to develop those [dynamic knowledge repositories] so that they integrated all of the available knowledge. By integrated I mean what's there that's relevant to what kind of issues, that one could find a pathway very directly. It's very easy for your friends to give you a link that will take you right to something, or give you a family or a network of links that put together a whole, put all this together and say, "See, there must have been a reason for all that."

The next step is to start to stitch all those pieces of knowledge and context together. The term *web*^{2} or *web squared* has been suggested by Tim O'Reilly and John Batelle to emphasize the harnessing of collective intelligence via the accumulation of users' contextual information.[18] A simple example of what a system that supports context accumulation[19] should do is that user's social web graph data tells that it is their close relative's, say, sister's or aunt's 25th wedding anniversary in a week; it knows that one is standing on the corner of Thirty fourth Street and Fifth Avenue in New York; it knows because of data about her and husband's taste that they like certain things; it tells which store to go to buy a gift for them; it also knows that there is a Federal Express office two blocks away; it knows their address; it knows where to send the gift.[20] The system would suggest, "It's time to think about their wedding anniversary. Here are suggestions for them." One would not even necessarily need to go and look at the gift. It could just say, "Here are potential gifts," and lay those all out for the user as suggestions and say, "Do you want me to send this to them?" That's all the user has to do. If one wants to write a handwritten card, one can of course do that, too. As a matter of fact, all of this information already exists in dozens of different places. It is just that it hasn't been put together in order to solve problems for people. There is nothing mysterious or even radically new in this, but it means providing deeper connections between different information systems and coordination between those systems. And yet that is one of the essential features in the next stage of social web to achieve better support for collective intelligence.

In the 1990s, the web's ability to bring together millions of previously unrelated buyers and sellers worldwide at a low price via electronic commerce helped give a boost for Customer Relationship Management (CRM) systems. Following the idea of CRM systems, Tim O'Reilly asks for a future personal CRM system in the social web in which one is able to manage their contacts in an asymmetric follow model. A simple example is that a system could recognize user's email contacts with someone else and show them in this system's context and it could list when others commented on one's blog posts or referred to one on Twitter. Yet, even though these future personal CRM systems and tools for managing contextual information are seemingly simple, we are still surprisingly far from seamless integration between different information channels and managing context accumulation. Although we are already seeing a massive increase in technology that supports group interaction and mobile multimedia, including taking pictures and video with mobile devices and allowing people to send real-time messages to each other, the current social web applications are still fairly weak for managing one's own connectedness and network awareness. An exciting aspect of the future web is that context accumulation might make the information space that needs to be managed from user's perspective "smaller" rather than larger through better finding of the target information, thus easing a user's cognitive overload. For understanding one's own overall social graph, connections and their consequences, more sense-making tools that build upon the idea of accumulated contextual information would be needed. Via context accumulation tools, people could track records for themselves, and in some special cases they would allow other people to see their behavioral patterns.

There is a big business opportunity for a "new Google" to make sense of people's social connections.[21] What is needed are tools for managing one's own social web, in which sophisticated data could include categories like location, movement, taste, sentiments, emotions, and perhaps even mood. In addition to establishing and maintaining online social network, successful products likely will be those that can aggregate and translate the incredible amount of data available into something useful and meaningful. Thus, tools for integrating and coordinating the related pieces of information will be needed. The provision of various types of novel collective intelligence technologies will help further humanize the web.

Increased interactivity

Caterina Fake:
We have gone from word-based culture to a very visual culture.

Ben Shneiderman:
A picture is worth a thousand words, but an interface is worth a thousand pictures.

Steve Jobs:
We are all born with the ultimate pointing device – our fingers – and iPhone uses them to create the most revolutionary user interface since the mouse.

A serious challenge in the original web was its limited interactivity, and there actually was a relatively high likelihood that the web would have died because of this. However, it survived and we have already begun to see the web becoming much more interactive. Companies used to present a lot of content, much of which was one-way, and the web was used mainly for searching information, whereas the social web by definition aims at engaging the user in a much deeper sense. People expect social interaction around the objects they have created, such as getting comments, and users seem to be ready to go an extra mile when they are engaged. To be able to support engagement, the technology has to be capable of not just pushing out information, but bringing it back in, storing it, and presenting it again. This whole new level of interactivity and participation is a major change that has already taken place in the web. However, there is still much to be done to reach even richer interactivity.

One might mistakenly think that the web is something that can be seen on a screen only. We already have seen mobile phones and other gadgets to incorporate new ways of interacting with the web. The Apple iPhone has been able to make a great business impact since January 2007, when it was announced with a slogan "Apple Reinvents the Phone with iPhone." Steve Jobs, Apple's CEO said at the time: "We are all born with the ultimate pointing device – our fingers – and iPhone uses them to create the most revolutionary user interface since the mouse."[22] iPhone is a physical user interface in which you move, shake, and speak to the device, and yet this is only a hint of future interactivity. But the web already has taken other forms and we can expect that there will be many more interesting devices for interacting with the web that we have not seen before. Tim O'Reilly forecasts futuristically that "The future UI [user interface] is a heads-up display. We're gonna get to a point where we're all gonna be wearing glasses. My heads-up, my application will recognize your face. It will bring up additional information about you, will look at my calendar or my address book and say 'oh yeah, this is where we met.'" Whether this happens remains to be seen, but it is likely that whole new ways of interacting with the web will be found.

In their search for social web innovations with increased interactivity, technology developers could learn a lot from the challenges of developing applications for disadvantaged users such as old people or those who have impaired hearing or eyesight. Removing any of the obstacles they face with could make the social web advance far beyond where we are now, which consecutively could open up many new business opportunities for the developers. In any case, using the web in everyday contexts and within our own actual social networks will benefit greatly from developing richer methods for interacting than we have today. Along with increasing interactivity response times are cutting shorter, and there can be massive transactions happening on the web in real time. Today, one can perform different actions one may have dreamt of 10 or 20 years ago.

One of the things that experts have spoken about over the past decades and that is happening today is interactive multimedia, perhaps more properly to be addressed as hypermedia. Hypermedia is not only photosharing and video but bandwidth in two directions, both downloading and the uploading with associative hyperlinks and notes. People are already exchanging video and movies on YouTube, but it is likely that we will see much more of this in the future.

Video-related information sharing opportunities have potential to grow into a new kind of full media for the future web. Video in many ways is in a similar situation as text was for the web in the late 1990s. Free homepage providers enabled people to post basically anything on their own, and interacting with text online little by little became easy and lightweight. Nowadays, people can post text into Wikipedia and others can immediately edit it, but videos mostly are still at the stage of making, uploading and commenting on (often silly) videos on YouTube, but not really collaborating. It is still difficult for a group of people to work together collaboratively on editing a longer video, partly because sending it back and forth requires quite a heavy workload and is rather slow. To some extent this is surprising, because Douglas Engelbart demonstrated collaborative multi-site real-time (text) editing in the well-known "Mother of All Demos" as early as in 1968, and this serves as a historical comparison point or baseline for all of this kind of collaborative knowledge work activities independent of the format of the data. With time, though, some of the ease of manipulation that text online has reached is likely to come to video. Sufficient bandwidth is needed for being able to edit video together without paying much attention to the actual process of sending and downloading. To achieve this, beyond many software-related issues, there is a lot of work to be done in figuring out the social norms for this new type of collaboration.

In overall, we as a society have shifted from a culture which was based on literacy and actual reading to one based on visuals, and this kind of visual culture does not seem to be disappearing anytime soon. This is particularly so because photos, pictures and video maintain enormous power – they have the ability to influence people. Much of this power lies in hypermedia's non-linear narrative structures. When one sees pictures in sequence, it creates a narrative in one's mind and in many cases it is this sequence which helps one to understand what is actually going on rather than single pictures. According to Ben Shneiderman, a big challenge in advancing interactive multimedia is that people are still currently trained to think in a textual and numeric way, and for this reason he requests for broader education that includes visual literacy as part of its program: "Training people to think visually will open up the possibilities. Education and practice in using maps and bar charts and more complicated tools should begin in high school. It would become a part of the culture and would [expand] people's capacity to deal with the complex world around us." Better educational use of relatively simple geographical maps and more generally conceptual maps, the latter of which provide spatial views to the web's hyperspace, could help improve students' and other social web users' navigational skills and it could also develop their conceptual thinking capabilities.

In parallel with the rich use of interactive multimedia, there is a different kind of trend taking place, microblogging, with very limited means of expressing oneself. It has been claimed that blog posts averaged about 255 words.[23] Interestingly, it is the amount up to which each ancillary packet can have words within a serial digital data stream, the length of multiple word message supported by the data monitor and the practical limit that captions were displayed on analog television receivers. Thus, it is possible that there might have been technical details without any intention and without a specific agenda resulting to this number of words. The length of 255 words is also the length of a short essay, the amount that court reporters must write per minute in shorthand in some training courses and the normal mean reading rate in a minute of high school students in the United States. Thus, there might also be a cognitive reason for this particular length. Whatever the case in reality is, texts online seem to be shortening even from this. Twitter is down to 140 characters. At the same time, some of the microblogging platforms such as tumblr.com allow posting images and videos in addition to text thus extending the capability to express ideas in this manner. Blauk.com, which encourages strangers to comment about topical issues and get in touch with each other,[24] builds upon a message system, which includes only 100 characters for the actual comment in addition to which a 64-character physical description of the user and another 64-character description of the time and place of the passing by is required.

In spite of their restricted length of messages, microblogging is a very powerful medium of communication. In a way, it is more of a basic technology, a platform, than full-fledged social networking systems, which means that there are very many ways to use it, and people are indeed using these services in ways which their developers never expected. Microblogging also opens up opportunities for people who face an information overload and rarely have time and energy to get deeper into the meanings behind massive amounts of information to be in the know of what is going on in their interest areas via this newsfeed type of stripped media approach. It is likely that rich media, such as video, and stripped media, such as microblogging, will both prosper and have their own uses in the future humanized web.

Persuasive user experiences

> *Ted Nelson:*
> *In software, you have effects on the screen that affect the heart and mind of the viewer and interact and have consequences. It's movies plus.*
>
> *Douglas Engelbart:*
> *What is it that motivates people, what makes them wonder, and what makes them put in some effort to try to think of solutions or innovations?*

Through increased interactivity and engagement of users, the social web has opened up many opportunities for developing new kinds of information systems for influencing their users' behaviors. For instance, through fostering healthier lifestyles the web is one of the most prominent areas for future healthcare improvement. Positive results have been reported in areas such as the management of anxiety and depression, asthma, complicated grief, diabetes, alcohol abuse, insomnia, obesity, smoking cessation, stress, and tinnitus.[25] Many other application areas within and beyond health-related ones include, for instance, directing users towards appropriate exercise behavior and promoting greener energy behaviors.

The key to behavior change through the social web is persuasive systems design. In their elaboration likelihood model, Richard E. Petty and John T. Cacioppo suggest that there are two routes for persuading people, either via "central" route or "peripheral" route. Approaching via central route underscores reason and argument, whereas approaching via peripheral route builds upon social cues and often on several arguments.[26] Robert Cialdini has suggested that there are six generic persuasive strategies, namely reciprocity, commitment and consistency, social proof, authority, liking, and scarcity.[27] Different kinds of persuasive software features which have psychological grounding can be implemented into the web,[28] supporting the user's primary activities, representing information fluently in the computer–human dialogue, and conveying the credibility of information being presented.[29] For instance, provision of positive feedback and virtual trophies after attaining a goal leverages the persuasive software features of praise and rewards. Leveraging social behaviors through software features that support social learning, comparison and facilitation, as well as recognition, competition, cooperation and normative influence have been found to provide highly persuasive user experiences. Implementations of persuasive software features may also apply game mechanics and gamification to engage users in target behaviors, for instance, boring tasks such as completing surveys, by rewarding users for their action with obtaining social badges.[30] Of course, nudging people to do small things is much easier than helping them to carry out a longer process of change through full-fledged behavior change support systems.[31]

In more general terms, the essence of persuasive technology is defined by Stanford-based psychologist B.J. Fogg as to "put hot triggers in the path of motivated people." This would mean that people need to have motivation, and they need to be in a primary process of doing something. At that case, the persuasive potential of information systems may trigger a user to change their behavior. These triggers may be real-time reminders, virtual rewards, social badges, or some other persuasive software features. Fogg suggests that persuasive technology should be metrics-driven to the extent that not only the actual change in behaviors, but also the facets of technology, such as the particular software features and their use, are easily measurable. Indeed, metrics have a lot of power even if they weren't that fancy. Of course, the challenge with metric-driven development is that they easily start to drive development efforts into one particular direction. This is because of the spot fallacy, the general tendency of focusing on things that will be measured rather than something that is of real insight or value. Nevertheless, the metrics have an enormous power to guide the design.

At the same time, both software developers and the general audience should be aware of the various ways in which people can be influenced through information technology designs. This is especially so because the contemporary and future web will keep opening up a myriad of opportunities for building software that aims at persuading people. Ethical considerations arise while developing persuasive user experiences, such as the actual voluntariness of users to use the application and potential ways for abusing it. There may even be situations where computer-mediated persuasion may take place without the user being aware of it. The motives and designer bias behind a web-based service, for instance, may remain not clearly explicated. According to Fogg, in the social web there has been a shift from the power being concentrated in a few companies and governments seeking their own interest to millions of people basically seeking good for themselves and people like them, and he sees this as a better arrangement than big companies dominating the whole software market: "All in all, it's a good thing that persuasive technology will be pervasive, because tools for creating those persuasive experiences will be in the hands of millions and not just a few powerful governments' organizations. If you have a million people creating persuasive experiences, the overall impact is going to be better than a few corporations seeking their own financial interest." Some people may still worry about a potential scenario in which people will be persuaded at every step. Yet Fogg believes that people will eventually learn to filter that out in such a manner that they will have channels that they listen to and the channels they don't. Experiences in a social medium eventually are only coming to a person through people they trust, which carefully fulfills the idea of social filtering.

In the social web it is often the case that simple less articulated mechanisms end up working better than more complex, even if perhaps logically better, ones. Thus, ideal solutions which do not work in practice must not become obstacles for less articulate but highly operational solutions. After all, it is the simplicity that makes many things with these systems useful, and their simplicity even has the power to change users' behaviors. But to be able to make things easy is often extremely difficult. Indeed, the capability to abstract things and to develop easy to use systems is not everyman's, or every web developer's, possession. Somewhat surprisingly, however, big brands no longer seem to have the clear upper hand in behavior change related services. In fact, in a way they have a disadvantage. Fogg puts forward a claim that it is not only understanding user behaviors that is important in the future web but that those who can think the clearest about behavior change and act the fastest will be winners. The success of Facebook and to some extent of Twitter, according to Fogg, is related to the persuasive experiences and yet simple interfaces they have been able to create. According to investor Reid Hoffman, there is strong interest and actual investment among venture capitalists in persuasive systems implemented in the social web arena. The interest is especially strong in questions such as how to measure the influence of people on each other,[32] determining the influence metrics through social and professional networks and leveraging those networks in order to market products or brands. Professor Henry Chesbrough from University of California Berkeley believes that persuasive systems design will soon gain great emphasis within academia and that it will be addressed in several fields such as information, engineering, technology management and business schools.

Nomadic social web

> *Tim O'Reilly:*
> *There's no question that the era of the PC is over and we really are in the era of mobile. All the rules about web applications that get smarter the more people use them applies a hundredfold in mobile.*
>
> *B.J. Fogg:*
> *Mobile phones are great for the close ties.*

The web has already gone mobile, and it seems clear that the device platform of the future is going to be mobile and handheld rather than PC-based and desktop. Professors Kalle Lyytinen from Case Western Reserve University and Youngjin Yoo from Temple University call the current generation of mobile systems as nomadic information environments in which the fundamental drivers are mobility and digital convergence as well as their massive scale. In their conceptual framework, the two key layers of these environments are services and infrastructure, both of which can be studied at the individual, team, organizational, and inter-organizational levels.[33] The big opportunity in the nomadic social web lies in that one can really do things with it at the point of interest without needing to be at one's desk; users do not have to go to a dedicated terminal or computer either for looking up a street address or sending a quick note to somebody; a medical doctor can obtain necessary information at the bedside of a patient. One can already do almost all of the same things on a smart phone than only recently with a laptop or even a desktop computer. Not everything that people now do on the web will be reasonable to do on the nomadic mode, but a great many things are transferring or will transfer. This nomadic social web can lend context and meaning for many different kinds of services. In fact and most importantly, it is not going to be just another opportunity, but the nomadic social web will be the major platform in the future web and it will still continue to evolve.

The mobile phone platforms have played a central role in the development of the nomadic social web. It is common to browse the web via mobile phones or use native mobile applications which are specifically designed and implemented for mobile devices. The mobile phone is ultimately a socially connected device. Regarding the development of nomadic social web applications, Henry Chesbrough suggests that "a lot of the content that's on the web, which is not today formatted for [mobile devices], is going to somehow have to transform. Somebody's going to make some money developing a product or technology that reformats all this content that was created in the PC-based era that will now be displayed on devices with [small] screens." The opposite view is, of course, that the data on the web will stay as it is and the mobile applications, devices and infrastructure have to adapt to it. Admittedly, native mobile applications can be useful for specific contexts, but most new mobile appliances will likely be web-capable. One of the things we are already seeing is that the web is being used less and less based on traditional channels and more and more through mobile devices such as Internet tablets.[34] Since an increasingly large percentage of web use is and will be mobile, web developers cannot assume that people would use web services only from PCs or laptops with fast connections.[35] In turn, new interfaces need to be created that are tuned to the size and nature of mobile devices and that in a true sense will utilize their core capabilities such as location awareness.

However, the technological features are only the tip of the iceberg. Geographical positioning systems, location-based software capabilities, and particularly the ability to filter and intelligently manage contextual information and context accumulation make it possible to benefit not only socially but economically in our daily lives. A simple example of the contextual information on top of Global Positioning System (GPS) is that one is able to put their phone up and point it to the Eiffel Tower or Empire State Building so that it recognizes the tower and gives them information about where they are and what all kinds of information is related to the object, much of which is created by other users. For another instance, technologies such as RFID (Radio Frequency IDentification) and NFC (Near Field Communication) enable in-store promotions and real-time coupon offers to be delivered for users in the aisle right while being there, This becomes especially powerful after the social web has enabled users to share information about specific products and retailers in this context between each other. As visible already now, majority of Foursquare users are willing themselves to check in at different geographical locations and let their friends see where they are at a given moment. The nomadic social web's potential can also be seen from the fact that many geographical positioning and location based information systems are being integrated with mobile devices and the social web. For instance, NAVTEQ, a subsidiary of mobile phone manufacturer Nokia, which it had acquired a few years earlier, was seamlessly integrated with Nokia's mainstream mobile and location-based service operations with an aim to develop "a new class of integrated social location products and services for consumers," and "platform services and local commerce services for device manufacturers, application developers, internet services providers, merchants, and advertisers."[36] Thus, companies expect that the next generation nomadic social web would have enough power to differentiate them from their competitors. Information about one's physical location is indeed an important part of the nomadic social web.[37]

Mobile phones are also becoming payment systems through which users could make peer-to-peer payment, for instance, by touching mobile phones to each other and entering the amount of money to be transferred. At the same time, in developing countries mobile phones have become the major channel of using the web rather than desktops or laptops, and this being on the leading edge for the mobile use of the web, even if the majority of mobile phones available there are by no means top-of-the-line models, could open up a surprising opportunity for businesses originating from these areas. Yet, for companies that may have had tremendous success in the desktop world or original web but who are weak in the mobile and handheld world, this development is becoming an existential challenge. Thus, nomadic social web is a central and already visible part of the humanized web, and the implications of this nomadic behavior are immense.

Giant sensor network

> *Paul Saffo:*
> *Cheap sensors are driving the web.*
>
> *Vint Cerf:*
> *The Internet operation will extend to outer space.*

The bondage between human values and hard technology is interesting. Something that in itself is very far from the humanized web but that makes it even more an integral part of people's everyday lives is the web as part of physical products and objects through sensors. Tim O'Reilly explains that "sensory model is a big part of [the future web], because what we're starting to build is a world in which our computers and our applications are driven increasingly by sensors." Many technological and business opportunities related to the humanized web have opened as different kinds of sensors have been developed and have become cheaper. An example of a local effect of a sensor would be that once you put a phone to your ear it recognizes the motion or gesture as the trigger to start listening and to go into speech recognition mode.

There are already social web applications that build upon networked sensor data. The Quake-Catcher Network, a joint collaborative initiative run by Stanford University and the University of California Riverside, is an earthquake detection network through which motion sensors in laptops can become part of a distributed monitoring system. On 21 February 2011, a 6.3 magnitude earthquake occurred just outside of Christchurch, New Zealand. Several Quake-Catcher Network stations installed in and around Christchurch succeeded in recording this earthquake.[38] In a similar manner, sensors connected to our bodies and then connected back to the web may provide meaningful quantitative data on our health.

Tim O'Reilly notes that "this whole area of thinking about the Internet as the backend for a giant sensor network leads you to just all kinds of interesting ideas." A company called AMEE in the United Kingdom provides web service and API for information systems based on various kinds of energy-related sensor data and an algorithm which converts energy factors into carbon dioxide emissions using data from millions of users in different countries. According to O'Reilly, the company is able to see from the connected electricity meters what make and model of refrigerator or washing machine somebody has in their home thanks to the unique energy signature of each appliance. All of a sudden, it is possible to upgrade one's hardware the same way that there is an upgrade cycle for the latest version of a piece of software. This means huge opportunities for marketing. It turns out that the data that one can get out those kinds of new web-based applications, such as connected electric meters and smart grid, is enormous. In just the same way that Google said "Oh, there's hidden data in the link structure of the web," somebody could come and say "Oh, there's hidden data in what's coming out of electric meters" or other similar areas.

The idea of the "Internet of Things" was presented in the late 1990s, referring to uniquely identifiable objects in a similar structure as in the Internet. From web perspective, an even more interesting development thread is collecting data from sensor networks and integrating it to the web. Web-specific version of the Internet of Things, the "Web of Things," means that everyday devices and objects are fully integrated with the web.[39] This results in a giant sensor network and in wide-scale connecting of the social web to the physical world. For example, heart rate monitors enable their measurement results to be brought into the web, individuals to share information to a restricted set of friends or perhaps someone to publish measurement results in aggregated forms from multiple people, teams, organizations or other entities to a wider audience. In addition to the outbound traffic from monitors, there are also many kinds of information that may be brought from the web to these wristbands, for instance, advice based on information harvested from the web to notify a user about a flu trend that has arrived in the very geographical area the day before; this could explain why his or her workout is going worse than normally, and the wristband would suggest to radically ease exercise at this time. The future web is indeed becoming a world in which millions of devices are reporting in with data. From the perspective of the web of things, the social web with its hundreds of millions of people linked to each other is only the first stage. Vint Cerf notes, "I expect to see more 'things' on the net than there are people. I expect to see an increasing amount of information flowing into the net from the edge, not just flowing out of the net to the edge." This would mean that more data on the web would be machine processable, in the best case turning much of that data into meaningful knowledge. Should this happen, many of the methods and techniques developed in the semantic web research would then become extremely useful. And yet having so many "things" on the net would increase opportunities to develop more sophisticated pervasive applications for people's everyday lives and in this manner contribute towards even more humanized web.

The web's future pervasiveness seems to be more than just words. The most extreme case is that NASA is committed to rapidly developing an internetworked model of space communications. NASA's Jet Propulsion Laboratory aims at extending Internet operation to outer space.[40] Tests of the deep-space communication have been carried out in Jokkmokk in northern Sweden.[41] Vint Cerf describes that the tests were made among the Sámi, reindeer herds because "it was a test to see whether or not this deep-space communication idea would work well in a disruptive local terrestrial environment and it did, in fact, work quite well." Whether the Internet operation in outer space will happen and if so in what form remain to be seen. Nevertheless, it demonstrates how serious the efforts of big players around extending the web beyond its current boundaries really are.

All in all, the web drives the convergence of many information technologies, all the way from outer space Internet communication to more down the earth integration between print media and the web, and the web is about to become present in all facets of modern life. The web and other technologies, whether it's media, entertainment, general information, or professional or personal communications, seem to be coming together so that the web as a distinction almost loses its power because the web is just a part of everything else. In other words, bringing the web into the living room, car and other places of everyday life may make it just a commodity or utility. According to B.J. Fogg, "It is fading to the background where we don't think about 'this is the web' anymore. Just like electricity inside the walls. All I need to know is how to plug-in, and then do what I want." Should this happen, the web would have made a similar lasting impact on people's lives as electricity has had. Regarding this, computer scientist and the head of the Computer Science Laboratory at Xerox PARC Mark Weiser famously said in 1991 that the most profound technologies are those that disappear, "those which weave themselves into the fabric of everyday life until they are indistinguishable from it."[42] The social web is as yet a distinguishable technology, but when we get to the humanized web, we may have reached an indistinguishable stage for the social web.

In sum, the major expectation of the future web is becoming more humanized. Technologically, this will be brought about by the nomadic social web as the major platform for the web use and the web becoming a giant sensor network. Supporting human sense-making and the growth of collective intelligence and guaranteeing users with highly engaging and persuasive user experiences will provide business opportunities in this humanized web. Core values for coping with and making successful business in this kind of an environment are very humane too. These will be discussed in the next chapter.

11
Core Business Values

It will be impossible to superimpose innovative thinking and then integrate it successfully into organization's business processes. To succeed in the new humanized web based economy requires a combination of core business values and competences that have to converge no matter what one's domain is. These core business values are watchfulness for technological shifts, ability to think outside the box, intrapreneurial spirit, and having an appetite to fail fast. A key to success is to have a balance among these core business values.

Core business values for thriving to create social web innovations

1. Watchfulness for technological shifts
   - recognizing an opportune moment
   - understanding the S-curve of technology adoption
   - aiming at being a fast follower
2. Thinking outside the box
   - openness to new ideas and serendipity
   - individual creativity
   - bringing ideas from one field to another
3. Intrapreneurial spirit
   - passion
   - persistence
   - persuasiveness
4. Appetite to fail fast
   - being able to innovate quickly and then revise
   - willingness and ability to fail fast
   - capability to recognize cost-to-failure

Watchfulness for technological shifts

Paul Saffo:
It is flat spot before takeoff. Most ideas take 20 years [to] become an overnight success.

Mårten Mickos:
There rarely is a first mover advantage.

Recognizing a moment at which there is a technological shift going on makes radically new things possible, and watchfulness for technological shifts helps companies to develop and even more importantly to introduce their offerings to the markets at an opportune *moment*. Terry Winograd explains: "When they started doing Google, the idea that you would be able to store all the web in memory, we were just crossing those boundaries. If that technology hadn't changed, they couldn't get you the answer back in one second. Xerox PARC and the early things there were just crossing technological boundaries for what a personal-size computer could do. The vision has to come along when you're at one of these shift points in the technology that enables you to really push." When an opportune moment comes, most people would say, "Oh, you can't do this, it's not practical," but the visionary would say, "No, I think I can make it practical," and then takes advantage of that shift.

There is a load of stories about businesses that once were working with similar ideas than what later became a large success by someone else, but who couldn't identify the shift in technology happening. What happened to Datapoint Corporation is an example of this. Before personal computing it designed a simple computer on a board, originally for the very successful Datapoint 2200 programmable terminal, and made a deal that Intel could put it on a chip. They sold it as a secretarial input device for digital systems, but in fact it was a completely functioning computer. They also created an operating system, but they were too high for the market and too expensive when the personal computer came in. Their management did not realize what the competition was until too late. However, the chip that they designed was eventually the 8008 and it was a start to a longer queue: 8080, 8086, 186/286/386/486 and then the Pentium.[1]

A key facet of being watchful for technological shifts is not only to recognize that an opportune moment has arrived, but also the timing of introducing the innovation to any larger audience. Innovation is a tough business to be in because the vast majority will never make it big. In fact, very few will, and it is not always based on skill. Right timing is extremely difficult since in most cases there are many who are trying to make exactly the same move. Nevertheless, the worst a company can do is to be indecisive; sometimes a clear-cut decision may be to put something on hold. But waiting because of reluctance is a symptom of the company not being either insightful or agile enough (or, in the worst case, both). Caterina Fake and Mårten Mickos admit that there is a lot of happenstance and serendipity involved in the timing. Fake explains that when they developed Flickr as a by-product of Game Never Ending "we didn't really know what we were doing at the outset." Yet, she proclaims that when technology developers have the attitude, "I know the answer," it actually means that their new idea probably is not a good investment for venture capitalists, because "if you're really inventing something, you shouldn't know what you're doing. You should actually lack confidence. You should feel like a failure for a good long time that so you've happened upon the thing that is solving the problem."

Even companies that move rapidly are still subject to what is called the *S-curve of technology adoption*.[2] The S-curve in this context relates to the effort put into improvements and the results achieved over time. Progress is often frustratingly slow, it is flat spot before takeoff, then the pace surges, and finally the progress slows down again; being able to create innovations at these different stages requires different levels of investments and funding. Even in businesses that combine hundreds or thousands of technologies, there are usually only a few technologies that are crucial to their key processes, and it is these core technologies that the managers should be able to identify and follow. Thus, understanding the natural patterns of S-curves of technological progress is an important way to be capable of recognizing technological shifts. Technologists should keep the natural pattern of S-curves in mind even in the period of growth, when they are forgotten easily, because the seeds of technological destruction are already being sown.

Generally people tend to overestimate the benefits in the short run and underestimate the benefits on the long run. This means that very soon after an innovation has been introduced, most developers get excited, think of the first mover advantage, get going, and forget to realize that the majority of the market quite likely isn't ready yet. Perhaps this is why in many cases there isn't necessarily any first mover advantage. At least Mårten Mickos claims that there rarely is such. There are examples of companies who have won because they were the first ones out, but in practice there are many more examples of just the opposite. For instance, with the PC, it wasn't the early leader in operating systems, Digital Research, that succeeded, but rather it was the second generation company Microsoft; Google was not the first search engine; Apple was not the first producer of a smartphone. They all succeeded to do it at the right time. For nearly every very successful company, you find others who tried it earlier on. It is like for every sportsman who succeeds in making a career, just think of how many thousands were nearly as good but didn't make it. The bad news in business is that there will be hundreds if not thousands of equally smart people, who just don't develop their ideas at the right time. In many cases, it makes sense to wait a little bit and contemplate what it is that really drives the business. It is not that one has to be the second or third, either – one just has to do it when the markets are ready to consume. Going out with a fantastic value proposition without realizing that the market isn't ready happens all the time, and still there isn't necessarily anything wrong with the value proposition other than the timing.

Because there is not necessarily any first mover advantage, a potential strategy to be integrated with the capability to identify technological shifts and to time introducing of innovations is being a *fast follower*. This fast-follower strategy is similar to the way many large companies adopt new versions of operational and office information systems. Very often they do so, say, six months after the first companies do, who have tried the new version right away and sometimes paid dearly for their experience. Based on the success of MySQL, Mårten Mickos advises considering this strategy also for developing new technology:

> At MySQL we had this saying that we are a fast follower. This sounds funny because people know us as a pioneer. And MySQL is a pioneer, but in terms

> of technology we were mostly fast followers. We observed the ecosystem and the open source world around us to see what was happening, and when the evidence was strong enough that there was something going, only then would we engage. So we kept our R&D costs very low. We learnt from what was happening around us, and once we got engaged we were ready to acquire software and pay for it proper money. Because they already had proven the technology and there was lower technology risk.

MySQL thus put into practice the userwatching and nic approaches. Tim O'Reilly notes how difficult it is to invent something totally new from scratch and to be able to commercialize it: "There are times when there's an explosive new platform and there are lots of opportunities for innovators, but even in the most explicit times, most innovators don't profit from their inventions, or they profit a lot less than people who came along later because the first people don't get it right." Being centrally located in an innovation ecosystem makes it easier to be a fast follower, which, in many cases, is a much safer business strategy than "deciding" to start creating Zero-to-One innovations from scratch. This fast follower approach is exactly what MySQL ended up doing. And indeed, often very little can be done with an innovation at the time of inventing it, instead components need to be added to the initial offering and the users will have to come and start co-creating value. In this manner, the industry as a whole tries to gradually improve the leading solutions. This means that even Zero-to-One innovation often needs further incremental innovations to fulfill the original idea's full potential, which again emphasizes the importance of developing platforms by using which others can try things out.

Thinking outside the box

Mark Granovetter:
Ways of thinking can become standardized in just a couple of years so that people become completely captured.

Caterina Fake:
We were busy inventing a game when we accidentally stumbled upon a photosharing idea.

Judy Estrin:
What was just a crazy idea yesterday is often a breakthrough of today.

Mårten Mickos:
Really smart innovators look around and combine things in a surprising way.

Innovation is ultimately never done by committees, and rarely does it come from large workforces either. In practice, almost all in-house innovation is driven by individuals or by small teams. As Reid Hoffman describes it, "Sometimes it's a small team where there's a maximum, say, three to six collaborators. But the essential idea is almost always born of one person or two to three. This concept could be anything from technology to process to an idea of how you pull financing and the market distribution together and all the rest of this stuff." Indeed, shared insight by small teams is critical. You need people such as Doug Engelbart, Alan Kay, Steve Jobs or Larry Page, or at least visionaries on some smaller scale. Typically, they have a particular vision, a direction, which is not necessarily completely against what is around them, but it is just pushing in a particular area that they are insistent on.

The root of any innovation is being in a frame of mind in which one could take advantage of unexpected events and turn lessons learned into new insight, but the challenge is that one easily gets locked in one's own thinking and breaking free is difficult. According to Mark Granovetter, "once people really have got the paradigm, it takes over thinking. It becomes hard to think outside the box." Yet, thinking outside the box is the only way people are able to create new avenues for thinking or make the kind of progress that is needed for creating something really new – Zero-to-One innovations. The key is to get out of a usual way of thinking and try to see the problem one is working at from a different point of view, potentially even from a view that has never been used before. If one is able to figure out other perspectives, then one has a great advantage over people who are stuck within standardized way of thinking.

A key business value that allows thinking outside the box is *openness to new ideas and serendipity*. Terry Winograd describes the atmosphere in MIT's Artificial Intelligence lab when he was a student there in the 1960s: "There was a sense that technology was available to approach in a sort of open and playful way to try out new things. It was very much an unstructured environment. It was very much not a sort of 'here's our goals you have to achieve by such-and-such a date.' Rather 'here's a bunch of equipment and you're a bunch of smart people, see what you can do with it.' That sort of open-ended feeling to it got me oriented towards [the question] how do you do research? You don't drive it down from its goals and sub-goals as much as [from] opportunities." In a similar manner, examples from penicillin to Ethernet tell stories of business people who were working in one direction, but who were willing to look at another direction. There has to be openness to imagining, collaborating, and listening to others; there has to be a questioning of the status quo; there has to be curiosity and self-assessment. Furthermore, the way one frames questions is essential; narrow questions may produce narrow answers without disruptive thinking. The questions that are being asked have to be wide enough so that general principles can be discovered.

There is a wide variety of opinions on what are the best ways to be able to think outside the box. Different approaches could be tried, but to a great extent thinking outside of the box is similar to creativity. Thus, *individual creativity* should be encouraged. Both companies and educators should be able to figure out ways to teach people to think creatively rather than to think only within paradigms. Ted Nelson advocates Walt Disney's kind of creativity: "Walt Disney had a signature. Everything that came out of the Disney studios while he was alive was the product of his own taste and judgment, which incorporated many suggestions and many ideas from many people. But it was unified by this taste and judgment." This kind of creativity could also be called being a visionary.[3] The general idea of trial and error relates closely with the spirit of creativity. In this way, one is continuously trying out and changing circumstances and viewpoints. And yet, experienced entrepreneurs and innovators have a clear understanding that failures happen all the time. In fact, according to B.J. Fogg, most innovation attempts fail. However, success stories also exist.

Imagine fashion house Prada's first Epicenter in Soho, New York. This fashion store was described as an exclusive boutique, a public space, a gallery, a performance space and a laboratory, all at the same time. Among other things, it installed "magic mirrors," consisting of cameras and displays, for letting people to see clothes on them front and back at the same time, dressing room doors turning opaque at the touch of a button, wireless RFID chips in the product labels tracking merchandize, and closets transmitting information about chosen garment onto a screen, and it enabled sales associates to utilize wireless devices for highlighting sketches and catwalk video clips for customers. Today all of this may sound like business as usual, but this all took place in December 2001.[4] IDEO, a human-centered design company which is widely regarded as one of the most innovative design consultancies in the world, had accepted the challenge for enhancing Prada's retail experience, and its human factor specialists were closely working with the Prada people for creating this novel experience.[5]

Creativity is often needed also to commercialize innovations. Commercializing is a multistage and complex process, but the ability to think outside the box has to be shown all the way from small business decisions. For simple instances, to name page rank company as "Google" after "googol" was fresh thinking. In a similar fashion, Mårten Mickos explains about the creation of the brand and dolphin logo for MySQL: "In the first proposal, the dolphin was jumping from left to right, which is typically the case in the western world. Everything has to go up to the right. But then we said, 'No, we actually want to be contrarian, so could you turn the dolphin around, so it surprisingly jumps from right to left.' And the logo started looking much more powerful. I don't know where we took that thinking, but we just had this thinking that 'hey, we don't need to be like everybody else.'"

Thinking outside the box crossbreeds with combining things in a fresh way. In some cases, that may be all it takes. It doesn't necessarily take a new invention *per se*, and one doesn't need to always have a new gadget that nobody has ever produced before. Many Zero-to-One innovations that change people's lives indeed are truly new, but since innovations happen in encounters on borderlines another proven innovation model in the high-tech space is the combination of two existing things. Many successful social web services have been able to perform this kind of a move. Take the Apple iPhone and its iTunes as an example. Most components that the phone is built of existed long before, but nobody had packaged them together as such a good user experience like

Apple did. The innovation there was to realize the advantage of combining what existed in different places in a smart way for an excellent user experience. Looking at it afterwards, many will say it is obvious that that is how it was going to be done.[6] In reality, it wasn't obvious, and many companies and individuals failed in trying to develop something similar to it. Considering it obvious would be historical determinism, which simplifies complicated events retroactively to make the story easier to understand. Rather there are often discontinuities in the historical processes and flows of information come together only at a later stage. Indeed, a glance at this development from a very wide perspective or after a longer time period may make events and the development appear as if they had been continuous without noteworthy breaks, and it may make the actual discontinuity lose its relevance to us.[7]

One important way to combine things freshly is to *bring ideas from one field into another field*. The creation of innovations has been found often to arise precisely as a by-product of the bridge-building process, when ideas are transferred from one social sphere to another, and it frequently turns out that a solution or process that is approved in one school of thought is quite unknown in another.[8] An example of bringing an idea from one field to another is inventing the communications technology known as frequency-hopping spread spectrum (FHSS). This invention from the first half of the twentieth century was aimed at protecting U.S. radio-guided torpedoes, but the technology held the potential to revolutionize the world of wireless communications as well. It was patented on 11 August 1942, by a team of two very unlikely innovators, namely voluptuous actress Hedy Lamarr (married name Hedy Kiesler Markey in the patent application) and an American *avant-garde* composer George Antheil in Hollywood. During the World War II, the Allied powers used different Identification Friend or Foe systems to protect their devices against eavesdropping and signal jamming attacks. The FHSS method transmitted signals by rapidly switching a carrier among several frequency channels using a pseudo-random sequence both the transmitter and receiver knew. Lamarr had been previously married to the CEO of one of the world's leading arms manufacturers, Fritz Mandl, before she ran away and escaped to the United States, and while married to Mandl she had been exposed to military technology plans and discussions attempting to design remote-controlled torpedoes. From this she got the idea of distributing the torpedo guidance signal over several frequencies and convinced Antheil, who was the "bad boy" of experimental music in the 1920s and had synchronized player pianos for the *Ballet Mécanique*, to construct a synchronized signal device based on 88 frequencies corresponding to the number of keys on a piano. Twenty years after its conceptualization, the FHSS system that had reached an operational state was implemented for secure communication during the Cuban Missile Crisis. The system was installed on ships sent to blockade Cuba in 1962. Some 30 years later, there were commercial applications of it along cordless and mobile phones utilizing CDMA technology.[9] All of this traces back to the interplay between an actress and a musician.

Another example of bringing an idea from one field to another, in this case interlinking between multiple scientific disciplines, is the idea of the strength of weak ties developed by Mark Granovetter. In this view, strong and weak bonds hold the members of society together, and weak ties are surprisingly powerful, for instance, when searching for a new job. Granovetter explains how he got the idea of "weak ties" for network theory and published his famous article "The Strength of Weak Ties" in *American Journal of Sociology* in 1973:[10]

> I learned chemistry. Hydrogen bonding is a very crucial part of a lot of chemical processes, but the bonds themselves are extremely weak. They barely hold anything together, but they still create the possibility for all these chemical reactions. Harrison White [Associate Professor of Sociology at the Harvard Department of Social Relations at the time] introduced me to some research by Rapoport and Horvath about junior high schools and where you can reach a lot more people through your seventh and eighth best friends than you could through your first-second best friends. So you kind of follow up the networks. When I saw that it did strike me: That's like weak ties knitting together large structure. That's just like chemistry.

In a similar manner, Flickr co-founder Caterina Fake explains that they started building a massively multiplayer game, which failed: "Then we built this fairly lame product which was conversation based on the game, where you could drag and drop photos into a conversation. Basically, we threw that [game] away and then just expanded the website, which this chat photosharing was based on." So they quickly adopted a new course of action after something unexpected happened and it was recognized. What happened to Flickr is an example of both openness to new ideas and bringing ideas from one field to another, namely Fake continues that Flickr's novelty was that they brought many of the principles from massively multiplayer gaming into photosharing:

> If we hadn't been working on the game, we wouldn't [have] ended up there. We wouldn't [have] been able to innovate. If we had actually thought about it, done research, and saw that photosharing was actually kind of a lame business [we wouldn't have done it]. It's just a lot of people putting photosharing out there. [It] is a loss-leader for photo finishing and printing services, which would not have been interesting to us at all. So the ability to actually innovate in that area was by taking a very different view on it, coming from a different background, a different set of experiences, and applying them to this particular problem.

The lesson is that open-minded and creative developers should look around and combine things in a surprising and fresh way perhaps bringing ideas from one field to another. Indeed, companies that look at business from non-traditional angles may see new opportunities much more clearly than those who are locked in their core business.

Intrapreneurial spirit

> *Terry Winograd:*
> *Having a passionate visionary seems to be close to most of these breakthroughs.*
>
> *John Lilly:*
> *You should ignore revenue that makes your product worse for the mission.*
>
> *Ted Nelson:*
> *New ideas are not welcome. People can't understand them no matter how clearly you state them. They cannot imagine it. It sounds to them like static noise or craziness.*

To facilitate innovation processes, organizations must cultivate a spirit in which creating innovations is truly appreciated. A core business value no matter whether one works for a company or owns a business is what we call intrapreneurial spirit – an entrepreneurial mindset as a loyal company employee. Having an entrepreneurial mindset could be an extremely strong learning experience. Peter Thiel, the CEO and co-founder of PayPal, said about being an entrepreneur that he has never learned so much except maybe between the ages of two and three.[11] An intrapreneurial spirit is needed from social web innovators or practically anyone who desires to succeed in the era of the social web whether they formally are entrepreneurs or not. This way of thinking is also needed from company employees, if they expect to be able to come up with social web innovations; thus, the name intrapreneurship rather than entrepreneurship.

Once developed, this intrapreneurial frame of mind often turns into *passion*. Ted Nelson explains: "You need to take a lot of ideas and unify them in the most elegant way possible. It's a matter of passion, focus and clarity." The passionate desire to build something new and to carry it through drives innovation. Ted Nelson illustrates innovating with the image of carrying a ball into the end zone in American football – one has to take charge of the idea and make sure it happens. Nelson frequently uses an expression "early adopters never switch," meaning that after having developed this type of passion people are extremely highly dedicated, perhaps sometimes also locked in into their idea, and keep working to achieve their goal. There isn't always any other business reason for thriving to innovate. Neal Sample exhorts companies to maintain the passion and to keep working despite setbacks:

> A lot of people will start something, it's not immediately successful, they get a little frustrated, and they put it aside. There're probably millions of fantastic ideas that don't make it simply because people either lose interest, or whatever [reason]. The more often we can encourage folks to take the craziest ideas they can and to carry them all the way to completion, to take them as far as they possibly can, the more likely we are to be successful. There are a lot of things that people will tell you, "No, somebody else has done that," "somebody's tried it before," "it won't possibly work in this market," and you find that it's just absolutely not true.

For example, consider Twitter in its early stages. It was basically a very simple short messaging system and there was nothing fundamentally new in the technology. There were doubts about who would "randomly" follow somebody else on Twitter, but its developers kept working with it. Referring to this kind of a phenomenon, Neal Sample advises those who work on innovating:

> Keep with it, take your ideas as outlandish as it might be. If it's different, it's entirely possible that it's gonna amount to something. The only people that'll fail are the people that don't start; you get the folks who are just kicking themselves for like, "Oh, I thought of that ten years ago." "Well if you would've kept on, you would've made something out of it." Let people be skeptical, let some people say no, maybe you don't get the funding you need, and maybe you don't get the financial support, but you will absolutely fail if you don't start, and the only way you'll be successful is if you keep on with it.

Even if almost everyone claims to appreciate new ideas, business environments in reality are often hostile to them. Innovation is often so different than the rest of the culture in a company that it faces something like an allergic reaction. It may also be that nobody is willing to adopt the new idea within the company, which makes decision-making climb into unnecessarily high level; all too often it goes up to the Vice President or CEO level. Reid Hoffman tells about founding and launching LinkedIn:

> Two thirds of my network, two thirds of my friends thought I was crazy. They'd say: "Look, it's not valuable for the first million people that are in it. Between the first person and the millionth person, what do they use it for? What do the first two people use it for? We know each other already, why are we connected on LinkedIn? It's useless, it'll never go anywhere." But I believe that I can get enough people who believe in the concept of it looking forward, that I can get the first million people in, I can make that happen. It was a valid critique. It was intellectually sound. I paid a lot of attention to how do I get to the first million users without them being active value proposition users.

In addition to passion also *persistence* is needed. Persistence can be described by a Finnish word, *sisu*, which, however, is difficult to translate to other languages. It would literally mean a combination of determination, perseverance, strength of will, and "having guts," and yet not only showing momentary courage but rather sustained action against all the odds and any repeated failures. Paul Baran, who gets most credit for inventing package switching for the field of telecommunications, was at first ridiculed by his audience, telephone engineers in phone companies and military. Baran has told that they thought him crazy or ignorant of telephony – or both.[12] Ted Nelson refers to a saying that "it takes 40 presentations before anyone hears your idea." And indeed, for instance, Firefox was for several years just floundering, and then they found the right angle, which was to get Firefox in *The New York Times*, before it took off. In addition to patience and persistence, one must also be able to *persuade* others of the validity of one's ideas, a capability that naturally ties in with the other two characteristics, as well as to develop and provide user experiences in the applications, platforms and ecosystems being built. In this media laden world one's message has to be delivered in a most persuasive way to obtain any attention. Thus, to make things happen, an innovator needs a combination of passion, persistence, and persuasiveness.

Appetite to fail fast

> *B.J. Fogg:*
> *The innovation that works today has two parts: launch small and fast, and measure the results. That means innovate very quickly. And revise, revise and revise.*
>
> *Paul Saffo:*
> *The thing about the Valley that really matters is we know how to fail in the right way.*
>
> *Judy Estrin:*
> *How much money do you have to put in before you know whether it works or not?*

Even if the world of innovating is for the most part thrilling, one of the traps that we as web developers may fall into is that we may like living in a state of dreams. We may think, for example, that we will "build the best software for our field ever" and "ship it in 18 months" instead of just putting it out next week and facing the consequences. The former daydreaming will not work in the social web, whereas the latter is the modern "social web thinking" that needs to be adopted: *innovate quickly and revise*. The attitude should be that one is ready to face the bad news immediately, because by doing so at least one will learn something real. It is not always pleasant, but one will learn. Moreover, once a company starts delivering, it almost always must revise the service offering and this causes progress.

As a rule, information systems are being developed to be too complicated. Based on his experience as a consultant, B.J. Fogg says that he cannot think of a single product, where he thought that the product was too simple or that it needed more features. Indeed, too often we try to overthink from the beginning instead of just getting our hands dirty trying. For this reason, one of Jimmy Wales's mottos is, "avoid excessive a priori thinking." Wales explains that creating Wikipedia could not have happened by sitting down ten years earlier and trying to design the perfect Wikipedia system, because one could never have been able to anticipate all the potential human interests nor all the "what if" questions. It is important to get started and figure out things along the way – if a product or service doesn't work, start it over. The challenge for many companies and perhaps even for some cultures is to worry less about keeping their ideas close and instead try them in practice, and letting them go if they really do not work.

Most innovations, even Zero-to-One innovations, innovations that provide something really new and can disrupt the existing markets, happen in stages, and a historical context is unavoidable to understand and explain them. Sociologist

Mark Granovetter participated in the first systematic analysis of the data in the *Silicon Valley Genealogy Chart* by using techniques of network analysis and network visualization. The group in which he took part aimed at illuminating the continuing significance of patterns laid down in the initial set of founded companies and spin-offs that gave the Valley its distinctive industrial organization. Their work was based on *Semiconductor Genealogy Chart* that was developed by journalist Don C. Hoefler, following a concept suggested by the Fairchild head of human resources Jack Yelverton.[13] This chart traces nearly forty-year-long lineage of major developments in Silicon Valley, the lineage beginning from the invention of the transistor by William J. Shockley and his collaborators at Bell Laboratories in New Jersey in 1947.[14] The lesson learned is that to name something as an innovation is often hindsight, and even innovations that finally make a breakthrough often do build on already existing innovations.

Risk-taking always goes hand in hand with creating innovations, in particular when hunting for a breakthrough. Judy Estrin emphasizes this: "Without risk, you have nothing, but it has to be intelligent risk. We have become too risk-averse as we've become more fearful of failure. The second thing is, we have to stop being so short-term focused, because when you are only focused on short-term returns, you eliminate the ability to get deep, broad innovation."[15] Risks, even intelligent ones, mean that the end-results by no means are guaranteed or that they would simply be achieved if enough time is given. There are many examples of inventors and innovators who did not get recognition while still alive. Nathan Beverly Stubblefield (1860–1928) carried out private "wireless telephone" demonstration in which sound was transmitted through the air via induction in 1892, broadcasting human voice using his telephone system based on metal rods buried in ground.[16] In 1902, he demonstrated novel communication from ship to shore using ELF (Extremely Low Frequency) and VLF (Very Low Frequency) band to transmit voice. Finally, on 12 May 1908, Stubblefield received U.S. patent 887,357 for his Wireless Telephone, using the voice frequency induction system. However, eccentric Stubblefield lived out his life as a hermit and starved to death in 1928.[17] For another example, the famous Johannes Gutenberg (1398–1468)[18] lost his printing press due to debts to a wealthy moneylender. As Paul Saffo states, "as an innovator you can do everything right and you can still die," and yet even though the inventors and trailblazers who create paths for others to follow would not achieve business success themselves, they cannot be deemed a failure as an innovator.

To be able to innovate, one has to have personal tolerance for risk and failure as an individual. Much of the work on innovations is risk-taking and means doing things beyond one's comfort zone. For this reason, a key success factor is indeed the willingness and ability to fail – or even more importantly, to *fail fast,* if need be. Something that really matters is knowing how to fail in the right way. According to Paul Saffo, Silicon Valley is built on the rubble of earlier failures rather than the spires of earlier successes.[19] Saffo ironically depicts the major difference between Silicon Valley's downturn and New York after the stock market crash of 1929 as the Valley's buildings being two stories high and surrounded by grass; when people jump in despair, they just sprain their ankles, they are lying there with an ice-bag on their foot, and then they realize they have a half-finished business plan on their computer and they start it again.

It gives a serious lesson to learn from this, however, to be able to measure the *cost to failure*. Figuring out the cost-to-failure means that we would know how long it takes and how much money we have to put in before we know whether something works or not. For instance, when investing in biomarker research, how could one figure out earlier that a drug may not work as opposed to getting to phase four trials and realizing only then that it has problem that can't be resolved. Judy Estrin explains that in the social web there is a very low cost-to-failure: "You throw something up, either it works or not, you do A/B switches, it's a very low cost. The cost of failure is you switch it back to the other way. If you are developing a new drug, the cost of failure is a loss of life. You really have to think about different industries from car, whether it's automobile to batteries, to med tech to biotech to consumer Internet." Thus, reducing the cost-to-failure would mean simply figuring out how to get to the failure earlier, if need be. Even if "the natural appetite for failures" may differ by geographical location or culture – of course none wants to fail, but in Zero-to-One innovation most attempts fail anyway – there is no question that being able to know the cost-to-failure, being able to fail fast, and being able to recognize that failure are critically important capabilities for any innovation hungry organization.

Balance of the core business values: case Silicon Valley

> *Judy Estrin:*
> *You can't just pick one [core business value] and decide you're creating an innovation; you need a balance.*

Striving to create an innovation needs a balance of all facets of core business values and competences rather than choosing to focus on one or some of them. Judy Estrin, CTO of Cisco and serial entrepreneur, puts forward a claim that core business values are constant across all innovative environments, and they also remain consistent across all types of persons, companies, or countries.[20] Yet, the core business competences and values can be cultivated in organizations, networks and teams as well as among individuals.

Losing the balance of core business values may explain many of the failures in the hunt for innovations. For instance, patience without risk-taking or trust without proper questioning does not encourage innovation. According to Judy Estrin, even weak economic situations often may be explained by losing the balance of core values, because financial crises are caused by impatient people taking risks without asking questions and without openness or transparency as to what they are risking. As a consequence of losing the balance between core business values trust is lost, and when banks cannot trust each other everything gets locked up and the result is a financial crisis. Central for the balance of core values in an innovation ecosystem is trust, whereas harmful to trust is fear. Judy Estrin emphasizes that influencing users through fear is highly questionable and slows down innovation: "One of the most fundamental forces against innovation, against change, is fear. People often say that threats motivate innovation, because they say that necessity is the mother of invention. It actually is not threats that motivate innovation, because if you're afraid, you close down. If you can turn a threat into a challenge, which then can be used to inspire people to get involved, it is challenges that motivate people, not threats." As Estrin notes, "there's a big difference between challenging people and scaring them."

The importance of balance between core business values is showcased by the rise of Silicon Valley over the Boston area as number one technology business area. In 1980s, Boston was the high-tech center of the United States, but by 1990s it was a distant second to Silicon Valley. What happened? According to futurologist Paul Saffo, the most important reason why Silicon Valley surpassed the Boston area and continues to innovate is its innovation ecosystem. The often-presented argument for the pole position of Silicon Valley in ICT business is that the model is the result of local culture, and indeed huge value comes from the people actually operating within its networks. This is what makes Silicon Valley so powerful. Sociologist AnnaLee Saxenian explains that innovations happen in a social context in which people learn from peers rather than from isolated experts who sit and think something up. The regional advantage comes from having clusters of people who are specialized but who learn from each other and who develop each other's talents and expertise.[21] With these clusters, it is much quicker to communicate, share, sell, and spread the ideas than in a closed environment. In a way Silicon Valley is like one big company. One of the advantages in Silicon Valley is also that the venture capitalists fund start-ups in a way that traditional bankers cannot do. Such venture capitalists often have technical backgrounds themselves; they know what is going on, they know people and they also knit together networks. They tell other people what is going on in other parts of the network, and they form focal points. The strength of this network is a great advantage for Silicon Valley compared to most other regions. Silicon Valley has also been a pioneer in combining scientific research, venture funding and social networks in a fluent way.

Many Silicon Valley entrepreneurs seem to have internalized the beauty of weak ties, and they appreciate the role of social networks and getting essential feedback from them. Reid Hoffman agrees with this view:

> Silicon Valley leverages open networks. People don't go, "Oh, it's my idea, can't talk to you about it." It's like, "Here's my idea, what do you think? Oh you have a variant? Oh, actually I like this aspect of your variant. Ok, I'm going to modify my idea now." They go around and talk to people constantly about what they're doing. It's the individual who can drive something, make it happen, have the initial seeding, kind of the ground zero event, but the way that the thing gets refined and taken to practice is by a lot of deployment of the network around you. The characteristics you need of the network are ability to find expertise, have people who would give good feedback, and find people and resources to deploy. This network feedback is very useful in refining innovation.

One of the things that historically has made Silicon Valley especially rich as an environment for innovation has been the balance of the core values in terms of its sharing of information, its willingness to take risks, and questioning of the status quo.[22] Regarding the cost-to-failure and the balance of core business values that Silicon Valley has, or at least has had, Paul Saffo speaks about the Goldilocks Zone: "If the risk is very high, it means that you die. If the risk is low, nothing really happens. Silicon Valley is right in the middle. There are consequences to failure, but they are not lethal. You get a chance to innovate again. That risk moves you forward." Judy Estrin emphasizes freedom as a key ingredient in the culture in Silicon Valley, which lets people question authority, and uses as an opposite example China, which has been producing a multitude of smart scientists and engineers but which does not have the same notion of individual freedom as Silicon Valley does and thus hasn't obtained balance between the core business values.

The balance also creates inducement for technology developers to set foot in the Silicon Valley. Sometimes innovations are invented somewhere else, but then their developers gravitate to the innovation center. This could be seen from what happened to the Mosaic browser. After being originally developed in the NCSA at the University of Illinois in Urbana-Champaign, key persons established Mosaic Communications Corporation, moved to Mountain View in the Silicon Valley, and the company became big as Netscape. Another example of an innovation that was originally invented somewhere else but which gravitated to the innovation center is the web itself. Even though the web was invented in Europe, it could be claimed that it was actually in Silicon Valley that it was able to grow into being the wonderful virtual innovation environment it is today.

Quite surprisingly, Silicon Valley itself is a creation by some of the very same people who originated many of the ideas behind the web. We particularly want to refer here to Vannevar Bush's role in the creation of Silicon Valley. Historian Margaret Pugh O'Mara calls this type of an environment as a "city of knowledge," which composes of a central university, a nice suburban area, and a desirable geographical location. She explains how "Stanford University went from a rich man's folly to being the institution perfectly situated to reap the benefits of postwar suburbanization and Cold War military spending." Individuals and institutions took advantage of the favorable conditions and federal policy with massive defense investments during the first two decades of the Cold War. These enriched the research university, enabled its growth, and prompted an explosion of high tech development.[23]

Frederick E. Terman (1900–82), Dean of Engineering and later Provost at Stanford University, sometimes referred to as "the Father of Silicon Valley," regarded immediate post–World War II Stanford University as an underprivileged institution when it came to defense projects. He and university President Donald Bertrand Tresidder (1894–1948) realized how important it was to draw closer to industry and emphasize high commercial relevance in the actions of the university. For instance, Stanford Research Institute (SRI) was established in 1946 to support this type of innovation and economic development. Stanford University also owned thousands of acres of land in affluent areas in which middle-class professionals desired to live. It was a pleasant and safe environment, and thus it was also a major landowner and a prime actor in social policy. A live-work community for scientific production that was an exclusive environment with a high degree of homogeneity, cultural vibrancy and distinctive architecture and design appealed to many scientists, professors, and engineers, who willingly adapted to what O'Mara calls Vannevar Bush-style meritocratic elitism. O'Mara further explains that Stanford was "blessed with so many institutional and geographic advantages that its administrators could have the luxury of focusing their energies on creating a community of science." This is no surprise since Terman had been a student of Vannevar Bush at MIT.

Vannevar Bush had been the one who had institutionalized the relationship between government, businesses and scientific communities in the United States. When being at the MIT, Bush was the leading candidate to become the President of Stanford University. However, Bush turned down the position and became instead the head of a new US agency, the Office of Scientific Research and Development, which started to coordinate and fund hundreds of military research projects.[24] What happened was that the amount of funding through federal grants and projects received by Stanford University more than quadrupled during the 1950s. Terman, among others, readily admitted that federal money served as seed money for further industrial innovation. Terman's protégés' companies such as Varian Associates and Hewlett-Packard were tenants for the Stanford Industrial Park established in 1951 and named later Stanford Research Park. Skipping the pivotal role of the federal contracts and the interaction between public and private is typical, in O'Mara's opinion, of "the enduring myth of the Silicon Valley entrepreneur." Nevertheless, the remarkable achievement was that the new innovation ecosystem, Silicon Valley, emerged.

So, many of the early Internet pioneers were operating in the physical innovation environment of Silicon Valley, which was built on the ideas of Bush, and they also paid attention to Bush's idea of extending human memory by imitating human associations and utilizing webs of trails for personal use. A prime example is Dr Douglas Engelbart who got inspiration for his inventions from Bush; he also took a position at SRI in Menlo Park in 1957 after a year as an acting assistant professor at University of California Berkeley. The emerging innovation environment in Silicon valley appeared to be a place for him more than traditional academic environments in order to pursue his vision, which was in his own words "that anybody could create a link pointing to any place, any paragraph of any single [piece of text] that's ever been written on the web... That was my dream." Engelbart's agenda, *Augmenting Human Intellect: A Conceptual Framework*, got its chance, and the U.S. Air Force Office of Scientific Research provided funding for it. Engelbart published the H/LAM-T conceptual framework in 1962, and later, his NLS system was the first to employ the practical use of hypertext links and many other modern computing concepts. A central issue in his lab, Augmentation Research Center, was to develop an approach for bootstrapping human collective intelligence for catalyzing and accelerating innovation, and DARPA was funding Engelbart's research center.[25] Thus, Vannevar Bush had left his mark in two ways: in the early Internet pioneers' ideas of free associative trails and personalized links behind the virtual environment, the web, as well as in the ideal of web-like physical innovation environment, Silicon Valley.

The Nordic Way

> *Henry Chesbrough:*
> *The whole world doesn't need to be like Silicon Valley.*
>
> *B.J. Fogg:*
> *Stay tuned to normal people.*

Thinking about the core business values and competences, Silicon Valley has had a great advantage over other regions in the world for about 30 years, and the healthy question is whether it will be able to maintain that. Silicon Valley seems to have lost some of its previous richness as an environment for innovation. It nearly dropped the ball already in the 1980s. One of Judy Estrin's key messages is that Silicon Valley should get back into a balance of core values, and that "one of the problems we have as a culture is, because the consumer Internet has become so hot in the Valley, people tend to look at it as the model of innovation."

Silicon Valley is often used as the business model also for any other region without much criticism. But the whole world doesn't need to be like Silicon Valley. Henry Chesbrough states that "there are too many people in the U.S. both in business and also in academia who seem to think that the U.S. way is the way: 'We are the model that everybody should follow. We're here in Silicon Valley. The whole world should be like Silicon Valley.' I don't believe that's possible. I don't believe it's desirable. I actually don't think it's factually accurate to say so." According to Chesbrough, ignorance of other countries that have also been tremendously successful, but with innovation models that are quite different from Silicon Valley's, is common in the United States. In general, people are not well-informed about these alternatives, and thinking that Silicon Valley by definition is number one in the innovation market causes people to be myopic. Understanding this is extremely important since it comes down to the questions we ask in our research. Chesbrough advises comparing the United States with other regions and noticing some of the successes different models have had in other regions of the world.

A very interesting different approach is the Nordic Way. Henry Chesbrough uses the small country of Finland as a positive example of having even higher trust in the economy than what is found in Silicon Valley: "As a smaller and more homogenous society, the Finnish society can establish very strong trust relations more rapidly than in the U.S. With more trust, you can achieve more social cohesion and social coordination without ownership, and you can do so more rapidly." Much of this with its pros and cons comes from the cultural level. Trust is a key ingredient in fully operational business ecosystem, whereas not being able to operate in a trusting environment is a huge overall problem in today's business and innovation. An erosion of trust is a global problem that hinders openness and willingness to take a risk, among many other problems.

Another difference between Silicon Valley and the Nordic Way is that in Silicon Valley one practically always has to approach business people, who are in key organizational positions, through multiple gatekeepers, whereas in Europe and particularly in Nordic countries there are fewer of these kinds of barriers, and the social structures are much flatter, so that one is able to reach key business people much more easily. It is also very easy when one is living in Silicon Valley, Boston or New York to think that everyone thinks like you do, but living outside of hotspots may put one in touch with ordinary people all the time. Thus, to avoid innovator's myopia in this sense, the message for developers who are located in technological hotspots or other extraordinary areas is to stay tuned to normal people.

To succeed in the humanized web the core business values are watchfulness for technological shifts, ability to think outside the box, intrapreneurial spirit and having an appetite to fail fast. A key to success is to have a balance between these core business values. To succeed in the innovation business, it is quintessential to cultivate these values throughout the organization.

12
Future Challenges

The Millennium Technology Prize is awarded every second year to inspire and recognize technological innovations that provide answers to some of the challenges of our time and particularly improve the quality of human life and sustainable development.[1] In terms of monetary value and public esteem, the prize ranks as one of the world's most prestigious scientific awards. The first Millennium prize in 2004 was awarded to Sir Tim Berners-Lee for inventing the Word Wide Web. The potential of the web to influence the lives of billions of people in a beneficial way was one of the key reasons for awarding the prize to him. However, in spite of an enormous number of applications having been and being built on top of Sir Berners-Lee's achievement, the future humanized web also holds many challenges and even threats for mankind. These include the failure, after all, to augment human intellect, unintended consequences and intended malicious action. It will be interesting to see whether the web can be elevated into a science of its own and whether it can help solve any of the really hard world-scale problems.

Failure to augment human intellect

> *Ted Nelson:*
> *The web is a threat. They are going the wrong way with structures that don't fit human life.... The web is hierarchical in every respect. You should be able to have two-way links, four-way links, seven-way links, and they shouldn't be embedded inside the document.*

According to Douglas Engelbart, the essence of any information technology is to support augmenting human intellect. Engelbart explained in the Augmented Knowledge Workshop in 1988 that he had "an intuitive conviction implanted in his head in the 1950s" to commit his career to "augmenting the human intellect."[2] In the early days of the web, promoting the magnitude of profundity, deep thinking, and users' chance to follow their inherent associative thinking – augmentation of human intellect – were emphasized. But as with any other new industry or new technology in the web, there has been some hiccups and adjusting such as in the form of hype during the takeoff or losing some control at a later stage.

The web is undeniably one of the greatest recent technological innovations of the mankind, but at the same time the social web is plagued by several in-built paradoxes to such a great extent that anyone who falls deeply in love with this new type of connectivity could actually end up losing human contact. Moreover, new challenges may arise with the future web. A specific threat in the future humanized web is that the solutions developed, contrary to all general expectations, would fail to augment human intellect and they would thus miss the mark from the original goal. To hypertext visionary but web critic Ted Nelson even the early web was just "FTP with lipstick" and Facebook is "e-mail plus the web in a new package."[3] According to Nelson, the whole computer world today is based upon two fundamental misunderstandings of human life and thought, and he thinks that the contemporary technologists have adopted these incorrect fixations. These two are the simulation of hierarchy and the simulation of paper. Nelson explains about the simulation of hierarchy that "the tradition since about 1947 is that computers are built around hierarchy. This is convenient for addressing files and directories. It is not convenient for human concerns, because human concerns are not hierarchical. They crisscross and interweave. Thus, we need crisscrossing and interweaving structures." According to Nelson, the computer field seems to go on with this hierarchical tradition, which compels users to figure out how to fit their work and personal concerns into the hierarchy of files and directories. In his view, attempts to correct this, such as a "My Documents" folder in Microsoft Windows or tags in pictures, do not solve the actual problem. Rather "all of this is because they don't have a decent structural system for the organization of information." Apple's Mac takes a step forward from this hierarchical thinking via offering users with new types of data structures, but it is still far from what Nelson thinks computers should offer.

In fact, Nelson thinks radically that also the web is hierarchical:

> This hierarchy has been extended to the World Wide Web. The World Wide Web is nothing but the extension of the hierarchical directory of one person's computer to the new hierarchical directories that include the hierarchical directories of millions of servers on networks. So now you have this mega-hierarchy to deal with and a so-called "web page" is what [is] to be found in one of these directories, either as the default directory, the default page, or a particular page within it. Now we just have the same problem of dividing things up multiplied by a million. That's the hierarchic problem. Within the format of documents, HTML and XML, everything is forced to be hierarchical. Cascading style sheets hierarchical. The tagging hierarchical. All of this represents a techie way of thinking that is completely incorrect from the point of view of human life.

Nelson, who about half a century ago coined the term *hypertext*, criticizes this hierarchical view by stating sharply that "my kind of hypertext has nothing to do with the web." He explains that the links he built originally were one-way links like in Douglas Engelbart's Augment system but then he branched out to transclusions,[4] which he views as very different and as much more powerful: "To me, that's the way to go: Links and transclusions at the same time. Hyperlinks as we know them today are one-way and they are embedded. All of that is wrong." In Nelson's personal vision, the ZigZag system[5] is such a construction set that allows amorphous databases that grow in any direction.

In a similar manner, the simulation of paper concerns Nelson: "Today's databases simulate paper in that they're made of rows and columns. Life is not made of rows and columns. One's concerns and connections are not made of rows and columns." What would be needed is rather keeping track of where you have been, whom you have met and other similar contextual information. When this kind of contextual information grows, accumulates, a conventional table can't help anymore. Nelson proclaims, "It goes in all directions and yet that is the structure and substance of the kinds of things I have to keep track of. The addresses and names connect with everything, that connects with everything, and that connects with everything." In Nelson's view, one should also be able to make marginal notes on web pages and side-by-side comments on documents on all document formats, and also the connections to every version should stay in place when documents are constantly modified and new versions are published.[6]

Admittedly, for the most part computers and the web are still based on user interface metaphors envisioned in 1960s by Douglas Engelbart, elaborated by PARC researchers, and commercialized by Apple. Paul Dourish confirms that traditional graphical user interfaces "look remarkable similar to that of the 1970s."[7] Ted Nelson criticizes the user interface controls and wags his finger at PARC: "Software today determines everything, making it fit in a window and then using pull-down menus and widgets to design your so-called interface. All you can have is what we have today. You're locked into the 'PUI.'"[8] Nelson refers to Stockholm Syndrome, claiming that sometimes the more difficult you make software to use, the more people become committed to it. This would also mean that the more difficult software is to use, the better it is for software vendors, because competition is stopped by the fact that people already are locked into it and overwhelmed to try something new. Something similar may happen with the web as well, if it gets stagnated. This might well happen since any change in the web's current infrastructure has already become extremely difficult to achieve. According to Paul Saffo, "the web's just become a particularly good layer in an intellectual rubble pile... [and] the pieces will stay." Being locked in certain user interface metaphors may indeed greatly limit our capability to think outside the box, and it might lead into failing to augment human intellect.

Unintended consequences

Judy Estrin:
The pendulum will swing back at some point.

John Lilly:
Things get out of control rather quickly now.

Paul Saffo:
Even a really dumb piece of software can be extraordinarily dangerous, if we make it autonomous.

History shows us that we can best enjoy benefits of a technology with as few negative implications as possible, when we get prepared for its consequences as early as possible. For this natural reason, it would be significant to direct portion of the research and design effort regarding the social web toward investigating its (often obvious but) unintended consequences.

A kind of a pendulum can already be noticed in the utilization of many different types of services, for instance electronic mail. In its early stages, email was a very positive and empowering experience for nearly anyone who started to learn to use it, and most people today would think that email is a must even for laymen or at least an absolutely necessary tool for any knowledge worker. However, spam in email frustrates more and more, requiring effort and wasting time deleting often half or more of the messages one gets.[9] All too often, email has changed from joy to pain. Similarly, in the usage of the social web, there are many things which affect user experience. Users can unwittingly end up visiting websites that can harm their computers. There are still issues which need to be addressed at the bottom technical layers, but at the same time better codes of practices to operate in and ways to patrol the social web are also needed. Content that many would consider annoying and content that was put on the web by users themselves in the past with poor judgment also affect their user experience. These may well result in a backlash amongst the large audience. This seems like an unimaginable situation for many as growth is by and large still expected, but people might well get tired of the negative implications in a medium from which they seek enjoyment but frequently get problems instead. People are also beginning to understand that the amount of time they're spending on the social web can be excessive, and that it in its current form doesn't always deliver the value they have been hoping to get from it. Thus, people start to face with the consequences of the value paradox.

The same thing happens with the friend and filter paradoxes. The fact that many of the connections that people have in the social web are based on semi-anonymous interaction may result in intensifying loneliness in the society. At some point, people may start to long for deeper connections and begin to seek for alternatives within or outside the social web. And even if the social web closes gaps for those capable of using it, it may generate gaps between them and those who are not capable of doing so. People may also start to realize that they have actually given an enormous power of influence over their lives to their social networks, perhaps unknowingly, since these networks filter out a lot of potentially useful information at the same time when they act as trust filtrating devices. All of this could result into that the social web starts to be perceived obsolete for satisfying basic needs of meaningful social connections which would erode the foundation of the social web.

The social web has started to become a powerful marketing media even though the reason why people went to these sites in the first place was non-commercial. Judy Estrin predicts that there is a threat of a setback due to excessive marketing operations directed at users who originally were not expecting to be targeted:

For a while, that's going to work, and they [companies] are going to get phenomenal viral marketing. At some point, there is going to be a backlash. The question we don't know is whether there's going to be a backlash from those kids and consumers that saw it and gravitated to it, just because it wasn't marketing. There's a lot of things about the social web that we don't know yet. We haven't seen the generation of kids who grow up using these tools, whether they'll stick with it as adults. As more and more companies use Facebook to get their products in front of all of your friends, will people accept [it] or will there be a backlash? When these kids grow up to be adults and suddenly people start realizing what they put on their Facebook pages as teenagers, are there going to be implications and backlash from that? This is an incredible opportunity and an incredible medium for collaboration, for marketing, for socialization, but there's a lot of people out there that take certain things for granted that we don't know yet. There's a lot of opportunities for positive and negative implications.

Terry Winograd believes that at some point there will be a major breakdown in the Internet, where some information that is really damaging will get out when it should not: "That will lead people to stop and think. Typically, if you ask people about privacy, it's like most security concerns. If it hasn't happened to you, you don't worry about it very much. You just say: 'Yeah, yeah, you're right. I should think about that.' But you know [people think] 'I don't actually lock my door when I walk out of the house, we don't have theft in our neighborhood. Well, if we had some thefts in our neighborhood I would start locking my door.' That's going to take some kind of an event like that before most people even think about it or care about it."

Due to tight coupling of information and services, almost any breakdown can have very wide implications. In such a situation, the key thing is what is made autonomous and what is left in the hands of people with good judgment. The potential future web becoming an environment that is primarily used by machines poses great dangers, when the biggest information providers and the biggest consumers of information on the web would be computers, the primary users of the web would not be people but bots. What is so challenging is that machines which do not have their own identity or morality may start echoing other machines with the speed of a rocket and thus hold all the potential to become a mob subject to groupthink. Machines also have a tendency to maintain errors. Futurist Paul Saffo also urges us not to take it for granted that revolutionary technologies are in any way egalitarian. Human history, however, does not bode well in this respect. Machines may fall into many of the pitfalls that a human is capable of avoiding and highly automated processes could cause an enormous backlash in the usage of the social web.

Intended malicious action

Caterina Fake:
A lot of antibodies need to be developed against bad behavior online.

Neal Sample:
There are lots of countries around the world that have their own restrictions. Those restrictions, if they're not understood by the people, make the web a tool of disinformation more than information.

In the envisioned humane social web, there will certainly be various types of network-based criminal, illegal and other malicious activities that will make use of the same technologies that are being used for productive activities to society. Ben Shneiderman explains that: "Any time you have a powerful technology, there are people who will misuse it. There's danger from criminals, terrorists, oppressive governments, and people [who] are simply troublemakers, to spammers and scammers and all kinds. Any time there's some change where people are inexperienced with the technology, then some people take advantage of their inexperience and manipulate that for their own gain." Indeed, every opportunity is a threat and every threat is an opportunity – they go hand in hand. Already now, there are people who are using their capability and the web's ease of use against one's interests. Spam and unwanted connections have become abundant over the past few years; phishing poses a threat for web users; there are people trying to sell unworthy products and services. Already today someone's reputation may be diminished significantly or someone's identity can be stolen in the social web, which no doubt results at the very least in more careful considerations of how to use the web at an individual level. In extreme cases, pedophiles and other criminal-minded people may use the web for horrific purposes. Thus, users of the social web face severe challenges related to the privacy and identity paradoxes. The web makes also deception very easy, which essentially is the credibility paradox, and it is only likely that many new ways for criminal activity in the web will emerge.

The intended malicious action by some people includes also activities such as cyberattacks, cyberwarfare and authoritarian social control. Cyberattacks from various types of hackers and criminals are already becoming more common. For example, although the details have not been distributed to the general population, it is known that the United States suffered cyberattacks since 2001, when Code Red worm infected over 300,000 computers in a few hours. These computers were turned into zombies, computers under remote control to carry out a programmed distributed denial-of-service attack against the White House website. Later, two of most wired countries faced similar serious challenges. In April 2007, Estonia faced a sophisticated cyberattack, being the largest ever distributed denial-of-service attack by the time,[10] and South Korea faced a similar kind of challenge in 2009, when approximately 166,000 computers located in 74 countries began carefully to attack websites in the country.[11]

It is noticeable that cyberwarfare between political powers is already being carried out with an unforeseen intensity. According to Ben Shneiderman, "The current interest in cyberwarfare, cyberdefence is an unfortunate but necessary sign of the importance and the maturation of the web." What is unknown is the real extent of cyberwarfare that is going on all the time. Cyberwarfare by no means is only about defenses; it is also about attacks. In a similar manner as the atomic bomb created a new political situation at the end of the World War II in which the superpowers never fought each other directly, the Internet and the web have also created a new political reality in the world. The political powers of today can easily find a place in the web arena, where they can harm their competitors without fighting each other overtly. For instance, they can use cyberthreats to convince other stakeholders to refrain from initiating their course of action. Distressingly, when cyberarsenals are large enough, almost any dispute of this kind could result in the disruption or collapse of the web.

The free web as such seems to be kind of *Mare Liberum* of the twenty-first century.[12] Quite understandably, freedom of the seas, *Mare Liberum*, was not a pleasant idea to each and everyone in the seventeenth century and it seems to be similarly today with the idea of free web. In the beginning of the twenty-first century, a stand towards it and its balance with other norms divides countries, groups and lobbies within individual countries, as well as international organizations and their actors. Some governments desperately try to restrict and control the web. In some places the web has been restricted as part of an existing system of strongly controlling people to the extent that entire countries and regions may be essentially firewalled and censored by their governments. Yet, it is not only those countries where Internet penetration has been lower that stand against the freedom of the web. The Organization for Economic Cooperation and Development (OECD) arranged a high-level meeting on the internet economy and policy making and published a communiqué on it in June 2011.[13] In this communiqué, 34 OECD member countries, Egypt, the OECD Business and Industry Advisory Committee, and its Internet Technical Advisory Committee reached an agreement regarding Internet policy making, and then in December 2011 published recommendations on it.[14] In these documents, OECD calls for light touch and non-government led regulating of the Internet for promoting economic growth. However, members of the OECD's Civil Society Information Society Advisory Council (CSISAC) consisting of more than 80 global civil society groups declined to support the communiqué and declared that its "principles are not compatible with CSISAC core values including respect for fundamental human rights and freedoms and, the rule of law, promotion of access to knowledge, promotion of open standards, Net Neutrality and balanced intellectual property policies and regimes." CSISAC also declared that the recommendation should promote more openness, be better grounded in respect for human rights, and strengthen the capacity to improve the quality of life for all citizens.[15] As can be seen from above, the freedom of the web divides opinions.

An internal arm wrestling about the freedom of the web and its norms also in the United States became a major piece of news around the world in January 2012. In the preceding May, the first U.S. *International Strategy for Cyberspace, Prosperity, Security, and Openness in a Networked World* was issued. The strategy called for respecting and protecting intellectual property, and declared: "States should in their undertakings and through domestic laws respect intellectual property rights, including patents, trade secrets, trademarks, and copyrights."[16] In the same month Democrat Senator Patrick Joseph Leahy from Vermont introduced *Preventing Real Online Threats to Economic Creativity and Theft of Intellectual*

Property Act of 2011 (PIPA) "to prevent online threats to economic creativity and theft of intellectual property, and for other purposes."[17] Less than a half year later in October 2011, Republican representative Lamar S. Smith from Texas introduced *The Stop Online Piracy Act* (SOPA) bill in the House of Representatives "to promote prosperity, creativity, entrepreneurship, and innovation by combating the theft of U.S. property, and for other purposes."[18] Both PIPA and SOPA, relying on copyright, received other co-sponsors in the Congress and support from companies. However, some legislators in the Congress, businesses, influential individuals, as well as human rights organizations strongly opposed PIPA and SOPA. Among the opponents were companies and organizations such as AOL, eBay, Facebook, Google, LinkedIn, Mozilla Corporation, Twitter, Yahoo!, YouTube, Wikipedia and the Wikimedia Foundation, and individuals, such as Vint Cerf, Caterina Fake, Reid Hoffman, Tim O'Reilly and Jimmy Wales, also stepped up to oppose the bills.[19] Prominent web sites displayed "black banners" over site logos with the words "Stop Censorship," and the English Wikipedia's 24-hour-blackout took place. Due to the extent of the protests, the U.S. administration responded and tried to calm down the general situation and Congress postponed consideration of the legislation.

Also authoritarian social control is one of the big challenges for the future web. On one extreme are criminals using the Internet without supervision, and on the other extreme are totalitarian states which block the Internet from their citizens. The question is that if one allowed supervision of the web, would they also allow totalitarian governments to block it. Those governments would then filter the amount of information that comes through and filter out specific sources, articles and topics. In such situations, the web would be turning into a tool for manipulation. This is far more than just a technical matter, it is fundamentally a social matter with political influences. Terry Winograd explains this dilemma:

> What is the nature of web systems which put you in danger of authoritarian social control, and what are the things which facilitate democratic social control? Sometimes that may be at a fundamental level, like, "What's the protocol?" One of the big questions that come up with the web is, what is the equivalent of phone wire tapping on the web? In general, the solutions aren't going to be based on a pure technical argument. They're going to be based on political and social arguments. What should the government be able to do, what shouldn't they be able to do? If you're worried about terrorists, shouldn't you be able to tap every wire, and if you're worried about privacy you shouldn't. You see this happening in a lot of countries, and the whole China approach, the censoring the web. People tend to think of the web as inherently open, because that's the way we've been using it. But in fact in China it's not open in the same way, and it's perfectly technically feasible for them to do that. People always say, "Well, the people will find a way around it." If you mean a hundred percent control, there will always be people who prevent it from being a hundred, but if you get 90 percent control over society, that still would be effective.

The potential uses of the web for authoritarian social control were not very carefully considered when the web was being created in the late 1980s and early 90s,[20] because the web was being developed by people who were committed to free-flow information distribution and open source type of thinking. Those people lived in democracies and could not really foresee the web's extraordinary world-scale impact on countries both developed and undeveloped, and even in countries under authoritarian control. In spite of all these great risks of authoritarian social control, cyberwarfare, cyberattacks, other criminal activity and bad behavior online, the biggest challenge for the humanized web to really succeed is how users can make sense of the information while information overload burdens them. The complexity in this is that one of the key ways to make sense out of the huge amount of information on the humanized web is the exercise of more control over what can be stored into it and how and when information can be retrieved. Even though doing so could help solve some of the design challenges at hand today, this would be against the freedom of the web ideal, and these types of restricted technical environments might also lead into many other challenges.

Most people seem to take the Internet for granted as a privilege that they are going to have forever. Ted Nelson is not so sure about that. He believes that many things could take down the Internet, and suddenly we would be without everything to which we have become accustomed in the web. What could cause such a collapse? Nelson argues: "Certainly the malware we're seeing. The people who are trying to stop these are much less smart and much less organized than the people who are building them. The governments could take it down very easily. The cutting the lines could take it down. Any of those three and perhaps other means. So there's no reason to be sure that the Internet is going to last forever."

Focus on really hard problems

> *Tim O'Reilly:*
> *It's time for people who've been working on consumer Internet or consumer technology in general to start taking their skills and applying them to hard problems.*

Despite the huge growth of interest in different variations of the social web such as social networking, social media systems and social computing, the full potential of the social web is still to be fulfilled. It has indeed demonstrated great success in playful, discretionary or personal projects, but many of the web visionaries request that more effort should now be directed toward making it effective as a civic social web, whether addressing healthcare, energy, education, disaster response, community safety or other such matters.[21] Shneiderman points out that "it's very satisfying to see in the time of tragedies, the floods or the earthquake, that programmers and others get together. They build software to help the aid workers coordinate their activities. These are noble efforts of contribution of software to support disaster response." For example, Google

Person Finder, an open-source web application, enables disaster victims and their families to search for displaced and missing persons.[22] It was first launched during the earthquake in Haiti in January 2010 and then used also after the Chile earthquake in February 2010, during the Pakistan floods in July 2010, after the New Zealand earthquake in Christchurch in February 2011, and in the immediate aftermath of the Tōhoku earthquake and tsunami in Japan in March 2011. To make it even more accessible, the application was embedded on various social networks. Another example is the Ushahidi Social Network Trends Map, a web server, which was utilized within hours of the devastating Japanese earthquake in March 2011 to enable disaster victims to upload information using the web or cell phones.[23] Also popular social web services such as Facebook and Twitter have been utilized extensively during disasters by victims to disseminate information. Indeed, the social web is already playing an increasingly important role in the response phase of emergency management, and it will have many more uses as a civic social web.

There are also many uses for the web in peaceful problem-solving situations. Hans Rosling's work with Gapminder has demonstrated how data visualization may give a better understanding of very large problems and potential solutions.[24] Gapminder developed the Trendalyzer software that converts international health statistical information into interactive graphics, applying the animation concepts from computer games to statistics. Trendalyzer was purchased by Google in March 2007, where it was further developed as Google Visualization API. Gapminder World continues to freely show and distribute important World trends in a visualized way in the Gapminder Foundation website.[25] There are also many challenges that are not on the agenda of the companies, but for which governments and other non-governmental organizations should help advance the technology.

Tim O'Reilly requests the use of the web for trying to resolve really hard problems:

> We have to apply our amazing skills and the amazing technology we're building to solve serious problems. We need to stop basically contributing to a world of waste. Just to give you one great example, look at healthcare. Each year we can expect that healthcare is going to cost more, we're going to spend more on it, there's more people who are going to require it, and we look ahead and we look at a bankrupt healthcare system. Now then, you contrast that with the technology industry where you have Moore's law. Every year we'll spend the same amount of money but we'll get a lot more for it. Maybe we'll even spend less money. So we're living in this sort of world of declining cost. And yet there are whole other sectors of our society where we're in increasing cost. We have to take that Silicon Valley Moore's law sort of economy into healthcare, into education, into energy, so that we're not saying, "Oh yeah, we're going to run into a point where we just can't keep up." We can't spend that much money. We have to be better. The whole lesson of technology is we can solve problems.

According to O'Reilly, the future web's greatest promise relates to this resolving of really hard problems especially through user self-services. The history of the telephone system provides an example how service problems have sometimes been solved through user self-services. A prediction in the early twentieth century was that the phone system could not grow anymore because every person would have to become a telephone operator to enable to sustain a full phone network. Whether the switching system should be semiautomatic or automatic rather than manual was an important issue in the communication technology in the first quarter of the twentieth century. The first-generation pioneering electromechanical telephone switching system, Strowger switching system, took off in LaPorte, Indiana in 1892, and the second-generation full commercial switching system, Rotary switching system, in Hague, the Netherlands in 1920. These steps helped define the role of the user and self-service. In a congress about telephones and the future held in Paris in 1910,[26] the audience was surprised by the anti-automatic remarks of the chief engineer of AT&T and the eighth recipient of the Edison Medal, John Joseph Carty (1861–1932), who had played a major role in developing the first transcontinental telephone line and who then stated: "The automatic system is not simple for the subscriber, who must take his telephone from the hook and perform a number of manual operations depending on the character of the call he wishes to make. Then he must press a button, which if all goes well rings the subscriber desired."[27]

As we would today know, the power of user self-services took Carty by surprise. The post–World War I era was a period of tremendously increasing urban telephone traffic in large towns with the subsequent routing of in tandem by operators in a number of exchanges. The manual effort performed by operators during the immediate postwar years was superseded by the automatization and user self-service, which relieved problems of labor shortage and increased labor costs. In a way, everybody was turned into a telephone operator through automatic or electronic switching, with the result that people could in fact dial from their own homes. This was an example of a kind of Moore's law in which the idea of having bank after bank of telephone operators was transformed into something completely different. This was a Zero-to-One innovation.

Similarly, Tim O'Reilly explains about applying user self-services and peer-to-peer (P2P) solutions to energy and healthcare: "I would love to see us figure out how to have an Internet-style electric grid, where I'm generating power, you're generating power, we're feeding ourselves, we feed our excess into the grid. But they're not really building it that way. Even when we're talking about the smart grid, it's still big central generation. We need P2P energy. How do we do that?" In O'Reilly's vision, breakthroughs need to be sought: "We need to think about Moore's Law in healthcare, where could we figure out interventions that are an order of magnitude cheaper, because we're able to apply the technology, we're able to have preventive care that's mediated by the sensor world." It would not be enough to meet the web's past or even present standards, but the idea of all-embracing user self-services and world-scale peer-to-peer solutions requires extensive adaptation and readjustment to the ideals of the future web. The humanized web would be something more in scale and in the way it is currently being carried out.

Attacking global scale problems

> *Judy Estrin:*
> *We have to stop being so short-term focused, because when you are only focused on short term returns, you eliminate the ability to get deep, broad innovation that we need to solve the planet's problems.*
>
> *Paul Saffo:*
> *The only solution is to flee into the future as fast as we can.*
>
> *Ben Shneiderman:*
> *I want to be part of a profession that is making the world a better place, and not just focused on the narrow technical.*

As we have already noticed, there is a plethora of challenges in the social and humanized web, and new challenges are prone to arise in the future. Douglas Engelbart showed his interest in the significance of solving world-scale problems already over half a century ago in his report of *Augmenting Human Intellect: A Conceptual Framework*. The first two of Engelbart's three original ideas, which he calls "flashes," were: "Flash 1: The difficulty of mankind's problems was increasing at a greater rate than our ability to cope. (We are in trouble.) ... Flash 2: Boosting mankind's ability to deal with complex, urgent problems would be an attractive candidate as an arena in which a young person might try to 'make the most difference.'"[28] Ted Nelson put Engelbart's level of interest in a form comprehensible to everyone when he dedicated his book *Geeks Bearing Gifts v.1.1: How the Computer World Got This Way* to "Doug" [Engelbart] and said about him: "And what he wants people to see is his overall vision of a world of accelerating team creativity – tackling the hardest problems of resources, pollution, population, crime, disarmament, global warming – and finding the solutions through deep collaboration."[29] The same commitment, or at least ideal, that Douglas Engelbart had in the early 1960s has been shared by many other web visionaries as well. Many experienced computer scientists such as Terry Winograd, Ben Shneiderman, Judy Estrin and Tim O'Reilly urge for computer science to aim more boldly at resolving the really challenging global problems rather than focusing only on relatively simple technological questions.

But the serious world-scale problems that humanity is facing seem abundant. For instance, the report *Vital Signs Online* published by the Worldwatch Institute at the end of 2010, revealed that global unemployment rose from 5.7 percent in 2007 to 6.6 percent in 2009 and that it is precarious employment which grows most prominently. In more general, it outlines a total of 24 challenging trends for nations to pay close attention to.[30] The *United Nations Millennium Declaration* in 2000 proposed eight chapters and a multitude of objectives for solving massive world-scale problems.[31] A deadline of 2015 set for the so called *Millennium Development Goals* was reconfirmed again in 2005 and 2010.[32] Ten years after the original declaration, they still suggested eight of initial goals; namely eradicate extreme poverty and hunger, achieve universal primary education, promote gender equality and empower women, reduce child mortality, improve maternal health, combat HIV/AIDS, malaria and other diseases, ensure environmental sustainability and develop a global partnership for development.

According to futurist Paul Saffo, the humankind is facing such great challenges that "the only way to solve [any of the big] problems today is to innovate our way out of the mess we've gotten into." The UN expects innovation in information and communication technology to play a key role in achieving said goals. For example, innovation is directly mentioned as one of the key factors to tackle extreme poverty and hunger and reach environmental sustainability. Information and communication technology is especially expected to be harnessed for universal primary education and in promoting global public health. Designing of modern ICT applications for developing countries is widely expected to happen. Thus, much hope has been placed by the United Nations and others on the role information and communication technology and innovation might play in solving global problems. Some people even seem to believe that technology has some intrinsic goodness that can be used to solve world-scale problems, which, however, may in itself lead to technological determinism or even a stage of lull with regards to the real challenges of the mankind.

In spite of these noteworthy calls for action, Tim O'Reilly is convinced that the recent economic crisis, which the previously mentioned UN resolution from September 2000 named as the worst since the Great Depression, was just an early warning to the world which is facing serious crises ahead. According to O'Reilly, many of the various world-scale problems could cause a collapse in the world economy. Whatever of these problems will be run into, he thinks that the most serious feature of the post-collapse future is that it will be a lot harder to build a technological civilization, if it's possible at all:

> You can't bootstrap up to the point where you can make, for example, solar cells. Wind is going to be available and so on, but you can't bootstrap back up to a nuclear plant. So if we had the equivalent of the fall of Rome today or 30 years from now, and we've used up all the easily available oil, we've used up all the easily available coal, you may never get back to technological civilization. That's something that I don't think people are fully coming to grips with. In that context, we have a chance in the next decade to tackle some big problems, and we've gotta get it right, because if we don't, we may never make it back to this level of civilization. So there's the energy stuff, there's a lot that could happen with global pandemics, there's stuff that could happen with genetic engineering gone awry, the nuclear specter is still out there. There are a lot of things that could knock us back a few centuries, and then we could never get back to where we are today.

In spite of his worry over the web's future challenges, Tim O'Reilly thinks that the future web could play an important role in the attempts to solve some of these world-scale problems. For instance, it could help to distribute useful and recuperating ideas. There are already websites and events, which proclaim to aim that purpose, such as the well-received "TED: Ideas worth spreading."[33] Ben Shneiderman goes one step further and suggests that the job of information technology professionals and computer scientists is to make the world a better place: "There are many people in my field, I wish there were more, who believe that computer science can change the world and that technologies can make the world a better place. It's our job to focus on how to make that a reality – in what ways can we shape the technology to make the world a better place?"

Shneiderman elaborates his motivation for resolving global problems through computer science by stating that:

> I want to be part of a profession that is making the world a better place, and not just focused on the narrow technical [aspect], not just the plumbing, as they say, but the delivery of water and the production of health, of creating a better world. We have to move toward a larger perspective. There's a great story of success of computer science after 50 years. As we mature, we should take on a larger role in the world in addressing the problems that are really critical in the world, whether it's health or disease, whether it's economic development, or civil rights and justice. These are all struggles for many people in the world and there's a role for computer science. We also need to think about energy sustainability and how we can use these social media to help people reduce their energy usage, preserve the environment. These are all central questions of our time. I would like my profession to be a leader in addressing those questions.

Thus, many web visionaries expect the social web to be able to help to resolve world-scale problems. To what extent it happens remains to be seen.

Science of the web

Now that the web has matured as an information and communication vehicle, it is no longer a newcomer to business. In spite of the noble efforts that web developers make, they may have still very little real influence on resolving the world-scale problems of the humanity. Yet, the web certainly has risen into such a prominent position that it can't be treated as a sidetrack of computer science anymore. Thus far, its development has been largely driven by computer scientists, but many in the computer science field have a very narrow and technologically focused conception of their discipline. However, science about the web is not only about computer networks or algorithms, or not even only about information systems development or computer–human interaction design, and yet according to James Hendler, Nigel Shadbolt, Wendy Hall, Tim Berners-Lee and Daniel Weitzner, the web is still surprisingly often studied just as a delivery vehicle for either technical or social content.[34] It is yet common that the web is regarded just as an application running on top of the Internet, or the web is treated only as a specific instantiation of more general principles of social networks and interconnected systems. But in fact much more is involved. For this reason, a new multidisciplinary science has been suggested called *web science*.[35] The proposed web science tackles both micro-level web properties and macro-level web phenomena and the relationships between these. Hendler and his colleagues declare that "a systems approach...is needed if we are to be able to understand and engineer the future web."

One of the key reasons why the web *per se* has been an understudied research area is the dominance of electrical engineering and hardcore computer science in both the ICT industry and academic education in recent years. The electrical engineering department is one of the largest in many technically oriented universities around the world. However, very often these departments possess little knowledge and capabilities, and in many cases even very little interest, in advancing the web as a science. All in all, the underlying theme of web science is that the web is socially embedded and can be used for many kinds of technology-mediated social participation.[36] Ben Shneiderman describes and prescribes the current era as a transition in the emphasis of research and education by stating that "the shift is from chips to clicks," or as we today might say from clicks to swipes. He describes web science as a new way of thinking about computer science, and encourages computer scientists to learn from design, usability engineering, teaching of innovations, media and games and to draw inspiration from e-commerce, medical informatics, information schools and services science. In his manifesto, what is needed is moving away from studying information technology to studying what users can do with the information technology.[37] Better descriptive theories to explain why some web-based services succeed and others do not and prescriptive models to guide implementers are needed. Web science aims at tackling these questions by treating the web as a primary focus of attention.

Part V

Final Remarks

13
Conclusion

The Black Swan theory about unexpected events of large magnitude and consequence, and their dominant role in history was published in 2007 by professor Nassim Nicholas Taleb. According to Taleb, almost all major scientific discoveries and historical events can be explained by them being "black swans," unpredictable and unplanned events, which are not esteemed for a long time even after their first sighting.[1] The social web can be considered as such. Its impact is of very large magnitude and even if it now does fulfill the original idea of the web, it was improbable in the early days of ARPANET, the Internet and the web, and it became highly esteemed long after its emergence.

And yet, the web has been social since its beginning. In the first wave of the web, the main interest of society and individuals focused on distributing information, and the people putting information onto the web tended to be institutionally trusted. It was an era of navigating the hyperlinks. With the acceptance of dangling links by the web community, the whole concept of navigating in hyperspace changed and "weak" hyperlinks won over the more complex, semantically-rich links. This paved the way for searching – associative hyperlinks generated automatically on the fly – to become a leading method for web use. Through the emphasis on search, a hidden layer of link structure and meaning in the web was discovered. Yet at the same time, both general population and software developers directed their attention for several years to expert-based content creation, which slowed the emergence of the social web. The Internet culture had originally been non-commercial, but the emergence of graphical web browsers changed the scene. The first IPOs by web companies, the Browser War I between NCSA and Netscape, and the Browser War II between Netscape and Internet Explorer directed the investors' and the general audience's attention to web-based services and energized start-ups. The rapid growth of these companies also helped many other companies to get their share of the emerging markets. Electronic commerce became the second wave of the web. Yet, communication was still mostly one-way. The burst of the dotcom bubble was a signal of the next major change taking place. Even if e-commerce and e-business applications did not disappear with the bust, the dominant force started to shift elsewhere.

After the bust, the web redirected from technology and business more toward people. The social web had begun with the first web, and it was only waiting to become fully developed. The social web is about people, an essential feature of the phenomenon being that people connect to others in their real-world lives, not only in a virtual world. Moreover, users contribute resources to social web services and interact with each other through them. Important technical development that helped make the social web a reality included seamless integration of relational databases with the web as well as the emergence of web-based software architectures, mashups, wireless protocols and the semantic web. Social networking, instant messaging, massively multiplayer online role-playing games, blogging, and online encyclopedias took place relatively early on and constituted the early sign of the social web. Surviving companies of the second wave began polishing the social aspects of their sites. Key social web applications and corporations started to become visible. The social web became the third wave of the web. In our modern society, the social web plays the roles of transformer, innovation accelerator and humanizer. It is transforming the way we perceive people and cultures; it is accelerating the pace with which innovations are being created, and as an overall result, it is humanizing the web.

Web as a transformer

For individual users, the most important promise of the social web is maintaining and establishing one's own social networks online. Establishing individual social networks online helps bring people together, and even far away people can feel ambient intimacy with each other. The promise of the social web also builds around its democratizing effect, including both access to diversity of viewpoints and capacity to communicate ideas, and resulting, for instance, in democratization of trade and household economics. In business, the most important benefit is that the social web is fertile for innovation. The support for social networks may act as a bridge builder, for instance, making newcomers more capable to get an access into new markets.

The emergence of the social web has caused changes in skills that are needed to succeed in this modern environment, in our view of others, their nature and abilities, and in how companies conduct business and design software. It is not only the skills needed from web developers that have changed, but also the skills needed from general population have dramatically changed. A way to describe the desired skill-set required from social web users is to think about them as T-shaped people, who have a broad interest but a deep area of expertise. It has become a core competence in today's information-laden world to be able to pick up relevant information and synthesize it. People also have to make choices in their life about how and with whom they will spend their time, and yet, it is unclear if people in general have the skills needed to make all these choices well. Digital natives, those who grow up with modern information technologies, and digital immigrants, those who have to unlearn previous methods of inquiry to learn to use newer ones, face different challenges in the social web. Digital natives obtain the idioms of the social web along with other social skills, whereas digital immigrants need to make an explicit effort to learn them. Radically new ways of thinking, such as ambient scheduling, may be natural for digital natives, whereas they are most unnatural for digital immigrants.

The web's breakthroughs have made it an integral part of our way of thinking and perceiving the world, and it is safe to say at the very least that the web changes how we perceive people, countries and cultures. People have even started to comprehend things that are new for them by comparing them with the web, asking "how is this similar to the web?" More importantly, the web has shown its capability to change people's lives. Some of the changes are troublesome such as the trend that people tend to think in shorter units and an increased desire for instant gratification, which lead into having short attention spans and craving interactivity and immediate responses to one's actions. The pronounced need for searching and picking up information has also led to a tendency to build on the work of others rather than aiming at creating truly new content and/or services.

The social web provides many opportunities for individuals, organizations and companies, who are up to date with it, but at the same time it has impacted even areas such as manufacturing, and it has revolutionized institutions and fields such as banking, media, music industry and electronic publishing. Newspaper, phone and telecommunication companies are transforming themselves into new kinds of companies. The web has also extensively changed professions, for instance, for the roles of librarians, journalists and software designers. Changes in software design have been more radical than is generally understood. Users can now participate in the actual development process, which is true participatory design, because it not only enables participation but it leads (at least to some extent) to distribution of power. In the social web, users are not only subjects who provide data, but they are actually helping to drive the whole procedure. The social web is also truly human-centered design, in which the focus of the designer is on the experience of the user rather than the technical construct itself. Big changes have been how rapid the development cycles have become and moving away from the user pay model in the software delivery. New business models have emerged and the social web has intensified the emergence of hybrid companies that combine the non-profit and profit sides of business and operations. In addition, software designers' increasing sensitivity to the issue of social responsibility has been most welcome.

Despite the social web's promise and the changes it already has caused, it is by no means unproblematic. Six paradoxes of the social web are the privacy, identity, credibility, friend, filter and value paradoxes.

The social web is about sharing information. Paradoxically, people have at the same time both the need to share information about oneself on the web and to keep their privacy, and they seem to be unsure what should be shared and what should be kept private. This is the privacy paradox. Users register and reveal their personal information and much of a user's online behavior and also purchasing behavior is automatically recorded by the information systems, which makes behavioral patterns much more easily analyzable by the user but also by others. Lack of judgment often causes additional problems, but what other people publish of a user is even more difficult to control; in some situations, anonymity adds to the challenge. The introduction of new information technologies is a Pandora's box, which seems to keep bringing in new challenges relating to the privacy paradox.

The social web is about one's real identity on the web, but paradoxically one of the most severe weaknesses of the social web is that even if a person's identity is acknowledged, it is not strongly represented. In most cases, users will know the person behind a web account only partially. This is the identity paradox.

It is relatively easy to be misled on the web. Almost anyone can say practically anything on the web, for instance to add anything to Wikipedia, and it appears just as authoritative as real facts. These epitomize the credibility paradox.

People who become enthusiastic about the power of the social web easily end up declaring social connections on very loose grounds, which epitomizes the friend paradox. This may lead into semi-anonymous interaction, when people are interacting with others whom they only know indirectly through online personas (even if they would partially reflect the person in real life). One may also become fixated on the number of ties they have in their social networks rather than the quality of the ties. Paradoxically, this may result in lightweight keeping in touch with one's true friends, thus diluting real relationships.

Although the social web in itself adds to the information explosion, one of its promises is that it can ease a user's information bloat through filtering out irrelevant information via social connections. Yes, to some degree people have started to use their networks as a trust filtration device, but the filter paradox lies in the possibility that people would pay attention to information only when it is coming through their social filters, thus limiting themselves to only a certain kind of information. This results easily into echo, which means that there are only likeminded people in the network or at least that there are very few others, and the same information is circulated again and again. With highly valuable information, this would not necessarily be much of a problem, but if the circulated information is also of low value it becomes a very severe problem.

Despite the social web's great promises, one often gets very little true personal value from using it, at least when the time used in it is considered. This value paradox lies in the fact that the social web tends to encourage focusing on surface-level activities and connections rather than those that have a high priority in one's life. One may even end up "talking to oneself" rather than to other people for social reasons, or perhaps even contributing to web pollution by obscuring the information people actually want to get from it. When fed by this self-centeredness of the social web, people may also easily fall into the illusion of individualism, thinking that they are different just because they act in a certain way, whereas in reality they actually just belong to a very carefully segmented market driven by business or other influential players. Yet another issue closely related to the value paradox is that of skills, since obtaining greater value out of the social web requires deep web skills.

Web as an innovation accelerator

Companies can pursue for two major types of innovations in the social web, incremental innovations and Zero-to-One innovations. Incremental innovation is about gradual betterment or next generation of products or services, the focus being to keep current products competitive or to leapfrog competitors, whereas Zero-to-One innovation has the capability to disrupt existing markets, and it aims at future growth in new markets and usually doesn't have anything to do with current products. The big opportunity for the social web is naturally how to create the latter. The key challenge for large companies is the innovator's dilemma. They may be busy feeding the cash cow to the extent that they can't grow any cash calves. However, it is even more difficult to recognize when a company falls into the pitfall of a false negative error. This happens when a falsely reassuring message that there is no business opportunity is given to innovators, based on thinking that the innovation is not a good fit with the existing business, when there actually is opportunity but only when considered outside of existing business. There has been a multitude of errors of this kind in the history of technology. Moreover, even if companies had insight into and expertise in the social web and they succeeded in creating something new, there still remains the question how to overcome inertia within the organization itself, making the innovation get over the threshold.

The highest payoff opportunity for companies happens in the social web, if they are able to develop and nurture innovation ecosystems. This implies building software platforms, by using which others can deploy their own ideas and products, as well as software developments kits and open application programming interfaces to support the use of these platforms. The web can even be considered as a new type of operating system. In any case, companies must be able to nurture business ecosystems on top of these software platforms and to motivate and to encourage the various stakeholders in these through powerful and positive user experiences.

It becomes essential for companies to choose their social web strategy. Traditionally, managers have been trained to think that it is the internal Divisions of Innovation in large companies that can generate innovations, but the social web has challenged this thinking. Newer outbound methods for searching and finding social web innovations are userwatching, including observing the Average Joe and watching the Alpha Geeks, crowdsourcing, open innovation, and initiation of and participation in networked improvement communities, nics. Large companies can also try out different kinds of organizational structures, incentives and other emerging ways for generating innovations, such as rapid experimentation and innovation timeoffs. No matter which of these strategies a company adopts, it should understand that in the social web there is premium on the youth, and yet when digital natives become the majority, it may be that digital immigrants are the ones who can think outside the box and bring ideas from one field to another.

Web as a humanizer

Understanding that the web is not frozen to stay where it is now but that it will keep evolving is important. The major expectation of the future web is that it will become even more humanized. In the epicenter of the humanized web will be new collective intelligence and sense-making technologies, including tools for context accumulation, trailblazing and tracing as well as ways for providing engaging and persuasive user experiences. The major platform for the humanized web will be nomadic, leading the web into becoming a giant sensor network.

The social and humanized web provides organizations and companies with tremendous opportunities to improve their operations. In order to succeed in this new web economy, a combination of core business values and competences must converge. By being watchful for technological shifts, thinking outside the box, showing intrapreneurial spirit and having an appetite to fail fast, all in balance with each other, one may succeed in web innovation.

In spite of the promises, the challenges of the future web are many, too. One big threat, contrary to all general expectations, is that the social web would fail to augment human intellect. The unintended consequences of the social web may also well cause a backlash in such a manner that masses of people would stop using major parts of the social web, and intended malicious action such as intense criminal activity no doubt would cause enormous trouble. Whereas many of the most popular social web applications thus far seem to relate to amusements or relatively trivial challenges, experienced web visionaries urge the field to put more focus on resolving hard or world-scale problems through developed technologies. For the academic world, these challenges on par with the desire to treat the web as a science offer an interesting future research agenda.

Final words

We have recognized the different waves of the web, how the web in spite of its social origins only later became the phenomenon that it is today, the social web, and how in our modern society it is playing the roles of transformer, innovation accelerator and humanizer. There is all the reason to believe that the web adventure will only continue. The web will keep boosting many of the changes in our lives and in the society, and it will continue to be centermost information and communication technology, which influences how innovations are being created. All in all, the web is getting humanized.

Notes

1 A Shift in Thinking about the Web

1. Print/DiNucci (1999), 32.
2. See, for example, Ankerson (2010).
3. Macnamara (2010).
4. Invention of the term web 2.0 is generally credited to web advocate Tim O'Reilly, but for his use of the term he credits Dale Dougherty: "One of my colleagues, Dale Dougherty, did come up with the term Web 2.0. I had been talking about the idea of the Internet operating system, how there's going to be open source paradigm shift, how commoditization of software was changing things. But the name Web 2.0 actually came in a brainstorming meeting that Dale had with Craig Klein. They were just brainstorming is there some kind of an event that we could do together. Dale said 'Yeah, we should do something – we could call it Web 2.0 – about the second coming of the web after the dot-com bust and what's different about it, why did some companies survive, why did some companies fail.' So it was Dale who came up with the name, and then I went 'Oh, this fits perfectly with my whole story about the Internet operating system, because what made some people succeed and some people fail was that they understood the rules of the new platform.'"
5. References to our interviewees are from the first-hand interviews unless otherwise specified. The interviews have been listed at the end matter of the book.
6. An example of web 2.0 technology is Ajax (Asynchronous JavaScript and XML), which enables the web browser and the server to communicate asynchronously. This means that the browser and server can transfer various kinds of data "behind the scenes" in such a way that the user is not informed about the data being transmitted between a server and browser. The goal of this is better user experience and responsiveness to user requests. See, for example, O'Reilly (2005).
7. For discussion of approaches to and definitions of user experience, see for example Law et al. (2009).
8. Krey (1955), 195–208.
9. Surowiecki (2004).
10. For value co-creation, see Prahalad and Venkatram (2000).
11. In later chapters, we call them Zero-to-One innovations.
12. See Schumpeter (1934).
13. See Drucker (1985).

2 Waves of the Web

1. The distinction between the waves is somewhat artificial, but it may become helpful for understanding how quickly industries and in particular high-tech industries evolve. The waves help make a distinction between what we have currently and what is being developed now.
2. Packet switching is a method that groups all transmitted data into "packets," which can move through any of the pathways in the communication network. Breaking communication down into packets also allows the same data path to be shared among many users in the network. The computer finally receiving these packets reassembles them to enable making sense of them.

3. According to Henry Chesbrough, the architecture and the infrastructure was not only developed in the United States with what was called ARPANET, but also through institutions like CERN and others around the world.
4. TCP/IP has played a key role in the development of the web. For instance, HyperText Transfer Protocol (HTTP), which lays the foundation for data communication on the web, has been build on top of TCP/IP. The first version of HTTP was documented in 1991. See for example Gillies and Cailliau (2000).
5. See for example Hillstrom (2005); Abbate (1999), 87.
6. See for example Bell et al. (2005); Clark (2003), 80; Silver (2005), 187–188, 196–197. One of the oldest known virtual communities in continuous operation is "The Whole Earth 'Lectronic Link," also known as the WELL (well.com), founded in 1985.
7. Telnet is a client-server protocol, which allows a user to establish a connection from one's own computer (client) with any networked computer (server) and use its resources remotely. In its early days, most users of networked computers operated from the computer departments of academic institutions or large private or government research facilities.
8. Bulletin Board System (BBS) is a computer system running software that allows users to connect and log in to the system using a terminal program. For the BBS story, see Senft (2003).
9. For Usenet, see Lueg and Fisher (2003).
10. Multi-User Dungeons Object-Oriented (MOO) and Multi-User Shared Hallucination (MUSH) were special types of MUDs. A noteworthy MUD that pre-dates the web is a Finland-based medieval fantasy BatMUD that has been online and available to players on the Internet since April 1990. During its first decade it was among the top three to five contenders with some 600+ players simultaneously online. In more general, some of the text-based MUDs are prominent still today, allowing users to create their own mental schemes and visualizations over what goes on, while graphically advanced versions, such as World of Warcraft, provide less room for imagination in this sense.
11. FTP is an acronym for File Transfer Protocol, which is a standard network protocol for transferring files from one networked host computer to another in a TCP network (like Internet).
12. For Unix see UT (1997).
13. CERN is an acronym for Conseil Européen pour la Recherche Nucléaire (in French).
14. DD/OC stands for Data Handling Division/On-Line Computing Group. See CERN/Berners-Lee (1989, 1990). As further reading see Berners-Lee with Fischetti (2000).
15. See for example SLAC (2006).
16. The Atlantic Monthly/Bush (1945); Life/Bush (1945). Life magazine added the subtitle "A Top U.S. Scientist Foresees a Possible Future World in Which Man-Made Machines Will Start to Think" into the article that Bush had authored.
17. Oinas-Kukkonen (2007); Oinas-Kukkonen et al. (2008), 193–195; Bardini (2000).
18. SRI/Engelbart (1962).
19. See ARC (1968).
20. The nickname appeared after the Persian Gulf War (1990–91), when the phrase "the mother of all battles" spread widely after being used in the war rhetoric.
21. For Xanadu™ Hypertext System, see xanadu.com; Oinas-Kukkonen (2002b).
22. See Nelson (1987a); Nelson (1987b).
23. See Halasz et al. (1986); Halasz (1988).
24. Frank Halasz (1988), 840, comments: "All of these first generation systems, however, included at least some support for medium to large teams of workers sharing a common hypermedia network." At about the same time, many other prominent hypertext systems were built too. These hypertext systems were relatively advanced in their computer–human interaction and computer-mediated communication features compared to other systems at that time. The ACM Hypertext Conference series, which started at 1987, played a central role in advancing both research and development into hypertext and hypermedia systems.

25. Hiltzik (2000); The New Yorker/Gladwell (2011).
26. With the "era" we mean here the massive scale use and dominance of the wave. All of the waves have similar "stages," namely the beginnings, massive use, and fading away (or transforming into the next wave). But the waves are not of the same length, value and shape. They are all different.
27. For the discussion of the web as fourth generation of hypertext, see Bieber et al. (1997).
28. Addressing web sites through the HTTP is based on the web-focused URLs (Universal Resource Locators), which are built upon the Internet's Domain Name System (DNS). The latter is a hierarchical naming system for data resources connected to the Internet, the advantage of which is that users do not need to know where computers or services actually locate and they can use names that imitate human language rather than computing. This idea and its derivatives are essential contributors to the web's usability. ICANN, Internet Corporation for Assigned Names and Numbers, is a nonprofit organization which coordinates the Internet protocol identifiers and domain name space.
29. Brin and Page (1998).
30. For the Google story, see for example Battelle (2008).
31. The Stanford Daily/Hanley (2003).
32. Kasner and Newman (1940); Pickover (2009), 338. Note also that Sergey Brin's father is a professor of mathematics at the University of Maryland and that Sergey Brin also had studied mathematics.
33. Google's IPO took place on 19 August 2004 with the market value of some $23 billion. This was less than some at the time were expecting, but its stock performance did very well for several years to come.
34. USPTO (2001).
35. Interactive television refers here to the possibility for viewers to interact with the television content while they are viewing it.
36. Kim (1999).
37. US Department of Commerce (1993); Kemppainen (2007).
38. See Faden (2001).
39. Burdman (1999).
40. Press (1993); Press (1994).
41. In 1999, when there were high expectations for server-based home network devices for interactive TV to appear on the US markets, TiVo was launched with its more sophisticated public digital video recorder approach than what was available by traditional video recorders.
42. Commercial were, for instance, Clarinet News Service, CARL UnCover for scholarly documents, and the Computists' Communique electronic newsletter.
43. Tim O'Reilly in interview by the authors.
44. According to David S. Evans (2009, 38–39) the first banner ad was sold to AT&T and displayed on the HotWired site in 1994.
45. This was one of the earliest signs of major dotcom transactions. It was still a few years later that Yahoo! built something similar but more sophisticated than GNN.
46. The first implementation of point-and-click interface had come out of PARC more than a decade earlier.
47. For the race between browsers, see for example Windrum (2004); Bresnahan et al. (2011), 36–55; Grunwald (2011), 417–419.
48. Version 1.0 of Netscape Navigator was released on 15 December 1994.
49. There were 60 publicly available plug-ins for Netscape Navigator as early as mid-1995.
50. Netscape Navigator 2.0 was released soon after the company's IPO on 18 September 1995.
51. See for instance Wired/Perkins (1995).
52. See Netscape (1995).
53. See Elliott (1997); compare with Infoworld/Wingfield (1995); Lach (1990).
54. Network World/Messmer (1994).

55. On 7 August 1995, which was just two days before the Netscape IPO, Spyglass announced about Enhanced Mosaic Version 2.1.
56. Microsoft Corporation was founded by Bill Gates and Paul Allen in Albuquerque, New Mexico already in April 1975. By the time of the Browser Wars Microsoft had moved to its present home area, Redmond, Washington, and it already had achieved its position as a dominant software provider for personal computers.
57. This estimate is according to technology research firm Wessels, Arnold & Henderson, LLC. See Network World/Nerney (1998); Elliott (1997), 49.
58. Microsoft made Internet Explorer for Windows 95 available also as an extended version known as Microsoft Plus! for $49.95.
59. NYT/Fisher (1998).
60. To succeed to its rights and to coordinate the development of the Mozilla application Netscape created the Mozilla Organization in February 1998.
61. NYT (1999).
62. Later, AOL scaled back its involvement with Mozilla Organization. The Mozilla Foundation was launched on 15 July 2003, and the Mozilla Foundation established the Mozilla Corporation on 3 August 2005 to coordinate releases of the Mozilla Firefox web browser. Another for-profit subsidiary of the Mozilla Foundation is Mozilla Messaging, Inc. founded in 2007.
63. Companies also developed different types of "push technologies" to send information to users without their explicit requests for obtaining it. For the most part, these were not very successful. Nevertheless, they can be considered as predecessors of so called RSS feeds as well as status updates in social networking systems to appear later.
64. See for instance Search Engine Guide/Hedger (2005).
65. Yahoo! was still the most visited website in 2008. The Guardian/Clark (2008).
66. For the Amazon.com story, see for example Kotha (1998). Compare with Filson (2004); Hennessey (2000), 39–40.
67. For instance, craigslist.org, an online community which enables trading of goods between regular people, originally confined to the San Francisco Bay Area, became very popular. It was launched in 1995, and it became web-based in 1996.
68. For eBay story, see Lewis (2004).
69. Ghosh (2006), 489.
70. Consider for an example an online fashion retailer, Boo.com, founded in September 1998 by three Swedes and based in the United Kingdom. The service attracted huge venture funding, and it was launched in November 1999. Despite employing 18 contractor companies to construct their website at different phases of development, Boo.com disregarded many usability conventions of the time and there was no source code control mechanism. In spite of these it might have had a chance, however, the response time was far below necessary. Boo.com had a potentially huge client base, which it failed to capitalize. Users fled, its IPO was postponed, and eventually investors refused to give it more cash. Only after seven months of operation Boo.com crashed and $135 million in investor's funds were wasted. Boo.com ended up in liquidation in May 2000. See NYT/Sorkin (2000); Owen (2001); Leitch and Warren (2003).
71. Ljungqvist and Wilhelm (2003); Ghosh (2006); Ofek and Richardson (2003); Ritter and Welch (2002), 1796. Battalio and Schultz (2006), 2096, state that it was not obvious to traders that stock prices were too high.

3 The Killer Wave: The Social Web

1. The IRC is based on TCP. See IRC (2005).
2. In fact, IRC enabled also file sharing. File sharing became later infamous due to peer-to-peer file sharing and its related lawsuits encountered by Napster, a service created by

Shawn Fanning, John Fanning, and Sean Parker in 1999 and focused on audio files. Napster had to be closed down, but other services have emerged instead of it.

3. See for example Sarvas and Frohlich (2011).
4. MySQL (2011, 2012).
5. Floyd et al. (2007).
6. Oxford English Dictionary (2012). The Octoroon means "one-eight blood." It was produced at The Winter Garden Theatre in New York on 5 December 1859, shortly before the American Civil War. This play, which was popular at the time, took an abolitionist stand against racial injustice and was an early play to treat seriously of the Black American population. The Octoroon was reworked as *Life in Lousiana. A Play, in Five Acts* in 1861. In this play, an Indian chief of the Lepan Tribe called Wah-no-tee was explained to speak "a mash-up of Indian, French, and Mexican." See Boucicault (1859); Hawera & Normanby Star (1894), 3; DeVere Brody (2000), 101–116.
7. ProgrammableWeb (2012).
8. An early example from both pre-web mashup era and the implementation of a mobile web application can be found from our research team in February 1999. A system was developed using Nokia WAP Software Development Kit 1.0 and utilized through a software emulator in the same development environment. The system collected information at 15 minute intervals from several charge-free sources on the web, including information about stocks, weather, movies, television programs, sports results, and restaurant menus, among others, and compiled the information into a mobile application to be used via mobile phones. Using this application, for example, a businessman travelling from one city to another could check weather conditions at the destination and (almost) real-time stock rates while on the go. See Oinas-Kukkonen (1999).
9. Compare InformIT/Schneiderman (2003).
10. For OMA and WAP, see WAP Forum (2001, 2002); OMAM (2012); Bulbrook (2001); Olsson and Hjelm (2003). Actually, it is said that the WAP Forum simply changed its name and scope to Open Mobile Alliance, and the last event WAP Forum announced in its web pages was Open Mobile Alliance Plenary in Brussels, Belgium on 9–14 November 2003. Working methods were entirely new in OMA compared to the WAP Forum even though their traditions like mobile profiles were brought into this new community. WAP Forum™, W@P Certified™ and W@P™ are now trademarks of the Open Mobile Alliance. See OMA (2012).
11. About the activity, see Pedrinaci et al. (2010). The acronym RDF stands for Resource Description Framework, which is a metamodel for specifying different kinds of web data resources.
12. Bizer et al. (2009).
13. theGlobe and GeoCities went public in 1998, and theGlobe made financial history as its stock experienced a 606 percent share price increase in its first day. theGlobe launched GloPhone, a VoIP phone service, and teamed up with networking site Friendster, but it ceased operations in March 2007. GeoCities was purchased by Yahoo! for $3.57 billion in stock in January 1999. Some ten years later, in October 2009, GeoCities' websites actually became unavailable except in Japan.
14. For an early history of networking sites, see an insightful article by Boyd and Ellison (2007); Kim et al. (2010), 217, 219.
15. During that same period many other important developments happened. Gmail was launched in 31 March 2004, and Yahoo! bought the web-based email system of OddPost on 12 July 2004 which resulted in a version of Yahoo! Mail.
16. Zephyr was developed at MIT in the late 1980s to aid system administrators to send messages to users in an easily noticeable format.
17. Grinter and Palen (2002).
18. For MMORPGs, see for example Achterbosch et al. (2008).
19. Wired/Kim (1998); Blizzard Entertainment (2010).
20. See for example The Economist (2006); Wired/Wortham (2007).

21. PHP is a general-purpose scripting language designed to produce dynamically generated web pages. It was originally created by Greenland-born Rasmus Lerdorf in 1995.
22. According to W3Techs, WordPress had a steady share of 54 percent of content management system market share in August 2012 (W3Techs, 2012; see also W3Techs, 2011). To get an idea about its popularity, WordPress.com was responsible for more than 10 percent of all websites in the world, it served 18 million publishers, and it saw about 300 million unique visits monthly. TechCrunch/Tsotsis (2011). For founder Matt Mullenweg's interview, see The Big Web Show (2010).
23. Other leading social networking services, such as Facebook and LinkedIn, also have their own microblogging features, often referred to as "status updates."
24. Rosenzweig (2006); Reagle (2010); Luethi and Osterloh (2010).
25. Gates (1993). PACS-L stands for Public-Access Computer Systems Forum.
26. Encyclopædia Britannica (1999).
27. Wales's company Bomis Inc. originally was an Internet search portal and a vendor of online erotic images.
28. Rosenzweig (2006); Luethi and Osterloh (2010); Reagle (2010).
29. USPTO (2001).
30. One of the most successful and popular social web services ever, Wikipedia, was already introduced in Chapter 2.
31. For MySpace, Facebook and SixDegrees, see Boyd and Ellison (2007); Kim et al. (2010), 216–217; Treadaway and Smith (2010).
32. BBC News (2011a).
33. "Six degrees of separation" originates from Hungarian author Frigyes Karinthy's volume of short stories *Everything is Different* in 1929. The concept was later extensively tested and popularized by American psychologist Stanley Milgram and others. See Karinthy (1929) and Milgram (1967).
34. Business Insider/Carlson (2011).
35. LinkedIn Press Center (2003).
36. LinkedIn Press Center (2007b).
37. LinkedIn Press Center (2007a).
38. Hoffman (2011).
39. NYT/Creswell, (2011); WSJ/Woo et al. (2011).
40. SMS is an acronym for Short Message System in mobile telecommunication.
41. Asymmetric follow model means that if A follows B it does not imply that B follows A. In the symmetric network model A following B would also mean B following A. Asymmetric follow is a very powerful metaphor which many other social networking system developers have now adopted. For instance, Facebook did not have it when it was launched but it soon added similar feature through their fan pages.
42. For example, Tim O'Reilly had 1,594,524 followers and YouTube celebrity Julian Smith had 112,145 followers in August 2012.
43. For a very compressed Twitter story, see the introduction in Sagolla (2009) or Kierkegaard (2010).
44. Dorsey (2006).
45. Stone (2007).
46. In May 2012, Alexa Web Information Company still ranked MySpace as 156th in the world. Alexa (2012a).
47. Google and Microsoft aggressively tried to purchase Twitter in 2009, but in vain. By this time its valuation had risen to $1.44 billion in SharesPost Inc., a marketplace for trading stocks of private companies.
48. See Ludicorp (2012).
49. GNE Museum (2012).
50. See Kunkle and Morton (2006).
51. Caterina Fake in interview by the authors; USA Today/Graham (2006, 2007).
52. USA Today/Hopkins (2006); YouTube (2011).

53. See Lapitsky (2005).
54. YouTube was the third most visited site among all websites, right behind Facebook and Google in August 2012. Alexa (2012b).
55. Reuters/Anupreeta (2009).
56. For instance, in 2012 the video Gangnam Style by Korean rap artist Psy achieved more than one million views in a bit more than five months from its uploading.
57. Vanity Fair/Etter (2011).
58. For Groupon, see WSJ/Weiss (2010); Reuters/Barr and Baldwin (2011); ABC News/ Liedtke (2011); TechCrunch/Lunden (2012).
59. See foursquare (2012a).
60. foursquare (2012b).
61. "4sqDays" is an acronym for "FourSquareDays." See foursquare (2012c).

4 The Promise

1. Conklin (1987).
2. Kling (2000). See also Conklin (1987).
3. See for example Crowston and Williams (2000). Yet, it was relatively late when any greater number of researchers started to focus their work on the web's potential for supporting people's social networks.
4. Mårten Mickos was the CEO of MySQL between 2001–08 and after the acquisition of MySQL Senior Vice President of the database group at Sun Microsystems till March 2009. After that he became CEO of Eucalyptus Systems, Inc., a company focusing on open source cloud computing, a Member of the Board of Directors of Nokia and venture capitalist.
5. The phrase "ambient intimacy" was launched by Leisa Reichelt on Twitter on 1 March 2007. See Reichelt (2007).
6. Mark Granovetter introduced the concepts of strong and weak ties in his seminal article in the American Journal of Sociology in 1973. See also Granovetter (1995).
7. See Wired/Kelly and Wolf (1997); Wired/Kelly (1999).
8. John Lilly was the CEO of Mozilla Corporation between 2008–10.
9. See Kiva (2010).
10. Titanic's "unknown child" was first falsely identified as Irish Eugene Rice, later as Swedish Gösta Leonard Pålsson, based on dental records as Finnish Eino Viljami Panula, and finally based on mitochondrial DNA molecule he was identified as English Sidney Leslie Goodwin. See Barczewski (2006); Maltin and Aston (2011).
11. BBC News (2010b). Later, the Finnish government has announced that every household within two kilometers of a fiber optic cable supplying superfast broadband running at 100 megabits per second has the right to it by 2015. Despite its ambitious goals all geographical areas have not progressed equally swiftly.
12. ITU (2010, 2011). It is interesting to note that already in 2008 half of search queries on Google came from outside of the United States. See NYT/Sorid (2008); NYT (2008).
13. Ben Shneiderman in interview by the authors.
14. Technorati (2011). These numbers from the survey should be considered indicative only. There may be big differences between different languages and between various geographical areas.
15. According to Technorati, 55 percent of hobbyist bloggers received fewer than 1,000 unique visitors per month. See Technorati/Sobel (2010).
16. Parkinson (2010). This quotation of Andy Warhol, which already has become a cliché, can often be found in various different forms, relatively often being misquoted. The first edition of the original publication has clearly achieved a very high status among collectors of rare publications. The first printing issue of Andy Warhol's Moderna Museet 1968 exhibition catalogue without dust jacket and original cardboard slipcase

was priced as high as $2,500 in an online marketplace for professional booksellers in December 2010.
17. Dave Carroll Music (2012); Carroll (2009); The Huffington Post (2009b).
18. Caterina Fake, chairman of the board of Etsy, in interview by the authors. Etsy is regarded as a financial success, valued at about $100 million, with 400,000 worldwide sellers and gross sales of $180.6 million in 2010. The World Economic Forum defined Etsy as one of Technology Pioneers. See Etsy (2012); The Telegraph/Salter (2010).
19. See for example The National/Sands (2008); silentwhisper2009 (2011); Al-Ahram Weekly Online (2011).
20. Al Jazeera English (2011).
21. The Times of India/Bagchi (2011).
22. Business Insider/White (2011).
23. A Swedish Internet service provider and web hosting company PeRiQuito AB (PRQ) has hosted WikiLeaks digital archives in Solna, Stockholm from its early years. See Dagens Nyheter (2010); Kauppalehti (2010).
24. Democracy Now! (2010).
25. The Washington Post/Miller (2010).
26. See The White House/Obama (2011a). The new apparatus included "Senior Information Sharing and Safeguarding Steering Committee," the "Classified Information Sharing and Safeguarding Office," the "Executive Agent for Safeguarding Classified Information on Computer Networks" and the "Insider Threat Task Force."
27. Denial of service is an attempt by a third party to make a service unavailable for its intended users.
28. BBC News (2010c).
29. WSJ/Whalen (2011).
30. Julian Assange had already been living a nomadic life and at one time declared his wish to get a political asylum in Switzerland. After Assange was alleged for sexual offensives in Sweden, he was bailed in the United Kingdom in December 2010 for a payment of £240,000 in cash and sureties, strict bail conditions including wearing an electronic tag, reporting to police every day and observing a curfew residing at the manor home owned by a supporting journalist. Assange declared being a victim of a sham. In late May 2012 Britain's Supreme Court ruled that Assange should be extradited to Sweden. Assange took a refuge in the Ecuadorean embassy in London in August 2012, where he was granted political asylum. See NZZ Online (2010); Tages Anzeiger/Diethelm (2010); BBC News (2010c); BBC News (2012).
31. Cross et al. (2001).
32. Saxenian (1994).
33. Steiny and Oinas-Kukkonen (2007).
34. See Oinas-Kukkonen (2008).
35. Cross et al. (2002).
36. See Hampton et al. (2011).
37. USC (1981).
38. See Reagle (2010).

5 The Change

1. Computerworld covered in 2005 that Katrina survivors needed Internet Explorer Version 6 or higher to apply for the Federal Emergency Management Agency (FEMA) for assistance online. See Rosencrance (2005).
2. See Donofrio et al. (2010).
3. Iansiti (1993).
4. Moggridge Associates in London merged with David Kelley Design and Matrix both in Palo Alto and ID Two in San Francisco and formed IDEO in 1991.

5. Standards for the 21st-Century Learner (2007).
6. See Prensky (2001a, 2001b).
7. Oinas-Kukkonen and Kurki (2009).
8. The first to use the term *edutainment* was Walt Disney in 1948. See Van Riper (2011).
9. Prensky (2003).
10. Roberts et al. (2005). The diagnosed numbers of ADD have increased, but most researchers attribute the rise to growing awareness and better screening of children. Jay Giedd, a neuroscientist in the child psychiatry branch of the National Institutes of Health commented in April 2011 that he sees "ADD much more as something caused by biology and not as something caused by the environment." For further information of the comment, see MSNBC/Carroll (2011).
11. Hallowell (2006).
12. Rideout et al. (2010).
13. Sparrow et al. (2011); See also The Atlantic/Carr (2008).
14. The web in itself is not intended for changing humans. Some web applications can, of course, be built with the intent of changing their users' attitudes and/or behaviors.
15. Prensky (2001a). It should be noted, however, that hypertext, in spite of Prensky's valuable definition, by no means is random access. Hypertext and hypermedia, by definition, mean associative access which is implemented through navigating the hyperlinks.
16. One of those who agree with this view is Nicholas Carr, the author of *The Shallows: What the Internet is Doing to Our Brains* published in 2010. Carr believes that the way we use the web to find, store and share information can literally re-route our neural pathways.
17. "Digital natives" and "digital immigrants" have been further discussed by John Palfrey and Urs Gasser in the book *Born Digital: Understanding the First Generation of Digital Natives* published in 2008.
18. Agarwal and Lucas (2005).
19. See McAfee (2006); Cook (2008).
20. For an instance of an enterprise social network service, see Yammer, originally launched in September 2008. Yammer is a microblogging system supporting private communication within intra-organizational or extra-organizational settings. Access to it is enabled by a user's Internet domain (email address). It could be described as an organizational Facebook or Twitter. Microsoft acquired Yammer in June 2012.
21. This refers to both organizational use of originally non-organizational social web tools and tools developed particularly for organizational use. For the former, see Kane et al. (2010) and Kane (2011). An example of the latter is Yammer.
22. Apple Press Info (2001); Patterson (2006).
23. The Guardian/Hammersley (2004).
24. Brick-and-mortar store is "a traditional business serving customers in a building as contrasted to an online business." First known usage in 1992. Merriam-Webster Dictionary (2012).
25. The New Yorker/Crouch (2011).
26. Much if not most of banking has shifted to the web. Scandinavian banks spearheaded in this process. More recently, also many developing countries have widely started to utilize mobile banking.
27. In the year 2009, Mozilla had about 350 million users worldwide, and it generated close to $100 million in revenue. In spite of these convincing figures, Mozilla has only about 250 employees spread around the world.
28. Mozilla Foundation placed two-page advocacy ad in *The New York Times*. Mozilla Foundation (2004); Cabello, P. (2008).
29. Scandinavian research on participatory design within systems development has its roots in the 1970s. The role of working unions has traditionally been exceptionally strong in the Nordic countries. For the Scandinavian participatory design approach, see for example Bødker (1996).

30. Bødker (1996).
31. Vodanovich et al. (2010).
32. A legacy system is an old software or information system, which still operates in the planned way and which continues to be used, even if newer technology or more efficient methods for performing the tasks already have become available. However, they may hinder or slow down starting to use newer and more effective methods or technologies.
33. See MobileWorks (2012); TechCrunch/Kincaid (2011).
34. See CPSR (2005).

6 Six Paradoxes

1. For instance, hackers stole personal details from approximately 77 million Sony PlayStation Network accounts and 1.3 million Sega Pass gameplayers' networked user data and system accounts in 2011. See Reuters/Reynolds and Baker (2011); BBC News (2011b).
2. CNBC (2009a), note also readers' comments on these pages; CNBC (2009b); The Huffington Post (2009a).
3. Oinas-Kukkonen (2000).
4. See The Huffington Post/Grieshaber (2011). Many other similar type of incidents have happened as well.
5. Challenges related to privacy in the social web are multilayered and grand, and they will to a growing extent be in the interest of billions of people. Numerous researchers have set up to work on the privacy paradox. For instance, the Workshop on Networked Privacy at the ACM CHI Conference on Human Factors in Computing Systems in 2011 proposed creating a Privacy Task Force to design interactional privacy features by an interdisciplinary multinational team of computer scientists, designers, human science experts, theorists and authorities. See CHI (2011).
6. Henry Chesbrough in interview by the authors.
7. See The Economist (2012).
8. See Goffman (1963).
9. What had happened was that a loose circle of young French mathematicians connected to the École normale supérieure in Paris met informally but regularly in "Café, grill-room, A. Capoulade" at 63 boulevard in Saint-Michel during the academic year 1934–35. It was usual among politicians, artists and scientists to meet in Parisian cafés. These young men felt that French mathematical research was lagging far behind that of other countries, and they formed a team which they called the "Committee on Analysis" or "Committee for the Analysis Treatise." They undertook collective writing without rendering any acknowledgment on individual contributions.In the summer of 1935, the Committee adopted a strange pseudonym, "Bourbaki," referring to a French general with Cretan ancestry, Charles Denis Sauter Bourbaki. As part of their freshmen initiation at the École in 1923, some of the committee members had been subjected to a hoax lecture describing the "theorem of Bourbaki," a mathematical theorem named after the general. One of the *bourbakists*, mathematician André Weil (1906–98), later Professor of Mathematics in the Institute for Advanced Study in Princeton University, relished the story and refined this imaginary figure at first as a former lecturer M. Bourbaki at the fictitious Royal University of Besse in fictitious Poldavia and later as a non-existent Russian mathematician named D. Bourbaki. But in fact the visiting cards of N. Bourbaki got Weil himself into a big trouble. As a conscientious objector, Weil had escaped into Finland to avoid being drafted into the French army during the World War II. However, Weil had also travelled in the Soviet Union, having had correspondence with Soviet mathematicians. He had been carrying around visiting cards of this imaginary N. Bourbaki. After the Soviet Union attacked Finland in 1939, he was

arrested on charge of being a Soviet spy. He was released and expelled to Sweden after Finnish mathematicians testified in his favor.

In any case, the *bourbakists'* work later became famous for its perpetually revised multi-volume treatise entitled *Eléments de Mathématique*, published under the pseudonym "Nicolas Bourbaki" from 1939 to the present. Bourbaki became a legal association, Association of the Collaborators of Nicolas Bourbaki, in August 1952. Bourbaki's most recent piece of work was published in 1998. An interesting additional detail is that according to Andre Weil's autobiography, diplomat Nicolai'des Bourbaki who was a legitimate member of the family of the general, tracked down the committee in 1948, thinking Nicolas Bourbaki might be a distant cousin. For more information on Bourbaki, see Beaulieu (1993); Knapp (1999); Clark (2005), 82–86; Corry (1996), chapter 7; Varadarajan (1999).

10. Halmos (1957).
11. Stara (2006); Stara/Podcast (2006); VG/Østbø (2006).
12. Companies and organizations that support the APWG include, for instance, Google, Yahoo!, Facebook, MySpace, Microsoft, Huawei, Symantec Technologies, McAfee, F-Secure, Telefónica, and SRI International.
13. APWG (2011).
14. UN (2000, 2010).
15. See, for instance, Hovland and Weiss (1951).
16. Of course, there are socio-technical mechanisms that to some extent help tackle this issue.
17. Later CTO at eBay and Senior Vice President of Technology at American Express. See All Things Digital/Swisher (2010).
18. The study by Ridings and McClure Wasko (2010) confirms the observation of power law distribution of participation: Only a few members of an online community will significantly contribute content when measured in message volume. The authors also show that these distributions change over time and that too "steep" of a distribution of participation may result in a decline in online participation.
19. Dunbar (1993); Research Intelligence (2003).
20. Gladwell (2000).
21. Conklin (1987).
22. See Roberts et al. (2005); Rideout et al. (2010).
23. Reid Hoffman in interview by the authors.
24. The biggest anime and *manga* magazine in Scandinavia is the *Anime* magazine in Finland. In 2007, it had 44,000 readers in a country of 5.2 million inhabitants. *Otakus* formed a community of likeminded people who utilize the web for their collaboration. The Finnish Anime Union defines itself as "a communications forum for joint operations among anime clubs and other related associations." The union produces "shared web content, services, resources and events." See Anime (2011); Animeunioni (2011); Valaskivi (2009).
25. See Sunstein (2007). Quite interestingly, Pew Internet study on American users of popular social networking systems found no evidence that the users were any more likely than others to cocoon themselves in social networks of likeminded and similar people. See Hampton et al. (2011).
26. Granovetter (1978).
27. Perceived value is of course a very personal matter. One way to describe the value obtained from the social web is to consider of it as either an utilitarian information system or an hedonic information system. See Heijden (2004).
28. See for example Poli and Agrimi (2012); Tonioni et al. (2012).
29. See for example chapter "Polarization and Cybercascades" in Sunstein (2007).
30. For a discussion of identity changes, see Goffman (1963).
31. The expression that "we amuse ourselves to death" was made popular by educator Neil Postman, whose book *Amusing Ourselves to Death: Public Discourse in the Age of Show Business* was published in 1985.

7 The Quest for Zero-to-One Innovation

1. See NSF (2011). The Office of Science and Technology Policy within the Executive Office of the President, strongly supports this program established in 2005. The Science of Science Policy is regarded as an emerging interdisciplinary and international field of research and community of practice that seeks to develop theoretical and empirical models of the scientific enterprise. This program has set three major goals: advancing evidence-based science and innovation policy decision making; building a scientific community to study science and innovation policy; and leveraging the experience of other countries. See OSTP (2011).
2. Estrin (2008).
3. Nonaka and Takeuchi (1995).
4. There is a long tradition in computer science to consider adoption into use as an approximate of success. See Davis (1989), Davis et al. (1989) and Venkatesh et al. (2003). However, more emphasis should be put into studying actual use and how to influence it rather than the adoption process only.
5. Caterina Fake in interview by the authors. At that time, Yahoo! already had about 13,000 employees.
6. Christensen (1997).
7. Mac Life/Ochs and Williams (2007).
8. See Juettemeyer (2008).
9. Wu (2011).
10. Henry Chesbrough in interview by the authors. See also Chesbrough (2003).
11. Xbox was launched in September 2005. It was developed as being compatible with online multiplayer gaming and digital media delivery service Xbox LIVE which had been available since in 2002. Both of these two were brought together with Windows Phone 7 Series in 2010. See Microsoft News Center (2010).
12. Carlos Fernando Flores Labra is a Chilean engineer, cognitive scientist, entrepreneur and politician. He was Director of state owned corporations and a Minister of Finance during Salvador Allende *régime* in 1970–73, a political prisoner during Augusto Pinochet *régime* in 1973–76, a doctoral student at the University of California at Berkeley 1976–79, a research fellow in the Computer Science department at Stanford University and a philosophy professor at the University of California at Berkeley. During a period of 20 years, between 1982–2001, Flores published several monographs; after that he entered into politics. He was a Chilean senator between 2002 and 2010. He has been the President of Chile's National Innovation Council for Competitiveness since 2010. See for instance strategy+business/Fisher (2009).
13. Winograd and Flores (1986).
14. David M. Kelley is an engineer, educator, entrepreneur and venture capitalist. He has Donald W. Whittier Professorship in Mechanical Engineering at Stanford University and is Director of Hasso Plattner Institute of Design at Stanford also known as d.school.
15. Kelley (2001, 2002, 2004).
16. DataPoint Corporation was originally known as Computer Terminal Corporation.
17. ARCnet stands for Attached Resource Computer network.
18. See Cross et al. (2001).
19. Oinas-Kukkonen (1998).
20. See for example Reuters/Anupreeta (2009).

8 Social Web as an Innovation Ecosystem

1. Davenport et al. (2006).
2. Various software engineering approaches have been suggested to help tackle these challenges including agile software development and extreme programming.

3. Neal Sample in interview by the authors.
4. Neal Sample in interview by the authors.
5. This transmission of key software functionality from the information system or application level to the operating system level was addressed in one of the authors' early keynotes. See Oinas-Kukkonen (1995).
6. Jimmy Wales in interview by the authors.
7. Tansley (1935).
8. See Microsoft News Center (2011); AdvertisingAge/Patel (2011).
9. For his doctoral dissertation, see Sample (2005). See also X.commerce (2011).
10. See for example Reuters/Anupreeta (2009).
11. Oinas-Kukkonen (2008).
12. Terry Winograd in interview by the authors.

9 Social Web Innovation Strategies

1. See Schumpeter (1934). In fact, Schumpeter distinguished between invention and innovation already during his European period. At this time, his major work was *Theorie der wirtschaftlichen Entwicklung*. See Frank (1998), 507–509.
2. See Kaes (2003).
3. Feldman (2011).
4. Caterina Fake, co-founder of Hunch, in interview by the authors. Hunch was acquired by eBay in November 2011. For another example of question-and-answer web services, see Quora (2012).
5. Professor of Linguistics David W. Maurer claimed in "Carnival Cant: A Glossary of Circus and Carnival Slang" in *American Speech* in June 1931 that Wagner of Charleston had been reputed to have originated a word "geek." See Maurer (1931), 327–337. Wagner of Charleston's or other sideshow star's epithet or definition geek depends on geck. It was originally a Lower Saxon word, which can be traced in 1385, when it meant a court jester. An itinerant medieval entertainer was called as *gauckler*, who could *gaukeln*, show tricks. Much later in the mid-twentieth century a geek meant clearly a socially eccentric person, who could get engrossed in a single subject. During the last quarter of the twentieth century a geek became a slang expression for an expert in scientific and technological pursuits but being short of social skills. See Nickell (2005); Liberman (2008).
6. The sensor trend in relation to the future web will be discussed in Chapter 10.
7. For another view, see the article by Jeff Howe, who made the term popular. Wired/Howe (2006).
8. Surowiecki (2004). Calling this approach "the wisdom of crowds" may be an exaggeration, and at least in this sense "crowdsourcing" is a more modest and accurate name for the approach discussed here.
9. An earlier analysis of ours on Surowiecki's work suggests that this wisdom of crowds, essentially the crowdsourcing approach, can be described and defined with eight conjectures, which are all put into the context of social web here. For the original presentation, see Oinas-Kukkonen (2008).
10. Nature (2005); Giles (2005).
11. See for example MobileWorks (2012).
12. Chesbrough (2003).
13. For University Hack Day Program, see Yahoo (2012).
14. See for example Lewis (2004).
15. Engelbart (1992).
16. According to Tim O'Reilly, the social web perspective on open source is quite different from the perspective of the Linux or the Free Software Foundation people.
17. Gehani (2003); Hiltzik (2000).
18. The same connection is naturally needed also from business managers in their relationship to employees and other subordinates. In her book *The Plugged-In Manager: Get*

in Tune with Your People, Technology, and Organization to Thrive, Terri Griffith describes how it is not enough for managers to understand organizational processes and technology only, but that they also have to be connected to real people in their organization. See Griffith (2011).

19. NYT/Mediratta (2007); Mayer (2006). In July 2012 Marissa Meyer became the CEO of Yahoo!
20. See Coase (2003).

10 The Next Generation of the Web: The Humanized Web

1. Copley (2009).
2. Mitcham and Schatzberg (2009).
3. Brian Parkinson suggests that emotions are often best viewed as social phenomena rather than simply individual reactions only. He argues that many cases of emotion are essentially communicative rather than internal and reactive phenomena and that many of the causes, consequences and functions of emotions in everyday life are interpersonally, institutionally or culturally related. See Parkinson (1996).
4. Hampton et al. (2011). Interestingly, similar results were not found with other social networking systems than Facebook.
5. "As We May Think" was an expanded version of Bush's essay "Mechanization and the Record," which he had tried to publish originally in *Fortune* magazine in 1939. It was also published in *Life*. See The Atlantic Monthly/Bush (1945); Life/Bush (1945).
6. The most extensive example of a Memex owner's trails that Bush gave was a historical survey of why the short Turkish bow was apparently superior to the English long bow in the skirmishes of the Crusades.
7. The Atlantic Monthly/Bush (1945).
8. The Atlantic Monthly/Bush (1945).
9. Bush (1967).
10. See Oinas-Kukkonen (1997). Another interesting but not well-known software feature is the "fatlink." Hyperlinks which are attached to an object can be grouped into a fatlink to ease the cognitive overload, and the activation of a fatlink gives, for instance, a menu of the links contained in it. Individual links can then be activated from this list.
11. Other examples are social bookmarking web services such as Delicious (earlier known as del.icio.us, later delicious.com), launched in 2003, and social news websites such as Digg (digg.com), started out in 2004.
12. The term "lurker" was originally used for people who utilized bulletin board systems in the mid-1980s but did not contribute anything to them.
13. See Nonnecke and Preece (2000) and Nonnecke et al. (2006).
14. Lurking has received relatively little quantitative study, because data collection in most information systems focuses on the activities of information producers.
15. Muller et al. (2010).
16. See Google (2012).
17. In fact, Engelbart showed frustration over the years when people widely jubileed the physical and easy-to-grasp parts of his conceptual framework, such the mouse as a way to provide user input, but neglected the framework and the heavier parts of it, such as collective intelligence.
18. O'Reilly and Battelle (2009).
19. The term *context accumulation* was introduced by Jeff Jonas in August 2006. See Jonas (2006).
20. Caterina Fake in interview by the authors.
21. In their pursuit for better applications, computer scientists could learn a lot from the past 40+ years of research into social network analysis and sociology.

22. Apple Press Info (2007).
23. Caterina Fake in interview by the authors.
24. Blauk.com began operating in India in January 2010. See The Hindu/Fredrick (2010); The Hindu/Niharika (2010).
25. Strecher (2007).
26. Petty and Cacioppo (1981).
27. Cialdini (2001).
28. Fogg (2003).
29. Oinas-Kukkonen and Harjumaa (2009).
30. For an example of social badges, see foursquare (2012a).
31. Oinas-Kukkonen (2012).
32. See, for instance, klout.com or peerindex.com.
33. Lyytinen and Yoo (2002).
34. The first really big success with Internet tablets was Apple iPad.
35. For an example of the fast growth and rapid changes in mobile markets, consider the sales numbers of smartphones. Research firm Gartner announced in February 2011 that sales of smartphones rose 72 percent in 2010 to 297 million units, while worldwide sales of all handset sales rose 32 percent. Nokia's Symbian platform, which previously had been a clear market leader, started rapidly to loose its position, when Google's market share increased almost tenfold in 2010. Soon, Apple's iPhone 4 achieved 16 percent share of the smartphone market in the fourth quarter of 2010. Partly due to these developments, Nokia and Microsoft formed a broad strategic partnership in February 2011, in which Nokia adopted Windows Phone as its principal smartphone platform. *WSJ*/Sandstrom (2011); Microsoft News Center (2011).
36. Nokia Corporation (2011); NAVTEQ (2011). NAVTEQ was bought by Nokia at approximately $8.1 billion on 10 July 2008. See NAVTEQ (2008)
37. For an interesting article on the development of mobile location-based services, see Dhar and Varshney (2011).
38. The Quake-Catcher Network (2011).
39. For more on the web of things, see for example EUREKA (2011) or visit greengoose.com.
40. IND Technology & Science News/Lamarra (2003). NASA plans to leverage the Internet into the deep-space domain via an Interplanetary Networking Architecture. The basis of the new techniques is the Delay and Disruption Tolerant Networking protocol developed by the Delay-Tolerant Networking Research Group, which is chartered as part of the Internet Research Task Force. Several of its members participate in the DARPA Disruption Tolerant Networking program (see dtnrg.org).
41. NASA (2010); Luleå University (2009).
42. Weiser (1991).

11 Core Business Values

1. Nelson (2009); Ted Nelson in interview by the authors.
2. The term S-curve has been in use at least since the late nineteenth century. However, it was Everett M. Rogers' *Diffusion of Innovations* in 1962 that rendered a broader use for it.
3. Regarding recognition and superstar status, which some designers have achieved in the innovation processes of successful companies, see Dell'Era et al. (2011), 36, 37, 44–46.
4. TIME Staff (2001); digital wellbeing labs (2012).
5. According to IDEO's general manager, Tom Kelley, the reason why companies look outside for product development can be compressed into four main keywords, namely capacity, speed, expertise and innovation. See Kelley (2004). Interestingly, IDEO had

earlier been working also with other successful products such as the first Apple mouse and the second Microsoft mouse as well as the Palm V handheld device.

6. Duncan J. Watts discusses this kind of hindsight in his book *Everything is Obvious Once You Know the Answer* (Watts, 2011).
7. Oinas-Kukkonen et al. (2008).
8. Hargadon (2003).
9. See Walters (2005); Goleniewski (2003), 434; Rieback et al. (2006), 67.
10. Granovetter (1973).
11. Quoted by Reid Hoffman, Executive Vice President of PayPal, in interview by the authors.
12. For example, see Misa (2011).
13. Hoefler wrote a series of articles "Silicon Valley, USA," which started with the 11 January 1971, issue in his weekly tabloid *Electronic News*. It was Hoefler's articles, which named the northern California area of Santa Clara as Silicon Valley as well as presented Semiconductor Genealogy Chart in the same year. Silicon Valley Genealogy Chart was later maintained in poster by the trade association, Semiconductor Equipment and Materials International foundation since 1995.
14. See Castilla et al. (2000).
15. To exemplify short-term planning activities (at a national level), Estrin explains that in 2006 large American drug companies doubled their research and development investments into China and India to $2.2 billion rather than investing domestically. Quite likely it guaranteed better return on investment without shake-up risks, but unlikely did it promote long-term innovation to be carried out within the United States.
16. Alexander Graham Bell and Charles Sumner Tainter had invented and patented the Photophone, which they used for wireless transmitting of speech signal on a beam of light in 1880.
17. O'Malley (2011); Alaiwi et al. (2009), 105; Scott (2008).
18. Johannes Gensfleisch zur Laden zum Gutenberg (c. 1398, Mainz – 3 February 1468, Mainz).
19. Paul Saffo in interview by the authors. See also Newsweek/Saffo (2002).
20. Judy Estrin emphasizes the balance of core values. In her book *Closing the Innovation Gap: Reigniting the Spark of Creativity in a Global Economy*, the core values are defined as questioning, patience, trust, openness and risk (Estrin, 2008).
21. Saxenian (1994).
22. Judy Estrin in interview by the authors.
23. For this and also ideas in the next paragraph, see O'Mara (2005); Lécuyer (2007); Zachary (1999).
24. It was in this position when Bush published his ideas that related to the origins of the web.
25. See Chapter 2 and Oinas-Kukkonen (2007).

12 Future Challenges

1. See technologyacademy.fi.
2. Engelbart (1988). Our interview(s) with Dr Engelbart confirm that his view has remained as determined as it was in the 1950s.
3. Other Nelson's similar type metaphors can be found in Oinas-Kukkonen (2001); Oinas-Kukkonen (2002a).
4. Transclusion means that rather than copying data from one place and storing it in another place, the data is stored only once and connected via a transclusion link in such a manner that the same data can be viewed in different contexts.
5. For a prototype implementation of ZigZag, see xanadu.com/zigzag.

6. Nelson has been working for five decades in order to develop his ideal Xanadu system, the ultimate documentation system. A demo of Xanadu can be found at xanadu.com and xanarama.net.
7. See Dourish (2001), 26.
8. Ted Nelson uses the acronym "PUI," or term *pooey*, for what he calls "PARC User Interface." See also Nelson (2012).
9. Fortunately, methods for filtering spam have been and are being developed. Yet, there seems to be no clear solution for the problem; spam filters ease the symptoms of the problem only.
10. Some called it the "Web War One."
11. See Clarke and Knake (2010).
12. Dutch philosopher and jurist Hugo Grotius (1583–1645) formulated a principle that the sea was international territory to be used freely by all nations for seafaring trade in his book *Mare Liberum* published in 1609.
13. OECD (2011a); US Department of State/Kornbluh (2012), compare with Rodriguez (2011).
14. OECD (2011b); US Department of State/Kornbluh (2012).
15. CSISAC (2011a, 2011b).
16. The White House/Obama (2011b, 2011c); The White House/Schmidt (2011).
17. US Congress (2011a). The bill was presented by Senator P.J. Leahy in the 1st Session of the 112th Congress for himself and nine others.
18. US Congress (2011b).
19. Protect Innovation (2012). It has been also suggested that requiring developing countries to conform to the IPR policies defined by developed countries to protect their assets prohibits developing countries from innovating and slows down their progress. For a discussion on this, see Lessig (2002).
20. For further discussion on the topic, see, for example, Morozov (2011).
21. For disaster response, see, for example, Majchrzak et al. (2007).
22. See google.org/personfinder.
23. PA Times/Collins and Milen (2011). Ushahidi is a non-profit software company that develops free and open-source software for information collection, visualization and interactive mapping. See ushahidi.com. For another example, see sahanafoundation.org.
24. Chairman of the Gapminder Foundation, Hans Rosling, is Professor of International Health at the Karolinska Institutet in Stockholm, Sweden, he has worked as a health adviser to WHO and UNICEF and co-founded Médecins Sans Frontières (Doctors Without Borders). Gapminder Foundation is a non-profit organization that aims to improve the use and understanding of statistical health information.
25. See for example Rosling (2007); Discover/Barone (2007).
26. The National Telephone Exchange Association of the United States as well as the International Congress of Telegraph and Telephone Engineers in Europe provided forums to discuss the issue of automatic switching, which smaller independent telephone companies actively used.
27. Huurdeman (2003).
28. SRI/Engelbart (1962); Engelbart (1988).
29. Nelson (2009).
30. Worldwatch/Engelman (2010); Worldwatch/Renner (2010); Worldwatch/Tung (2010).
31. The Declaration was adopted by the UN General Assembly in September 2000 after its three-day-long Millennium Summit, which was the largest gathering of world leaders in history by that date. See UN (2000).
32. The UN General Assembly resolution of "Keeping the promise: United to achieve the Millennium Development Goals" stated in September 2010: "We, Heads of State and Government, gathered at United Nations Headquarters in New York from 20 to 22

September 2010, welcome the progress made since we last met here in 2005 while expressing deep concern that it falls far short of what is needed." See UN (2005, 2010).

33. See ted.com.
34. Hendler et al. (2008).
35. The Web Science Research Initiative was established by the MIT and the University of Southampton in 2006. Later, the Web Science Trust (WST) was launched to promote research and education in Web Science in 2009. See Web Science Trust (2011, 2012).
36. Preece and Shneiderman (2009).
37. Shneiderman (2007).

13 Conclusion

1. See Taleb (2007). According to Taleb, the rise of the Internet and Google are examples of black swan events. Of course, the Black Swan theory does not claim that black swan events would not have been planned at any level.

Primary sources

Governmental, research and international organizations' documents

APWG (2011) *Counter-eCrime Operations Summit 2011*, 26–29 April 2011 – Kuala Lumpur, Malaysia. The Anti-Phishing Working Group. http://www.antiphishing.org/events/2011_opSummit.html, date accessed 24 April 2011.

ARC (1968) "1968 Fall Joint Computer Conference demo of the Augment Research Center," 9 December 1968, *In the Demo*. MouseSite. Stanford University, Stanford, CA. http://sloan.stanford.edu/mousesite/1968Demo.html#complete, date accessed 30 March 2012.

CERN/Berners-Lee, T. (1989,1990) "Information Management: A Proposal," CERN, March 1989, May 1990. http://www.w3.org/History/1989/proposal.html, date accessed 30 March 2012.

CSISAC (2011a) "CSISAC Issues Statement on OECD Communiqué on Principles for Internet Policy-Making." *Civil Society Information Society Advisory Council (CSISAC), OECD*. Press release, Paris, 29 December 2011. http://csisac.org/CSISAC_PR_06292011.pdf, date accessed 13 February 2012.

CSISAC (2011b) "CSISAC Welcomes OECD Recommendation on Principles for Internet Policy Making." *Civil Society Information Society Advisory Council (CSISAC), OECD*. Press release, Paris, 19 December 2011. http://csisac.org/CSISAC-PR-191211/CSISAC-PR-191211.pdf, date accessed 13 February 2012.

EUREKA (2011) *Low-cost wireless sensor networks open new horizons for the Internet of things*. EUREKA Secretariat. Published on: 2011–04–12, http://www.eurekanetwork.org/showsuccessstory?p_r_p_564233524_articleId=868372&p_r_p_564233524_groupId=10137, date accessed 7 April 2012.

ITU (2010) *The World in 2010: ICT facts and figures*. International Telecommunication Union. http://www.itu.int/ITU-D/ict/material/FactsFigures2010.pdf, date accessed 13 December 2010.

ITU (2011) *The World in 2011: ICT facts and figures*. International Telecommunication Union. http://www.itu.int/ITU-D/ict/facts/2011/material/ICTFactsFigures2011.pdf, date accessed 22 August 2012.

NASA (2010) *DISCOVERY 2010*. NASA's Mission Operations and Communications Services, January 2010, AO NNH10ZDA003J, Revised: 1–05–10, D-22674. http://deepspace.jpl.nasa.gov/advmiss/docs/NASA_MOCS_Dis10.pdf, date accessed 25 April 2011.

NSF (2011) Science of Science and Innovation Policy (SciSIP). *The National Science Foundation*. http://www.nsf.gov/funding/pgm_summ.jsp?pims_id=501084, date accessed 25 April 2011.

OECD (2011a) *Communiqué on Principles for Internet Policy-Making*. OECD High-Level Meeting. The Internet Economy: Generating Innovation and Growth, 28–29 June 2011. OECD Conference Centre, Paris. http://www.oecd.org/dataoecd/40/21/48289796.pdf, date accessed 13 February 2012.

OECD (2011b) *OECD Council Recommendation on Principles for Internet Policy Making*. Organisation for Economic Co-Operation and Development, OECD. 13 December 2011. http://www.oecd.org/dataoecd/11/58/49258588.pdf, date accessed 13 February 2012.

OMAM (2012) "2002–2003 Schedule of Events," *Open Mobile Alliance Meeting Ltd*. http://www.wapforum.org/new/sched.htm, date accessed on 7 April 2012.

OSTP (2011) "About SoSP," *The Executive Office of the President, the Office of Science and Technology Policy, the Science of Science Policy Policy*. http://scienceofsciencepolicy.net/blogs/sosp/pages/sospabout.aspx, date accessed 25 April 2011.

SEC (2005) Yahoo! Inc. Form 10-k. Annual Report Pursuant to Section 13 or 15(d) of the Securities Exchange Act of 1934 for the Fiscal Year Ended December 31, 2005. United States Securities and Exchange Commission. Washington, DC 20549. http://www.scribd.com/doc/277067/Yahoo-2005-Annual-Report, date accessed 18 July 2011.

SRI/Engelbart, D.C. (1962) *Augmenting Human Intellect: A Conceptual Framework*, Summary Report AFOSR–3223 under Contract AF 49(638)–1024, SRI Project 3578 for Air Force Office of Scientific Research, Stanford Research Inst., Menlo Park, Calif., Oct. 1962.

UN (2000) Resolution adopted by the General Assembly [without reference to a Main Committee (A/55/L.2)]. 8th plenary meeting, 8 September 2000. 55/2, *United Nations Millennium Declaration*. United Nations, A/RES/55/2, General Assembly, Fifty-fifth session, Agenda item 60 (b). Distr.: General 18 September 2000.

UN (2005) Resolution adopted by the General Assembly [without reference to a Main Committee (A/60/L.1)], 60/1. *2005 World Summit Outcome*. United Nations, Sixtieth session, A/RES/60/1, General Assembly, Agenda items 46 and 120. Distr.: General 24 October 2005.

UN (2010) Draft Resolution Referred to the High-level Plenary Meeting of the General Assembly by the General Assembly at its Sixty-Fourth Session. Resolution adopted by the General Assembly. *Keeping the Promise: United to Achieve the Millennium Development Goals*. United Nations, A/65/L.1, General Assembly, Sixty-fifth session, Agenda items 13 and 115. Distr.: Limited 17 September 2010.

US Congress (2011a) *To Prevent Online Threats to Economic Creativity and Theft of Intellectual Property, and for Other Purposes*. A Bill, S. 968. 112th Congress, The Senate of the United States, 1st Session, 12 May 2011. http://frwebgate.access.gpo.gov/cgi-bin/getdoc.cgi?dbname=112_cong_bills&docid=f:s968is.txt.pdf, date accessed 13 February 2012.

US Congress (2011b) *To Promote Prosperity, Creativity, Entrepreneurship, and Innovation by Combating the Theft of U.S. Property, and for Other Purposes*. A Bill, H.R. 3261. 112th Congress, House of Representatives, 1st Session. 26 October 2011. http://frwebgate.access.gpo.gov/cgi-bin/getdoc.cgi?dbname=112_cong_bills&docid=f:h3261ih.txt.pdf, date accessed 13 February 2012.

US Department of Commerce (1993) *The National Information Infrastructure: Agenda for Action* (1993) Department of Commerce, Washington, DC. Information Infrastructure Task Force. 15 September 1993.

US Department of State/ Kornbluh, K. (2012) U.S. Ambassador to the OECD. OECD Adopts Recommendation for Internet Policy Making Principles. *Ambassador Kornbluh's Blog*. 4 January 2012, http://blogs.state.gov/index.php/site/entry/oecd_internet_policy_making_principles/, date accessed 16 August 2012.

USC (1981) *Transmission Control Protocol: DARPA Internet Program Protocol Specification* (1981). September 1981. Postel Jon (ed.). Information Sciences Institute, University of Southern California. http://tools.ietf.org/html/rfc793, date accessed 6 May 2012.

USPTO (2001) The United States Patent and Trademark Office. United States Patent. Method for node ranking in a linked database. Patent No.: 6,285,999 B1, date of Patent: 4 September 2001.

UT (1997) *Introduction to UNIX*. Academic Computing and Instructional Technology Services. The University of Texas at Austin. Austin, Texas 78712–1110. CCUG-1, Revised, November 1997. http://www.utexas.edu/cc/docs/ccug1/, date accessed 6 February 2012.

WAP Forum (2001) "WAP Forum™ Releases WAP 2.0 Specifications for Public Review." Mountain View, Calif. The WAP Forum™, 1 August 2001. http://www.wapforum.org/new/wap2.0.pdf, date accessed 18 August 2012.

WAP Forum (2002) *Wireless Application Protocol. WAP 2.0 Technical White Paper*. Wireless Application Protocol Forum Ltd, January 2002. http://www.wapforum.org/what/WAPWhite_Paper1.pdf, date accessed 18 August 2012.

The White House/ Obama, B. (2011a) Executive Order – Structural Reforms to Improve the Security of Classified Networks and the Responsible Sharing and Safeguarding of Classified

Information. Barack Obama, The White House, 7 October 2011. The White House, Office of the Press Secretary. http://www.whitehouse.gov/the-press-office/2011/10/07/executive-order-structural-reforms-improve-security-classified-networks-, date accessed 8 October 2011.

The White House/Obama, B. (2011b) *International Strategy for Cyberspace, Prosperity, Security, and Openness in a Networked World*. The President of the United States, Barack Obama, The White House, Washington. May 2011. http://www.whitehouse.gov/sites/default/files/rss_viewer/internationalstrategy_cyberspace.pdf, date accessed 13 February 2012.

The White House/Obama, B. (2011c) *International Strategy for Cyberspace, Prosperity, Security, and Openness in a Networked World*. A fact sheet on the strategy. The President of the United States, Barack Obama, The White House, Washington. May 2011. http://www.whitehouse.gov/sites/default/files/rss_viewer/International_Strategy_Cyberspace_Factsheet.pdf, date accessed 13 February 2012.

The White House/Schmidt, H. A. (2011) "Launching the U.S. International Strategy for Cyberspace," *The White House, President Barack Obama, The White House Blog*. White House Cybersecurity Coordinator, 16 May 2011. http://www.whitehouse.gov/blog/2011/05/16/launching-us-international-strategy-cyberspace, date accessed 13 February 2012.

Worldwatch/Engelman, R. (2010) "World Population Growth Slows Modestly, Still on Track for 7 Billion in Late 2011," *Vital Signs Online*. Worldwatch Institute. 17 December 2010. http://vitalsigns.worldwatch.org/vs-trend/world-population-growth-slows-modestly-still-track-7-billion-late-2011, date accessed 27 January 2011.

Worldwatch/Renner, M. (2010) "Unemployment and Precarious Employment Grow More Prominent" *Vital Signs Online*. Worldwatch Institute. 22 November 2010. http://vitalsigns.worldwatch.org/vs-trend/unemployment-and-precarious-employment-grow-more-prominent, date accessed 27 January 2011.

Worldwatch/Tung, A. (2010) "World Population Growth Slows Modestly, Still on Track for 7 Billion in Late 2011," *Vital Signs Online*. Worldwatch Institute. 2 December 2010, http://vitalsigns.worldwatch.org/vs-trend/meat-production-and-consumption-continue-grow, date accessed 27 January 2011.

Press releases

Apple Press Info (2001) "Apple Presents iPod," *Apple Press Info*, press release, Cupertino, California, 23 October 2001. http://www.apple.com/pr/library/2001/10/23Apple-Presents-iPod.html, date accessed 13 February 2012.

Apple Press Info (2007) "Apple Reinvents the Phone with iPhone," *Apple Press Info*, press release, Macworld San Francisco, 9 January 2007. http://www.apple.com/pr/library/2007/01/09Apple-Reinvents-the-Phone-with-iPhone.html, date accessed 13 February 2012.

Blizzard Entertainment (2010) "WORLD OF WARCRAFT®: CATACLYSM™ SHATTERS PC-GAME SALES RECORD," *Blizzard Entertainment, Inc.*, Paris, France, 13 December 2010. http://eu.blizzard.com/en-gb/company/press/pressreleases.html?id=2443931, date accessed 8 April 2012.

Encyclopædia Britannica (1999) "Britannica.com Site Launched," *Encyclopædia Britannica News Releases*, Chicago, 19 October 1999. http://corporate.britannica.com/press/releases/launch.html, date accessed on 28 March 2011.

Google Investor Relations (2011) "Google Announces Fourth Quarter and Fiscal Year 2010 Results and Management Changes," *Google Investor Relations*, Mountain View, California, 20 January 2011. http://investor.google.com/earnings/2010/Q4_google_earnings.html, date accessed 21 January 2011.

LinkedIn Press Center (2003) "Sequoia Capital 'Links In' with $4.7 Million Investment," *LinkedIn Press Center*, press release, Palo Alto, CA, 12 November 2003. http://press.linkedin.com/press_center/?id=25, date accessed 24 April 2011.

LinkedIn Press Center (2007a) "LinkedIn Network Announces Obama to Launch New Q and A Series," *LinkedIn Press Center,* press release, Palo Alto, CA, 12 September 2007. http://press.linkedin.com/press_center/?id=49, date accessed 24 April 2011.

LinkedIn Press Center (2007b) "LinkedIn Professional Network Reaches 10 Million Users," *LinkedIn Press Center,* press release, Palo Alto, CA, 11 April 2007. http://press.linkedin.com/press_center/?id=59, date accessed 24 April 2011.

Microsoft News Center (2010) "Microsoft Unveils Windows Phone 7 Series," *Microsoft News Center,* press release, Barcelona, Spain, 15 February 2010. http://www.microsoft.com/presspass/press/2010/feb10/02–15MWC10PR.mspx, date accessed 13 February 2012.

Microsoft News Center (2011) "Nokia and Microsoft Announce Plans for a Broad Strategic Partnership to Build a New Global Mobile Ecosystem," *Microsoft News Center,* press release, London, 11 February 2011. http://www.microsoft.com/presspass/press/2011/feb11/02–11-partnership.mspx, date accessed 25 April 2011.

Mozilla Foundation (2004) "Mozilla Foundation Places Two-Page Advocacy Ad in the New York Times," *Mozilla Foundation,* press release, Mountain View, California, 15 December 2004. http://www.mozilla.org/en-US/press/mozilla-2004–12–15.html, date accessed 14 April 2012.

NAVTEQ (2008) "Nokia Completes Its Acquisition of NAVTEQ," *NAVTEQ,* press release, 10 July 2008. http://corporate.navteq.com/webapps/NewsUserServlet?action=NewsDetail&newsId=645&lang=en&englishonly=false, date accessed 6 February 2012.

NAVTEQ (2011) "Library of Congress Selects NAVTEQ to Provide Map Data and Content," *NAVTEQ,* press release, Chicago, 12 January 2011. http://press.navteq.com/index.php?s=4260&item=23528, date accessed 12 February 2012.

Netscape (1995) "Netscape and Sun Announce JavaScript, the Open, Cross-platform Object Scripting Language for Enterprise Networks and the Internet. 28 Industry-leading Companies to Endorse JavaScript as a Complement to Java for Easy Online Application Development," *Netscape Communications Corporation,* press release, Mountain View, Calif., 4 December 1995. http://web.archive.org/web/20070916144913/http://wp.netscape.com/newsref/pr/newsrelease67.html, date accessed 4 September 2012.

Nokia Corporation (2011) "Nokia renews mission for mobile and location based services; appoints Michael Halbherr Executive Vice President," *Nokia Corporation,* stock exchange release, 22 June 2011. http://press.nokia.com/2011/06/22/nokia-renews-mission-for-mobile-and-location-based-services-appoints-michael-halbherr-executive-vice-president/, date accessed 12 February 2012.

OMA (2012) "Trademarks and Affiliate Logos," *Open Mobile Alliance Ltd.* http://www.openmobilealliance.org/AboutOMA/Trademarks.aspx, date accessed 8 February 2011.

News items

ABC News/Liedtke, M. (2011) "Hot Deal: Groupon Files for Highly Anticipated IPO," *ABC News,* technology, 2 June 2011. http://abcnews.go.com/Technology/wireStory?id=13745895, date accessed 6 February 2012.

Al-Ahram Weekly Online (2011) "Unblocked but not unmonitored," *Al-Ahram Weekly Online.* 24 February–2 March 2011, No. 1036. http://weekly.ahram.org.eg/2011/1036/re153.htm, date accessed 21 July 2011.

Al Jazeera English (2011) "Calls for weekend protests in Syria. Social media used in bid to mobilise Syrians for rallies demanding freedom, human rights and the end to emergency law," *Al Jazeera English,* Last Modified: 04 February 2011 03:51 GMT. http://english.aljazeera.net/news/middleeast/2011/02/201122171649677912.html, date accessed 14 April 2012.

BBC News (2010a) "Anonymous hacktivists say Wikileaks war to continue," *BBC News,* 17 December 2010. http://www.bbc.co.uk/news/technology-11935539, date accessed on 31 December 2010.

BBC News (2010b) "Delivering Finland's web 'human right'," *BBC News*, 24 January 2010. http://news.bbc.co.uk/2/hi/8477572.stm, date accessed 14 April 2012.

BBC News (2010c) "Wikileaks' Julian Assange 'fears extradition to US'," *BBC News*, 17 December 2010. http://www.bbc.co.uk/news/uk-12020063, date accessed 31 December 2010.

BBC News (2011a) "MySpace sold to Specific Media by Murdoch's News Corp," *BBC News*, Business, 29 June 2011. http://www.bbc.co.uk/news/business-13969338, date accessed 12 July 2011.

BBC News (2011b) "Sega says hackers stole data of 1.29 million users," *BBC News*, 19 June 2011. http://www.bbc.co.uk/news/technology-13829690, date accessed 27 October 2011.

BBC News (2012) "Profile: Wikileaks founder Julian Assange." BBC News, 17 August 2012. http://www.bbc.co.uk/news/world-11047811, date accessed 24 August 2012.

CNBC (2009a). "Google CEO Eric Schmidt on privacy," A CNBC interview by Maria Bartiromo, 3 December 2009. http://www.youtube.com/watch?v=A6e7wfDHzew, date accessed 18 August 2012.

CNBC (2009b). "Google's Privacy." Google's CEO Eric Schmidt interviewed by Maria Bartiromo. *CNBC Video*, Tue 29 December 2009 | 01:00 AM ET. http://www.cnbc.com/id/15840232?video=1372176413&play=1, date accessed 14 April 2012.

Dagens Nyheter (2010) "Wikileaks. Svensk tryckfrihet lockar omstridd sajt," *Dagens Nyheter*, Updated 2010–05–04, Published 30 April 2010. http://www.dn.se/kultur-noje/nyheter/svensk-tryckfrihet-lockar-omstridd-sajt-1.1087835, date accessed 5 November 2010.

Democracy Now! (2010) "EXCLUSIVE: WikiLeaks Prepares Largest Intel Leak in US History with Release of 400,000 Iraq War Docs," *Democracy Now!*, Friday, 22 October 2010. http://www.democracynow.org/2010/10/22/wikileaks_prepares_largest_intel_leak_in, date accessed 5 November 2012.

The Economist (2006) "It's the links, stupid," *The Economist*, 20 April 2006. http://www.economist.com/node/6794172?story_id=6794172, date accessed on 7 April 2012.

The Hindu/Fredrick, P. (2010) "Micro is the new macro," *The Hindu*. http://www.thehindu.com/life-and-style/metroplus/article91295.ece, date accessed 7 April 2012.

The Hindu/Niharika, M. (2010) "Are you being Blauked," *The Hindu*. 2 June 2010. http://www.thehindu.com/life-and-style/nxg/article444350.ece, date accessed 13 December 2010.

The Huffington Post (2009a) "Google CEO On Privacy (VIDEO): 'If You Have Something You Don't Want Anyone To Know, Maybe You Shouldn't Be Doing It.' (2009)" *The Huffington Post*, http://www.huffingtonpost.com/2009/12/07/google-ceo-on-privacy-if_n_383105.html. Posted December 7, 2009. Updated 11 December 2009, date accessed 14 April 2012.

The Huffington Post (2009b) "'United Breaks Guitars': Did It *Really* Cost The Airline $180 Million?" *The Huffington Post*, Updated 24 August 2009. http://www.huffingtonpost.com/2009/07/24/united-breaks-guitars-did_n_244357.html, date accessed 14 April 2012.

The Huffington Post/ Grieshaber, K. (2011) "Facebook Party Gets Out of Control after German Girl Forgets Privacy Setting," *The Huffington Post*, 5 June 2011. http://www.huffingtonpost.com/2011/06/05/facebook-party-out-of-control_n_871473.html, date accessed 6 February 2012.

The Guardian/Clark, A. (2008) "How Jerry's guide to the world wide web became Yahoo," *The Guardian*, 1 February 2008, http://www.guardian.co.uk/business/2008/feb/01/microsoft.technology, date accessed 6 February 2012.

The Guardian/Hammersley, B. (2004) "Audible Revolution: Online Radio Is Booming Thanks to iPods, Cheap Audio Software and Weblogs," *The Guardian*, 12 February 2004. http://www.guardian.co.uk/media/2004/feb/12/broadcasting.digitalmedia, date accessed 14 April 2012.

Hawera & Normanby Star (1894) "The Octoroon," *Hawera & Normanby Star*. XXVII(2757), 27 June 1894, 3.

IND Technology & Science News/ Lamarra, N. (2003) "Space-Based Middleware Technology," *IND Technology & Science News*, Interplanetary Network Directorate, Jet Propulsion Laboratory, May 2003, Issue 17. http://tmot.jpl.nasa.gov/Program_Overview_Information/IND_Program_News/IND_17-newsletter.pdf, date accessed 25 April 2011.

Luleå University (2009) "EU-project on Delay Tolerant Network (DTN) technology and test beds approved by European Commission," News/Press. Luleå University of Technology. 11 May 2009. http://www.ltu.se/press/d2958/1.38034?l=en, date accessed 25 April 2011.

MSNBC/Carroll, L. (2011) "Will teen multitasking give rise to ADD? Study may offer answer," Don"t fear, says researcher, young brains are amazingly able to adapt," *Nightly news. msnbc.com.* updated 12 April 2011. http://www.msnbc.msn.com/id/42557051/ns/nightly_news/t/will-teen-multitasking-give-rise-add-study-may-offer-answer/, date accessed 17 August 2011.

The National/Sands, P. (2008) "Syria tightens control over internet," 30 September 2008. *The National.* http://www.thenational.ae/news/worldwide/middle-east/syria-tightens-control-over-internet, date accessed 21 July 2011.

Network World/Nerney, C. (1998) "The Up and Coming. Get to know five companies that would shake up the NW200 in years to come," *Network World*, 20 April 1998, 15(16), 57–62.

The New Yorker/Crouch, I. (2011) "Books without Borders," *The New Yorker*, 19 July 2011. http://www.newyorker.com/online/blogs/books/2011/07/borders-books-bankruptcy.html, date accessed 6 February 2012.

The New Yorker/Gladwell, M. (2011) "Creation Myth. Xerox PARC, Apple, and the truth about innovation," *The New Yorker*, 16 May 2011. http://www.newyorker.com/reporting/2011/05/16/110516fa_fact_gladwell, date accessed 13 February 2012.

NYT (1999) "U.S. Versus Microsoft: Part 5 of 7; Setback for a Software Giant: Key Sections of Judge's Findings of Fact," *New York Times*, November 7, 1999. Updated 1 March 2012. http://www.nytimes.com/1999/11/07/us/us-versus-microsoft-part-5–7-setback-for-software-giant-key-sections-judge-s.html, date accessed 2 May 2012.

NYT (2008) "The Globalization of Web users," *New York Times*, 31 December 2008. http://www.nytimes.com/imagepages/2008/12/31/business/ 31hindi.gfx.ready, date accessed 13 February 2012.

NYT/Creswell, J. (2011) "Analysts Wary of LinkedIn's Stock Surge," *New York Times*, 22 May 2011. http://www.nytimes.com/2011/05/23/technology/23linkedin.html, date accessed 6 February 2012.

NYT/Fisher, L.M. (1998) "Netscape Reports Losses, and Its Shares Tumble," *New York Times*, January 6, 1998. http://www.nytimes.com/1998/01/06/business/netscape-reports-losses-and-its-shares-tumble.html, date accessed 2 May 2012.

NYT/Mediratta, B. (2007) "The Google Way: Give Engineers Room," *New York Times*, 21 October 2007. http://www.nytimes.com/2007/10/21/jobs/21pre.html, date accessed 13 February 2012.

NYT/Sorid, D. (2008) "Writing the Web's Future in Numerous Languages," *New York Times*, 30 December 2008. http://www.nytimes.com/2008/12/31/technology/internet/31hindi.html, date accessed 13 February 2012.

NYT/Sorkin, A. R. (2000) "International Business; Fashionmall.com Swoops in for the Boo.com Fire Sale," *The New York Times*, Technology, 2 June 2000. http://www.nytimes.com/2000/06/02/business/international-business-fashionmallcom-swoops-in-for-the-boocom-fire-sale.html, date accessed 3 October 2011.

NZZ Online (2010) "Wikileaks-Gründer appelliert an die USA," 4 November 2010, *NZZ Online.* http://www.nzz.ch/nachrichten/kultur/medien/autx_wikileaks-gruender_appelliert_an_die_usa_1.8273519.html, date accessed 5 October 2010.

PA Times/Collins, M.L. and Milen, D. (2011) "The Use of Social Network Applications in the Japanese Earthquake and Tsunami Response Efforts," *PA Times.* American Society for Public Administration (ASPA). Published 27 March 2011. http://patimes.eznuz.com/

article/Commentary/General_Commentary/The_Use_of_Social_Network_Applications_in_the_Japanese_Earthquake_and_Tsunami_Response_Efforts/22727, date accessed 24 April 2011.

The Quake-Catcher Network (2011) "February 21, 2011 M6.3 Earthquake in Christchurch Recorded on QCN Stations." Recent News. *The Quake-Catcher Network*. http://qcn.stanford.edu/press/news.php, date accessed 19 April 2011.

Reuters/Anupreeta, D. (2009) "Google sees YouTube profitable in near future," *Reuters*, New York, 17 July 2009. http://www.reuters.com/article/idUSTRE56F75P20090717, date accessed 16 January 2011.

Reuters/Barr, A. and Baldwin, C. (2011) "Groupon's IPO biggest by U.S. Web company since Google," *Reuters*, 4 November 2011. http://www.reuters.com/article/2011/11/04/us-groupon-idUSTRE7A352020111104, date accessed 12 February 2012.

Reuters/Reynolds, I. and Baker, L.B. (2011) "Furor at Sony after hackers steal Playstation user data." *Reuters*, Tokyo, New York, 27 April 2011. http://www.reuters.com/article/2011/04/27/us-sony-stolendata-idUSTRE73Q0D820110427, date accessed 27 October 2011.

The Stanford Daily/ Hanley, R. (2003) "From Googol to Google," *The Stanford Daily*, 12 February 2003. http://www.stanforddaily.com/2003/02/12/from-googol-to-google/, date accessed 7 April 2011.

Tages Anzeiger/Diethelm, R. (2010) "Assange will Asyl in der Schweiz," *Tages Anzeiger*, published 04 November 2010, 14:23. http://www.tagesanzeiger.ch/ausland/amerika/Wegen-Wikileaks-wurde-niemand-getoetet-/story/30352297, date accessed 5 November 2012.

The Telegraph/Salter, J. (2010) "Craft website Etsy brings big sales to small businesses," *The Telegraph*, 17 June 2010, Retail and Consumer. http://www.telegraph.co.uk/finance/newsbysector/retailandconsumer/7832080/Craft-website-Etsy-brings-big-sales-to-small-businesses.html, date accessed 23 April 2011.

The Times of India/Bagchi, I. (2011) "Tunisia to Egypt, an Arab upheaval," *The Times of India*. 29 January 2011. http://timesofindia.indiatimes.com/world/middle-east/Tunisia-to-Egypt-an-Arab-upheaval/articleshow/7382198.cms, date accessed on 4 February 2011.

USA Today/Graham, J. (2006) "Flickr of idea on a gaming project led to photo website," *USA Today*, Posted 27 February 2006 and Updated 28 February 2006. http://www.usatoday.com/tech/products/2006–02–27-flickr_x.htm, date accessed 8 April 2012.

USA Today/Graham, J. (2007). "Yahoo Photos going dark as Flickr shines on," *USA Today*, Updated 5 April 2007. http://www.usatoday.com/tech/webguide/2007–05–03-yahoo-photos-flickr_N.htm, date accessed 8 April 2012.

USA Today/Hopkins, J. (2006) "Surprise! There's a third YouTube co-founder," *USA Today*, Posted 10 November 2006. http://www.usatoday.com/tech/news/2006–10–11-youtube-karim_x.htm, date accessed 9 March 2011.

VG/Østbø, S. (2006) "Båten Anna." *VG Nett*. 22 August 2006. http://www.vg.no/musikk/artikkel.php?artid=127402, date accessed 11 January 2011.

The Washington Post/ Miller, G. (2010) "CIA launches task force to assess impact of U.S. cables' exposure by WikiLeaks," *The Washington Post*, 22 December 2010. http://www.washingtonpost.com/wp-dyn/content/article/2010/12/21/AR2010122104599.html, date accessed 8 October 2011.

WSJ/Sandstrom, G. (2011) "Android Leads Handset-Sales Surge," *The Wall Street Journal*, Technology, 9 February 2011, http://online.wsj.com/article/SB10001424052748704858404576133500949762720.html, date accessed 9 February 2011.

WSJ/Weiss, B. (2010) "Groupon's $6 Billion Gambler. The 30-year-old CEO in Chicago is changing the way we buy from local businesses. And trying to make billions doing it," *The Wall Street Journal*. 20 December 2010. http://online.wsj.com/article/SB10001424052748704828104576021481410635432.html, date accessed 6 February 2012.

WSJ/Whalen, J. (2011) "WikiLeaks Blames Paper for Breach. The Document-Leaking Group Says It Has Lost Control of Its Trove of U.S. Papers, Calling Disclosure 'Reckless'," *The*

Wall Street Journal, World News, 2 September 2011. http://online.wsj.com/article/SB10001424053111904716604576544153956483900.html, date accessed 8 October 2011.

WSJ/Woo, S., Cowan, L. and Tam, P.-W. (2011) "LinkedIn IPO Soars, Feeding Web Boom," *The Wall Street Journal*. Technology. 20 May 2011. http://online.wsj.com/article/SB10001424052748704816604576333132239509622.html, date accessed 18 July 2011.

Interviews

Cerf, Vinton. A telephone interview by Henry Oinas-Kukkonen, Mountain View, California, USA, 10 December 2009.

Chesbrough, Henry. An interview by Harri and Henry Oinas-Kukkonen, University of Berkeley, California, USA, 16 December 2009.

Engelbart, Douglas. An interview by Harri and Henry Oinas-Kukkonen, Stanford Research Institute, California, USA, 25 March 2009.

Estrin, Judy. An interview by Harri and Henry Oinas-Kukkonen, JLabs, LLC, Menlo Park, California, USA, 10 December 2009.

Fake, Caterina. An interview by Harri and Henry Oinas-Kukkonen, San Francisco, California, USA, 8 December 2009.

Fogg, B.J. An interview by Harri and Henry Oinas-Kukkonen, Petaluma, California, USA, 12 December 2009.

Garcia-Molina, Hector. An interview by Harri and Henry Oinas-Kukkonen, Computer Science Department, Stanford University, California, USA, 15 December 2009.

Granovetter, Mark. An interview by Harri and Henry Oinas-Kukkonen, Department of Sociology, Stanford University. California, USA, 9 December 2009.

Hoffman, Reid. An interview by Harri and Henry Oinas-Kukkonen, LinkedIn, Mountain View, California, USA, 26 March 2009.

Lilly, John. A telephone interview by Henry Oinas-Kukkonen, Oulu, Finland/Mountain View, California, USA, 13 January 2010.

Mickos, Mårten. An interview by Harri Oinas-Kukkonen, Los Altos, California, USA, 1 June 2009.

Nelson, Ted (Theodore H.). A telephone interview by Henry Oinas-Kukkonen, Oulu, Finland/Sausalito, California, USA, 30 April 2009.

O'Reilly, Tim (Timothy). An interview by Harri Oinas-Kukkonen, Sebastopol, California, USA, 15 April 2009.

Saffo, Paul. An interview by Harri and Henry Oinas-Kukkonen, San Mateo, California, USA, 9 December 2009.

Sample, Neal. An interview by Harri and Henry Oinas-Kukkonen, Yahoo!, California, USA. 17 December 2009.

Saxenian, AnnaLee. An interview by Harri and Henry Oinas-Kukkonen, University of Berkeley, California, USA,16 December 2009.

Shneiderman, Ben. An interview by Henry Oinas-Kukkonen, Bethesda, Maryland, USA, 27 August 2010.

Wales, Jimmy. An interview by by Harri and Henry Oinas-Kukkonen, Wikia Inc., San Francisco, California, USA, 8 December 2009.

White, Bebo. An interview by Harri and Henry Oinas-Kukkonen, The Center for the Study of Language and Information (CSLI), Stanford University, 31 December 2009.

Winograd, Terry. An interview by Harri and Henry Oinas-Kukkonen, Computer Science Department, Stanford University. California, USA, 19 March 2009.

Non-scholarly journals and magazines

AdvertisingAge/Patel, K. (2011) "Nokia: We'll Astound with Our Comeback. Finnish Marketer Begins Bid to Reclaim North American Market with Major New Handset Push,"

AdvertisingAge, News, 11 April 2011. http://adage.com/article/news/nokia-reclaim-north-american-market-astound/226912/, date accessed 25 April 2011.

All Things Digital/Swisher, K. (2010) "Exclusive: Yahoo Social Platforms Head Neal Sample Departs for eBay," *All Things Digital*, 27 August 2010. http://allthingsd.com/20100827/exclusive-yahoo-social-platforms-head-sample-departs-for-ebay/, date accessed 6 February 2012.

The Atlantic/Carr, N. (2008) "Is Google making us stupid?" *The Atlantic*, July/August, 302(56).

The Atlantic Monthly/Bush, V. (1945). "As We May Think," *The Atlantic Monthly*, 176(1), 101–108.

Business Insider/Carlson, N. (2011) "Insiders Tell the Story of LinkedIn's Stunning Success," *Business Insider*, 15 June 2011. http://www.businessinsider.com/the-story-of-linked-ins-stunning-success – as-told-by-the-people-who-were-there-2011–6, date accessed 6 February 2012.

Business Insider/White, G. (2011) "This Is the Wikileak That Sparked the Tunisian Crisis," *Business Insider*, 14 January 2011. http://www.businessinsider.com/tunisia-wikileaks-2011–1, date accessed 8 October 2011.

Discover/Barone J. (2007) "Hans Rosling," *Discover*, December, 28(12), 46–49.

InformIT/Schneiderman, R. (2003) "Don't Believe the Hype: Good Technology Gone Bad," InformIT, 10 January 2003. http://www.informit.com/articles/article.aspx?p=30498&seqNum=2, date accessed 6 February 2012.

InfoWorld/Wingfield, N. (1995) "Spyglass to challenge Netscape browser domination," *InfoWorld*, 21 August, 17(30), 31.

Kauppalehti (2010) "Piraattisatamasta suurpolitiikan näyttämöksi" (2010), *Kauppalehti*, Debatti, 30 August, 14. http://www.kauppalehti.fi/5/i/talous/uutiset/avoinarkisto/index.jsp?xid=3897828&date=2010/08/30, date accessed 5 November 2010.

Life/Bush, V. (1945). "As We May Think: A Top U.S. Scientist Foresees a Possible Future World in Which Man-Made Machines Will Start to Think," *Life*, 19(11), 112–124.

Mac Life/Ochs, S. and Williams, J. (2007) "Your Mac: The Great Communicator," *Mac Life*, October, 1(9), 30–37.

Network World/Messmer, E. (1994) "Spyglass captures Mosaic licensing," *Network World*, 29 August, 11(35), 4.

Newsweek/Saffo, P. (2002) "Failure is the best medicine," *Newsweek*, 25 March 2002. http://www.saffo.com/essays/failure-is-the-best-medicine/, date accessed 8 February 2012.

Print/DiNucci, D. (1999) "Fragmented Future," *Print*, 53(4), 32, 221–222. http://darcyd.com/fragmented_future.pdf, date accessed 9 April 2012.

Research Intelligence (2003) "The ultimate brain teaser," *Research Intelligence*. University of Liverpool. Business Gateway. Issue 17, August. http://www.liv.ac.uk/researchintelligence/issue17/pdf/resint17.pdf, date accessed 28 December 2010.

Stara (2006) "Kesähitti Boten Anna villitsee meillä ja maailmalla," *Stara*, 21 July 2006. http://www.stara.fi/2006/07/21/kesahitti-boten-anna-villitsee-meilla-ja-maailmalla/, date accessed 13 February 2012.

strategy+business/Fisher, L.M. (2009) "Fernando Flores Wants to Make You an Offer." *strategy+business*, 24 November 2009/ Winter 2009 / Issue 57. http://www.strategy-business.com/article/09406, date accessed 18 October 2011.

TechCrunch/Kincaid, J. (2011) "YC-Funded MobileWorks Aims to Be a Hands-Off Mechanical Turk," *TechCrunch*. 12 August 2011. http://techcrunch.com/2011/08/12/yc-funded-mobileworks-aims-to-be-a-hands-off-mechanical-turk/, date accessed 12 February 2011.

TechCrunch/Lunden, I. (2012) "Beyond the Daily Deal: Groupon's 170M Deals and 33M Users; Aims to Be "the OS for Local Commerce"," *TechCrunch*. 7 May 2012. http://techcrunch.com/2012/05/07/beyond-the-daily-deal-groupon-has-170m-deals-33m-users-aims-to-be-the-os-for-local-commerce/, date accessed 28 August 2012.

TechCrunch/Schonfeld, E. (2010) "Facebook Overthrows Yahoo to Become the World's Third Largest Website," *TechCrunch*, 24 December 2010. (http://techcrunch.com/2010/12/24/facebook-yahoo-third-largest-website/, date accessed 6 February 2012).

TechCrunch/Tsotsis, A. (2011) "WordPress.com Suffers Largest DDoS Attack in Its History," *TechCrunch*. 3 March 2011. http://techcrunch.com/2011/03/03/wordpress-com-suffers-major-ddos-attack/, date accessed 13 February 2012.

Time/Wallis, C. (2006) "genM: The Multitasking Generation," *TimeFrames*. Monday, 27 March 2006. http://www.time.com/time/magazine/article/0,9171,1174696,00.html, date accessed 3 October 2011.

TIME Staff (2001) "Top 10 Everything 2001. Design. 10. Prada Epicenter Store, New York City," *Time Specials*, 21 December 2001. http://www.time.com/time/specials/packages/article/0,28804,2005583_2005624_2005605,00.html, date accessed 13 February 2012.

Vanity Fair/Etter L. (2011) "Groupon Therapy," *Vanity Fair*, Business, August 2011. http://www.vanityfair.com/business/features/2011/08/groupon-201108, date accessed 24 August 2012.

Wired/Howe, J. (2006) "The rise of Crowdsourcing," *Wired*, Issue 14.06, June 2006. http://www.wired.com/wired/archive/14.06/crowds.html, date accessed 19 August 2012.

Wired/Kelly, K. (1999) "The Roaring Zeros," *Wired*, Issue 7.09, September 1999. http://www.wired.com/wired/archive/7.09/zeros.html, date accessed 14 April 2012.

Wired/Kelly, K. and Wolf, G. (1997) "PUSH! Kiss your browser goodbye: The radical future of media beyond the Web," *Wired*, Issue 5.03, March 1997. http://www.wired.com/wired/archive/5.03/ff_push_pr.html, date accessed April 14, 2012.

Wired/Kim, A.J. (1998) "Killers Have More Fun," *Wired*, Issue 6.05, May 1998. http://www.wired.com/wired/archive/6.05/ultima.html, date accessed 16 August 2012.

Wired/Perkins, A.B. (1995) "Netscape? Wake Up and Smell the Java," *Wired*, Issue 3.11. November 1995.

Wired/Wortham, J. (2007) "After 10 Years of Blogs, the Future's Brighter Than Ever," *Wired*, 17 December. http://www.wired.com/entertainment/theweb/news/2007/12/blog_anniversary, date accessed 11 March 2011.

Blogs, tweets, emails and videoclips

Cabello, P. (2008) "Firefox reaches 500 million downloads milestone," *Mozilla Links*, Posted on 22 February 2008. http://mozillalinks.org/2008/02/firefox-reaches-500-million-downloads-milestone/, date accessed 18 August 2011.

Carroll, D. (2009) "Statement" by Dave Carroll, Posted by sonsofmaxwell in *YouTube* on 10 July 2009. http://www.youtube.com/watch?v=T_X-Qoh__mw, date accessed 14 December 2010.

Dave Carroll Music (2012) "United Breaks Guitars Trilogy," http://www.davecarrollmusic.com/music/ubg/, date accessed 24 August 2012.

Dorsey, J. (2006). Tweet by Jack Dorsey, 21 March 2006. *Twitter*. http://twitter.com/#!/jack/statuses/20, date accessed 8 April 2012.

Feldman, D. (2011) "The Myth of the Average User: Your Mom Knows How to Click and Drag," *operationproject*, 11 August 2011. http://operationproject.com/2011/myth-of-the-average-user/, date accessed 15 April 2012.

Gates, R. (1993). Message by Rick Gates, "The Internet Encyclopedia," Mon., 25 October 1993 13:47:40 CDT, PACS-L Archives, October 1993, week 4 (#13. University of Houston. Listserv.UH.Edu. http://listserv.uh.edu/cgi-bin/wa?A2=ind9310d&L=pacs-l&T=0&P=1418, date accessed 28 March 2011.

Hoffman, R. (2011). Co-Founder and Chairman, LinkedIn, Reid Hoffman to Frank Reed. Email on 25 March 2011. http://www.marketingpilgrim.com/wp-content/uploads/2011/03/LinkedIn-Thanks.jpg, date accessed 24 April 2011.

Jonas, J. (2006) "Accumulating Context: Now or Never," *A collection of thoughts on information management and privacy in the information age, injected with a few personal stories*, 20 August 2006. http://jeffjonas.typepad.com/jeff_jonas/2006/08/accumulating_co.html, date accessed 4 September 2012.

Lapitsky, Y. (2005) "Me at the zoo," *YouTube*, video by by Yakov Lapitsky of Jawed Karim. Posted on 23 April 2005. http://www.youtube.com/watch?v=jNQXAC9IVRw, date accessed 9 March 2011.

Nelson, T. (2012) "Computers for Cynics 2 – It All Went Wrong at Xerox PARC," *TheTedNelson*, 28 May 2012. http://www.youtube.com/watch?v=c6SUOeAqOjU, date accessed 4 September 2012.

Reichelt, L. (2007) "Ambient Intimacy, *disambiguity*, social & community, 1 March 2007. http://www.disambiguity.com/ambient-intimacy/, date accessed 3 September 2012.

Rodriguez, K. (2011) "EFF Declines to Endorse OECD Draft Communiqué on Principles for Internet Policy-Making," *Electronic Frontier Foundation (EFF), Deeplinks blog*, 28 June 2011. https://www.eff.org/deeplinks/2011/06/eff-declines-endorse-oecd-communiqu-principles, date accessed 13 February 2012.

silentwhisper2009 (2011) "Syrian Revolution 2011 – Homs – Clock Tower – April 18 04–18," *YouTube*, loaded by silentwhisper2009. 5 May 2011. http://www.youtube.com/watch?v=YVMl4VsGxqQ, date accessed 21 July 2011.

Stone, B. (2007). Tweet by Christopher Isaac "Biz" Stone, "Incorporating Twitter," Posted by @Biz at 4:44 PM, 18 April 2007. *Twitter*. http://blog.twitter.com/2007/04/incorporating-twitter.html, date accessed 24 August 2012.

Academic and research websites

CHI (2011) *CHI 2011 Workshop on Networked Privacy*. http://networkedprivacy.wordpress.com/, date accessed 12 February 2012.

CPSR (2005) "CPSR History" *Computer Professionals for Social Responsibility*. http://cpsr.org/about/history/. Last modified 1 June 2005, date accessed 31 December 2010.

ProgrammableWeb (2012). http://www.programmableweb.com/, date accessed 24 August 2012.

SLAC (2006) "The Early World Wide Web at SLAC: Documentation of the Early Web at SLAC (1991–1994)," http://www.slac.stanford.edu/history/earlyweb/history.shtml. Page Owner Jean Marie Deken. Last modified 31 May 2006, date accessed 30 March 2012.

W3Techs (2011) "Usage of content management systems for websites," *W3Techs – World Wide Web Technology Surveys*. http://w3techs.com/technologies/overview/content_management/all, date accessed 17 July 2011.

W3Techs (2012) "Usage statistics and market share of WordPress for websites," W3Techs – World Wide Web Technology Surveys. http://w3techs.com/technologies/details/cm-wordpress/all/all, date accessed 24 August 2012.

Web Science Trust (2011) "WebScience Trust." *Web Science Trust Review 2011*. http://webscience.org/2011/WSRIa2291%20A4%2020pp%20Annual%20Review.pdf, date accessed 6 February 2012.

Web Science Trust (2012) "About the Web Science Trust." http://webscience.org/trust.html, date accessed 6 February 2012.

Xanadu (2012a) "PROJECT XANADU®. Founded 1960 * The Original Hypertext Project." http://www.xanadu.com/, date accessed 30 March 2012.

Xanadu (2012b) Welcome to Xanadu® SpaceTM. www.xanarama.net, date accessed 14 April 2012.

X.commerce (2011) "Neal Sample," *X.commerce Innovate Developer Conference 2011*. http://www.innovate-conference.com/speaker/neal-sample. http://www.innovate-conference.com/speaker/neal-sample, date accessed 12 February 2012.

ZigZag (2012) The ZIGZAG® DATABASE and VISUALIZATION SYSTEM. The true generalization of structure (still in prototype). http://www.xanadu.com/zigzag/, date accessed 13 February 2012.

Commercial and other websites

Alexa (2012a) "Top Sites," Alexa Web Information Company. http://www.alexa.com/siteinfo/myspace.com, date accessed 3 May 2012.

Alexa (2012b) "Top Sites," Alexa Web Information Company. http://www.alexa.com/topsites, date accessed 24 August 2012.

Anime (2011) *Anime*. http://animelehti.fi/, date accessed 14 January 2011.

Animeunioni (2011) *Portti Animeen ja Mangaan Suomessa*. http://www.animeunioni.org/index.html, date accessed 14 January 2011.

The Big Web Show (2010) "The Big Web Show #29: Matt Mullenweg." Interview by Jeffrey Zeldman and Dan Benjamin, 2 December 2010. http://5by5.tv/ bigwebshow/29, date accessed 13 February 2012.

digital wellbeing labs (2012) "Prada Flagship Store, NY 2001," *digital wellbeing labs*. http://digitalwellbeinglabs.com/dwb/concepts/prada-flagship-store-ny-2001/, date accessed 13 February 2012.

The Economist (2012) "About us." *The Economist*. http://www.economist.com/help/about-us#About. *The_Economist*, date accessed 6 May 2012.

Etsy (2012) "Community." http://www.etsy.com/community, date accessed 14 April 2012.

foursquare (2012a) "About foursquare," *foursquare*. https://foursquare.com/about/, date accessed 8 April 2012.

foursquare (2012b) "About foursquare," *foursquare*. last updated April 2012. https://foursquare.com/about/, date accessed 24 August 2012.

foursquare (2012c) "The 4SQDay Story," *4SQDay*. http://blog.4sqday.com/about/, date accessed 6 February 2012.

GNE Museum (2012). Curated by Cal Henderson. http://www.gnespy.com/museum/, date accessed 8 April 2012.

Google (2012) "Our mission: Organize the world's information and make it universally accessible and useful." http://www.google.com/about/company/, date accessed 13 February 2012.

IRC (2005) "IRC History by Jarkko Oikarinen,"*Internet Relay Chat: Information about IRC*. http://www.irc.org/history_docs/jarkko.html, date accessed 8 April 2012.

Kiva (2010) "Facts & History," *Kiva: Loans That Change Lives*. http://www.kiva.org/about/facts, date accessed 31 December 2010.

Ludicorp (2012), http://www.ludicorp.com/index.php, date accessed 8 April 2012.

MobileWorks (2012) "We're changing the way the world works," http://www.mobileworks.com/about.html, date accessed 14 April 2012.

MySQL (2011) "About MySQL." http://www.mysql.com/about/, date accessed 17 July 2011.

MySQL (2012) "MySQL Customers by Industry: Web: Social Networks," *MySQL*. http://www.mysql.com/customers/industry/?id=85, date accessed 6 February 2012.

Protect Innovation (2012) "Stop SOPA/PIPA." http://protectinnovation.com/downloads/Opposition_Dec16.pdf, date accessed 14 April 2012.

Search Engine Guide/ Hedger, J. (2005) "Yahoo! Celebrates Ten Years." *Search Engine Guide. The Small Business Guide to Search Marketing*, 3 March 2005. http://www.searchengineguide.com/jim-hedger/yahoo-celebrates-ten-years.php, date accessed 7 April 2012.

Stara/Podcast (2006). "An interview of Basshunter," *Stara.fi*, 15 September 2006. Podcast 34 – Basshunter. http://www.stara.fi/2006/09/15/starafi-podcast-34-basshunter/, date accessed 11 January 2011.

Technorati/Sobel, J. (2010) "HOW: Technology, Traffic and Revenue – Day 3 SOTB 2010." *Technorati™ State of the Blogosphere 2010*. 5 November 2010. http://technorati.com/

blogging/article/how-technology-traffic-and-revenue-day, date accessed 7 February 2012.

Technorati (2011) "State of the Blogosphere 2011: Part 3 – Page." Technorati™ Media State of the Blogosphere 2011. 4 November 2011. http://technorati.com/social-media/article/state-of-the-blogosphere-2011-part3/page-2/, date accessed 24 August 2012.

WikiLeaks (2010) "Iraq War Logs," http://www.wikileaks.org/, date accessed 5 November 2010.

Yahoo (2012) "University Hackdown at Hack Day!" – *Yahoo! Developer Network.* http://developer.yahoo.com/hacku/, date accessed 13 February 2012.

YouTube (2011) "A Brief History of YouTube," *YouTube5Year.* https://sites.google.com/a/pressatgoogle.com/youtube5year/home/short-story-of-youtube, date accessed 9 March 2011.

References

Abbate, J. (1999) *Inventing the Internet* (Cambridge, MA: MIT Press).

Achterbosch, L., Pierce, R. and Simmons, G. (2008) "Massively Multiplayer Online Role-Playing Games: The Past, Present, and Future," *Computers in Entertainment (CIE) – Theoretical and Practical Computer Applications in Entertainment Archive*, 5(4), Article 9, 9:1–9:33.

Agarwal, R. and Lucas, H.C. (2005) "The Information Systems Identity Crisis: Focusing on High-Visibility and High-Impact Research," *MIS Quarterly*, 29(3), 381–398.

Alaiwi, A., Sibley, M.J.N., Mather, P. and Holmes, V. (2009) "Extremely Low Frequency Based Communication Link," *Proceedings of Computing and Engineering Annual Researchers' Conference 2009: CEARC'09*, 105–110.

Ankerson, M.S. (2010) "Web Industries, Economies, Aesthetics: Mapping the Look of the Web in the Dot-com Era" in N. Brügger (ed.) *Web History* (New York: Peter Lang Publishing), 173–193.

Barczewski, S. (2006) *Titanic: A Night Remembered* (London and New York: Hambledon Continuum).

Bardini, T. (2000) *The Personal Interface: Douglas Engelbart, the Augmentation of Human Intellect and the Genesis of Personal Computing* (Stanford, California: Stanford University Press).

Battalio, R. and Schultz, P. (2006) "Options and the Bubble," *The Journal of Finance*, 61(5), 2071–2102.

Battelle, J. (2008) *The Search: How Google and Its Rivals Rewrote the Rules of Business and Transformed Our Culture*, reprinted (London, UK and Boston, MA: Nicholas Brealey Publishing).

Beaulieu, L. (1993) "A Parisian Café and Ten Proto-Bourbaki Meetings (1934–1935)," *The Mathematical Intelligencer*, 15(1), 27–35.

Bell, D.J., Loader, B.D., Pleace N. and Schuler, D. (eds) (2005) "Community Memory" in *Cyberculture: The Key Concepts* (London and New York: Routledge, Taylor & Francis Group).

Berners-Lee, T. with Fischetti, M. (2000) *Weaving the Web: The Original Design and Ultimate Destiny of the World Wide Web by Its Inventor* (New York: HarperBusiness).

Bieber, M., Vitali, F., Ashman, H., Balasubramanian V. and Oinas-Kukkonen, Harri (1997) "Fourth Generation Hypermedia: Some Missing Links for the World Wide Web," *International Journal of Human Computer Studies*, 47(1), 31–65.

Bizer, C., Heath, T. and Berners-Lee, T. (2009) "Linked Data – the Story So Far," *International Journal on Semantic Web and Information Systems* (IJSWIS), 5(3), 1–22.

Bødker, S. (1996) "Creating Conditions for Participation: Conflicts and Resources in Systems Design," *Human Computer Interaction*, 11(3), 215–236.

Boucicault, D., ESQ (1859) *The Octoroon*. A play, in four acts. http://library.marist.edu/diglib/english/americanliterature/19c-20c%20play%20archive/octoroon-index.htm, date accessed 28 March 2011.

Boyd, D.M. and Ellison, N.B. (2007) "Social Network Sites: Definition, History, and Scholarship," *Journal of Computer-Mediated Communication*, 13, 210–230.

Bresnahan, T., Greenstein, S. and Henderson, R. (2011) "Schumpeterian Competition and Diseconomies of Scope; Illustrations from the Histories of Microsoft and IBM," Harvard Business School Working Paper, No. 11–077.

Brin, S. and Page, L. (1998) "The Anatomy of a Large-Scale Hypertextual Web Search Engine," *Proceedings of the Seventh International Conference on World Wide Web*, Brisbane, Australia, 107–117.

Bulbrook, D. (2001) *WAP : A Beginner's Guide* (Blacklick, OH, USA: McGraw-Hill Professional Publishing).
Burdman, J.R. (1999) *Collaborative Web Development: Strategies and Best Practices for Web Teams* (Reading, Mass.: Addison Wesley Professionals).
Bush, V. (1967) "Memex Revisited" reprinted in W.H.K. Chun and T. Keenan (eds) *New Media, Old Media: A History and Theory Reader* (New York and London: Routledge, Taylor & Francis Group, 2006).
Castilla, E.J., Hwang, H., Granovetter, M. and Granovetter, E. (2000) "Social Networks in Silicon Valley" in C.-M. Lee, W.F. Miller, H. Rowen and M. Hancock (eds) *The Silicon Valley Edge: A Habitat for Innovation and Entrepreneurship* (Stanford, California: Stanford University Press).
Chesbrough, H.W. (2003) *Open Innovation: The New Imperative for Creating and Profiting from Technology* (Boston, Mass.: Harvard Business School Press).
Christensen, C.M. (1997) *The Innovator's Dilemma: When New Technologies Cause Great Firms to Fail* (Boston, Mass.: Harvard Business Press).
Cialdini, R.B. (2001) *Influence: Science and Practice*, 4th edn (Boston, Mass.: Allyn & Bacon).
Clark, C. (2005) "The Author Who Never Was: Nicolas Bourbaki," *Science Editor*, 28(3), 82–86.
Clark, N. (2003) "Community Networking" in S. Jones (ed.) *Encyclopedia of New Media: An Essential Reference to Communication and Technology* (Thousand Oaks, California: Sage Publications).
Clarke, R.A. and Knake, R. (2010) *Cyber War: The Next Threat to National Security and What to Do About It* (New York: Ecco).
Coase, R.H. (2003) "2003 Coase Lecture by Ronald Coase – Part 2/6." Ronald H. Coase, Clifton R. Musser Professor Emeritus of Economics lecture "The Present and Future of Law and Economics." The University of Chicago Law School, 17th Annual Coase Lecture, 1 April 2003. www.youtube.com/watch?v=r5kSrkilLoI, date accessed 24 April 2011.
Conklin, J. (1987) "Hypertext: An Introduction and Survey Computer," *Computer*, 20(9), 17–41.
Cook, N. (2008) *Enterprise 2.0 : How Social Software Will Change the Future of Work* (Aldershot: Gower).
Copley, B. (2009) *The Semantics of the Future* (New York: Routledge).
Corry, L. (1996) *Modern Algebra and the Rise of Mathematical Structures*, 2nd revised edn (Basel: Birkhäuser).
Cross, R., Borgatti, S.P. and Parker, A. (2002) "Making Invisible Work Visible: Using Social Network Analysis to Support Strategic Collaboration," *California Management Review*, 44(2), 25–46.
Cross, R., Parker, A., Prusak, L. and Borgatti, S.P. (2001) "Knowing What We Know: Supporting Knowledge Creation and Sharing in Social Networks," *Organizational Dynamics*, 30(2), 100–120.
Crowston, K. and Williams, M. (2000) "Reproduced and Emergent Genres of Communication on the World Wide Web," *Information Society*, 16(3), 201–215.
Davenport, T.H., Leibold, M. and Voelpel, S. (2006) *Strategic Management in the Innovation Economy: Strategic Approaches and Dynamic Tools for Innovation Capabilities* (Erlangen: Publicis).
Davis, F.D. (1989) "Perceived Usefulness, Perceived Ease of Use, and User Acceptance of Information Technology," *MIS Quarterly*, 13(3), 319–339.
Davis, F.D., Bagozzi, R.P. and Warshaw, P.R. (1989) "User Acceptance of Computer Technology: A Comparison of Two Theoretical Models," *Management Science*, 35(8), 982–1003.
Dell'Era, C., Buganza, T., Fecchio, C. and Verganti, R. (2011) "Language Brokering: Stimulating Creativity during the Concept Development Phase," *Creativity and Innovation Management*, 20(1), 36–48.

DeVere Brody, J. (2000) "The Yankee Hugging the Creole. Reading Dion Boucicault's *The Octoroon*" in Sybil Kein (ed.) *Creole: The History and Legacy of Louisiana's Free People of Color* (Baton Rouge: Lousiana State University Press).

Dhar, S. and Varshney, U. (2011) "Challenges and Business Models for Mobile Location-Based Services and Advertising," *Communications of the ACM*, 54(5), 121–129.

Donofrio, N., Spohrer, J. and Zadeh, H.S. (2010) "Research-Driven Medical Education and Practice: A Case for T-Shaped Professionals," *Viewpoint MJA*, Collegiate Employment Research Institute, T-Shaped Professionals, http://www.ceri.msu.edu/wp-content/uploads/2010/06/A-Case-for-T-Shaped-Professionals-20090907-Hossein.pdf, date accessed 1 October 2010.

Dourish, Paul (2001) *Where the Action Is: The Foundations of Embodied Interaction* (Cambridge, Mass.: MIT Press).

Drucker, P.F. (1985) *Innovation and Entrepreneurship: Practice and Principles* (New York: Harper & Row).

Dunbar, R.I.M. (1993) "Coevolution of Neocortex Size, Group Size and Language in Humans," *Behavioral and Brain Sciences*, 16, 681–694.

Elliott, C. (1997) "Underdog: Rapid Refocusing Saves Spyglass – For Now," *Journal of Business Strategy*, 18(6), 49–51.

Engelbart, D. (1988) "The Augmented Knowledge Workshop" in Adele Goldberg (ed.) *A History of Personal Workstations* (New York, New York: ACM Press).

Engelbart, D. (1992) "Toward High-Performance Organizations: A Strategic Role for Groupware" in D. Coleman (ed.) *GroupWare '92* (San Mateo, California: Morgan Kaufmann Publishers), 77–100.

Estrin, J. (2008) *Closing the Innovation Gap: Reigniting the Spark of Creativity in a Global Economy* (New York: McGraw-Hill).

Evans, David S. (2009) "The Online Advertising Industry: Economics, Evolution, and Privacy," *Journal of Economic Perspectives*, 23(3), 37–60.

Faden, E. S. (2001) "The Cyberfilm: Hollywood and Computer Technology," *Strategies: Journal of Theory, Culture & Politics*, 14(1), 77–90.

Filson, D. (2004) "The Impact of E-Commerce Strategies on Firm Value: Lessons from Amazon.com and Its Early Competitors," *The Journal of Business*, 77(S2), S135–S154.

Floyd, I.R., Jones, M.C., Rathi, D. and Twidale, M.B. (2007) "Web Mash-ups and Patchwork Prototyping: User-driven Technological Innovation with Web 2.0 and Open Source Software," *Hawaii International Conference on System Sciences*, 40th Annual Hawaii International Conference on System Sciences (HICSS'07), 86c.

Fogg, B.J. (2003) *Persuasive Technology: Using Computers to Change What We Think and Do* (San Francisco, CA: Morgan Kaufmann Publishers).

Frank, M.W. (1998) "Schumpeter on Entrepreneurs and Innovation: A Reappraisal," *Journal of the History of Economic Thought*, 20(4), 505–516.

Gehani, N. (2003) *Bell Labs: Life in the Crown Jewel* (Summit, NJ: Silicon Press).

Ghosh, A. (2006) "The IPO Phenomenon in the 1990s," *The Social Science Journal*, 43(3), 487–495.

Giles, J. (2005) "Internet Encyclopaedias Go Head to Head," Special Report, *Nature*, 438(15), 900–901.

Gillies, J. and Cailliau, R. (2000) *How the Web Was Born: The Story of the World Wide Web* (Oxford and New York: Oxford University Press).

Gladwell, M. (2000) *The Tipping Point–How Little Things Make a Big Difference* (Boston: Little, Brown).

Goffman, E. (1963) *Stigma: Notes on the Management of Spoiled Identity* (New York: Simon & Schuster Inc.)

Goleniewski, L. (2003) *Telecommunications Essentials. The Complete Global Source for Communications Fundamentals, Data-Networking and the Internet and Next Generation Networks* (Boston: Addison Wesley).

Granovetter, M.S. (1973) "The Strength of Weak Ties," *The American Journal of Sociology*, 78(6), 1360–1380.

Granovetter, M.S. (1978) "Threshold Models of Collective Behavior," *The American Journal of Sociology*, 83(6), 1420–1443.

Granovetter, M.S. (1995) *Getting a Job: A Study of Contacts and Careers* (Chicago: University of Chicago Press).

Griffith, T.L. (2011) *The Plugged-In Manager: Get in Tune with Your People, Technology, and Organization to Thrive* (San Francisco: Jossey-Bass).

Grinter, R.E. and Palen, L. (2002) "Instant Messaging in Teen Life," *Proceedings of the 2002 ACM Conference on Computer Supported Cooperative Work (CSCW '02)*, ACM, New York, NY, USA, 21–30.

Grunwald, D. (2011) "The Internet Ecosystem: The Potential for Discrimination," *Federal Communications Law Journal*, 63(2), 411–443.

Halasz, F.G. (1988) "Reflections on NoteCards: Seven Issues for the Next Generation of Hypermedia Systems," *Communications of the ACM*, 31(7), 836–852.

Halasz, F.G., Moran, T.P. and Trigg, R.H. (1986) "Notecards in a Nutshell," *SIGCHI Bull.*, 18(4), 45–52.

Hallowell, E.M. (2006) *CrazyBusy: Overstretched, Overbooked, and About to Snap! Strategies for Coping in a World Gone ADD* (New York: Ballantine Books).

Halmos, P. (1957) "Nicolas Bourbaki," *Scientific American*, 196(5), 88–99.

Hampton, K.N., Sessions Goulet, L., Rainie, L. and Purcell, K. (2011) *Social networking sites and our lives: How people's trust, personal relationships, and civic and political involvement are connected to their use of social networking sites and other technologies*. Pew Internet Study, 16 June 2011. http://pewinternet.org/Reports/2011/Technology-and-social-networks.aspx, date accessed 8 February 2012.

Hargadon, A.B. (2003) *How Breakthroughs Happen: The Surprising Truth about How Companies Innovate* (Boston, MA: Harvard Business School Publishing).

Hartley, S.E. (2010) *Kiva.org: Crowd-Sourced Microfinance and Cooperation in Group Lending*. HLS Scholarly Articles. March 2010. http://dash.harvard.edu/bitstream/handle/1/3757699/Hartley_Kiva_DASH.pdf, date accessed 15 August 2012.

Heijden, H. van der (2004) "User Acceptance of Hedonic Information Systems," *MIS Quarterly*, 28(4), 695–704.

Hendler, J., Shadbolt, N., Hall, W., Berners-Lee, T. and Weitzner, D. (2008) "Web Science: An Interdisciplinary Approach to Understanding the Web," *Communications of the ACM*, 51(7), 60–69.

Hennessey, A. (2000) "Online Bookselling," *Publishing Research Quarterly*, 16(2), 34–51.

Hillstrom, K. (2005) *The Internet Revolution*, Series: Defining moments (Detroit, Mi: Omnigraphics).

Hiltzik, M.A. (2000) *Dealers of Lightning: Xerox PARC and the Dawn of the Computer Age* (New York, NY: Harper paperbacks).

Hovland, C.I. and Weiss, W. (1951) "The Influence of Source Credibility on Communication Effectiveness," *Public Opinion Quarterly*, 15(4), 635–650.

Huurdeman, A.A. (2003) *The Worldwide History of the Telecommunications* (Hoboken, New Jersey: John Wiley & Sons, Inc.).

Iansiti, M. (1999) "Real-World R&D: Jumping the Product Generation Gap" in *Harvard Business Review on Managing High-Tech Industries* (Boston, Mass.: Harvard Business School Press).

Juettemeyer, T. (2008) "Blogger: Your Thoughts Here," *Journal of Library Administration*, 46(3–4), 119–138.

Kaes, A. (2003) "A Stranger in the House: Fritz Lang's 'Fury' and the Cinema of Exile," *New German Critique*, 89, 33–58.

Kane, G.C. (2011) "A Multimethod Study of Wiki-based Collaboration," *ACM Transactions on Management Information Systems*, 2(1), 1–16.

Kane, G.C., Majchrzak, A. and Ives, B. (2010) "Editors' Comments – Special Issue on Enterprise and Industry Applications of Social Media," *MIS Quarterly Executive*, 9(4), iii–iv.

Karinthy, F. (1929) "CHAIN-LINKS" in *Everything is Different*. Translated from Hungarian and annotated by Adam Makkai. Edited by Enikö Jankó. http://djjr-courses.wdfiles.com/local – files/soc180%3Akarinthy-chain-links/Karinthy-Chain-Links_1929.pdf, date accessed 30 November 2012.

Kasner, E. and Newman, J. (1940) *Mathematics and the Imagination* (New York, Simon and Schuster, 1940).

Kelley, D. (2001) "Design as an Iterative Process," *Entrepreneurial Thought Leader Speaker Series*, 3 October 2001. http://ecorner.stanford.edu/authorMaterialInfo.html?mid=686, date accessed 25 April 2011.

Kelley, D. (2002) "David Kelley on human-centered design," *TED2002*. http://www.ted.com/talks/david_kelley_on_human_centered_design.html, date accessed 13 February 2012.

Kelley, T. (2004) *The Art of Innovation: Lessons in Creativity from IDEO, America's Leading Design Firm* (London: Profile Books).

Kemppainen, J. (2007) *Talouskasvu, kilpailukyky ja informaatioteknologian läpimurto: Yhdysvaltain, Euroopan unionin, Ruotsin ja Suomen informaatioteknologia-ohjelmat ja niihin liittyvät poliittiset suunnitelmat sekä tulevaisuuskuva vuosina 1993–1995*, Lisensiaatintyö (Oulu: Oulun yliopisto, historian laitos, yleinen historia).

Kierkegaard, S. (2010) "Twitter thou doeth?" *Computer Law & Security Review*, 26(6), 577–594.

Kim, P. (1999) "A Story of Failed Technology: Deconstructing Interactive TV Networks," *Javnost-The Public*, 6(3), 87–100.

Kim, W., Jeong, O. and Lee, S. (2010) "On social Web sites," *Information Systems*, 35(2), 215–236.

Kling, R. (2000) "Letter from the Editor-in-Chief," *Information Society*, 16(3), 167–168.

Knapp, A.W. (1999) "André Weil: A Prologue," *Notices of the American Mathematical Society*, 46(4), 434–439.

Kotha, S. (1998) "Competing on the Internet: The Case of Amazon.com," *European Management Journal*, 16(2), 212–222.

Krey, A.C. (1955) *History and the Social web: A Collection of Essays* (Minneapolis: The University of Minnesota Press).

Kunkle, R. and Morton, A. (2006) *Building Flickr Applications with PHP* (Berkeley, CA: Apress).

Lach, E. (1990) "Program Helps Scientists Create Images from Data," *InfoWorld*, 12(9), 36.

Law, E., Roto, V., Hassenzahl, M., Vermeeren, A. and Kort, J. (2009) "Understanding, Scoping and Defining User Experience: A Survey Approach," *Proceedings of Human Factors in Computing Systems conference*, CHI'09, 4–9 April 2009, Boston, MA, USA (New York, NY, USA: ACM), 719–728.

Lécuyer, C. (2007) *Making Silicon Valley: Innovation and the Growth of High Tech, 1930–1970* (Cambridge, Massachusetts: The MIT Press).

Leitch, S. and Warren, M. (2003) "Designing Systems for E-Commerce," *Australasian Journal of Information Systems*, 10(2), 139 –143.

Lessig, L. (2002) *The Future of Ideas: The Fate of the Commons in a Connected World* (New York: Vintage Books).

Lewis, E. (2004) *GBS: Ebay* ([S.l.]: Marshall Cavendish Limited), Business Source Complete, EBSCOhost, date accessed 7 March 2011.

Liberman, A. (2008) *Analytic Dictionary of English Etymology: An Introduction* (Minneapolis, MN: University of Minnesota Press).

Ljungqvist, A. and Wilhelm, W.J., Jr. (2003) "IPO Pricing in the Dot-Com Bubble," *The Journal of Finance*, 58(2), 723–752.

Lueg, C. and Fisher, D. (eds) (2003) *From Usenet to CoWebs: Interacting with Social Information Spaces* (London and New York: Springer).

Luethi, R. and Osterloh, M. (2010) "Wikipedia: Ein neues Produktionsmodell und seine rechtlichen Hürden," Version: 28, April 2010. https://www.uzh.ch/iou/orga/ssl-dir/wiki/uploads/Main/wikipedia_und_recht.pdf, date accessed 28 March 2011.

Lyytinen, K. and Yoo, Y. (2002) "Research Commentary: The Next Wave of Nomadic Computing," *Information Systems Research*, 13(4), 377–388.

Macnamara, J. (2010) "Public Relations and the Social: How Practitioners Are Using, or Abusing, Social Media," *Asia Pacific Public Relations Journal*, 11(1), 21–39.

Majchrzak, A., Jarvenpaa, S.L. and Hollingshead, A.B. (2007) "Coordinating Expertise among Emergent Groups Responding to Disasters," *Organization Science*, 18(1), 147–161.

Maltin, T. and Aston, E. (2011) *101 Things You Thought You Knew about the Titanic…but Didn't!* (New York, N.Y. : Penguin Books).

Maurer, D.W. (1931) "Carnival Cant: A Glossary of Circus and Carnival Slang," *American Speech*, 6(5), 327–337.

Mayer, M. (2006). Vice President of Search Products & User Experience at Google, "License to Pursue Dreams." *Stanford Technology Ventures Program*, 17 May 2006. http://pr-lead.com/license-to-pursue-dreams-marissa-mayer-from-google/, date accessed 7 April 2012.

McAfee, A.P. (2006) "Enterprise 2.0: The Dawn of Emergent Collaboration," *Engineering Management Review, IEEE*, 34(3), 38.

Merriam-Webster Dictionary (2012) http://www.merriam-webster.com/dictionary/brick-and-mortar, date accessed 22 August 2012.

Milgram, S. (1967) "The Small World Problem," *Psychology Today*, 2, 60–67.

Misa, T.J. (Spring 2011) "Paul Baran (1926–2011)," *Charles Babbage Institute Newsletter*, 33(1). http://www.cbi.umn.edu/about/nsl/v33n1.pdf, pp. 3–6, date accessed 6 February 2012.

Mitcham, C. and Schatzberg, E. (2009) 'Defining Technology and Engineering Sciences in Philosophy of Technology and Engineering Sciences' in Anthonie Meijers (ed.) *Handbook of the Philosophy of Science*, Vol. 9 (Amsterdam and London: Elsevier and North Holland).

Morozov, E. (2011) *The Net Delusion: The Dark Side of Internet Freedom* (New York: Public Affairs).

Muller, M., Shami, N.S., Millen, D.R. and Feinberg, J. (2010) "We are all Lurkers: Consuming Behaviors among Authors and Readers in an Enterprise File-Sharing Service," *Proceedings of the 16th ACM international conference on Supporting group work (GROUP '10)*, 7–10 November 2010, Sanibel Island, Florida, USA (New York, NY, USA: ACM), 201–210.

Nature (2005) "Wiki's wild world," An Editorial. *Nature*, 438, 15 December 2005, 890.

Nelson, T. (2009) *Geeks Bearing Gifts v.1.1: How the Computer World Got This Way* (Lulu.com: Mindful Press).

Nelson, T. H. (1987a) *Computer Lib / Dream Machines: New Freedoms through Computer Screens – a Minority Report* (Redmond, Wash.: Tempus).

Nelson, T.H. (1987b) *Literary Machines : The Report on, and of, Project Xanadu Concerning Word Processing, Electronic Publishing, Hypertext, Thinkertoys, Tomorrow's Intellectual Revolution and Certain Other Topics Including Knowledge, Education and Freedom*. Edition 87.1. (N.J.:Schooleys).

Nickell, J. (2005) *Secrets of the Sideshows* (Lexington, Kentucky: The University Press of Kentucky).

Nonaka, I. and Takeuchi, H. (1995) *The Knowledge-Creating Company – How Japanese Companies Create the Dynamics of Innovation* (New York, New York: Oxford University Press).

Nonnecke, B., Andrews, D. and Preece, J. (2006) "Non-public and Public Online Community Participation: Needs, Attitudes and Behaviour," *Electronic Commerce Research*, 6(1), 7–20.

Nonnecke, B. and Preece, J. (2000) "Lurker Demographics: Counting the Silent," *Proceedings of CHI 2000. The Hague, The Netherlands* (New York: Addison-Wesley/ACM Press), 73–80.

Ofek E. and Richardson, M. (2003) "DotCom Mania: The Rise and Fall of Internet Stock PricesAuthor," *The Journal of Finance*, 58(3), 1113–1137.

Oinas-Kukkonen, Harri (1995) "Developing Hypermedia Systems – the Functionality Approach," *Proceedings of the Second Basque International Workshop on Information Technology (BIWIT '95)*: Data Management Systems, San Sebastian, Spain, July 1995, keynote paper (Los Alamitos, CA, USA: IEEE Computer Society Press), 2–8.

Oinas-Kukkonen, Harri (1997) "Towards Greater Flexibility in Software Design Systems through Hypermedia Functionality," *Information and Software Technology*, 39(6), 391–397.

Oinas-Kukkonen Harri (1998) "Evaluating the Usefulness of Design Rationale in CASE," *European Journal of Information Systems*, 7(3), 185–191.

Oinas-Kukkonen, Harri (1999) "Mobile Electronic Commerce through the Web," *Second International Conference on Telecommunications and Electronic Commerce (ICTEC '99)*. Nashville, USA, 6–8 October 1999, 69–74.

Oinas-Kukkonen, Harri (2000) "Balancing the Vendor and Consumer Requirements for Electronic Shopping Systems," *Information Technology and Management*, 1(1&2), 73–84.

Oinas-Kukkonen, Harri (2008) "Network Analysis and Crowds of People as Sources of New Organisational Knowledge" in A. Koohang, K. Harman and J. Britz (eds) *Knowledge Management: Theoretical Foundation* (Santa Rosa, CA, US: Informing Science Press), 173–189.

Oinas-Kukkonen, Harri (2012) "A Foundation for the Study of Behavior Change Support Systems," *Personal and Ubiquitous Computing*.

Oinas-Kukkonen, Harri and Harjumaa, M. (2009) "Persuasive Systems Design: Key Issues, Process Model, and System Features," *Communications of the Association for Information Systems*, 24, Article 28, 485–500.

Oinas-Kukkonen Harri and Kurki, H. (2009) "Internet through the Eyes of 11-year Old Children: First-Hand Experiences from the Technological Environment the Children Live," *Human Technology: An Interdisciplinary Journal of Humans in ICT Environments*, 5(2), 146–162.

Oinas-Kukkonen, Henry (2001) "Hypermediaguru Ted Nelsonin mietteitä 2000-luvun alussa," *Tietojenkäsittelytiede*, kesäkuu/15, 12–13.

Oinas-Kukkonen, Henry (2002) "Ted Nelsonin näkemys median ja markkinoiden sähköisestä ihmemaailmasta," *Tiedepolitiikka*, 27(2), 23–30.

Oinas-Kukkonen, Henry (2002) "World Wide Webin – kummisedän näkemyksiä ja kokemuksia uuden median maailmasta," *Tekniikan Waiheita*, 20(2), 16–26.

Oinas-Kukkonen, Henry (2007) "From Bush to Engelbart: 'Slowly, Some Little Bells Were Ringing'," *IEEE Annals of the History of Computing*, 29(2), 31–39.

Oinas-Kukkonen, Henry, Pulkkinen, J. and Anttila, T. (2008) "Continuity and Discontinuity in the History of Discoveries and Innovations," *Faravid. Acta Societatis Historicae Finlandiae Septentrionalis*, XXXII, 185–201.

Olsson, M.L. and Hjelm, J. (2003) "OMA – Changing the Mobile Standards Game," *Ericsson Review*, 1, 12–17.

O'Malley, M. (2011) *It Happened in Kentucky* (Guilford, Ct.: Globe Pequot Press).

O'Mara, M.P. (2005) *Cities of Knowledge: Cold War Science and the Search for the Next Silicon Valley* (Princeton: Princeton University Press).

O'Reilly, T. (2005) "What Is Web 2.0: Design Patterns and Business Models for the Next Generation of Software," *O'Reilly Network*, 30 September 2005. http://www.oreillynet.com/pub/a/oreilly/tim/news/2005/09/30/what-is-web-20.html, date accessed 17 November 2009.

O'Reilly, T. & Battelle, J. (2009) "Web Squared: Web 2.0 Five Years On," *O'Reilly Network: In: Web2.0 summit*. 20–22 October 2009. http://www.web2summit.com/web2009/public/schedule/detail/10194, date accessed 17 November 2009.

Owen, S. (2001) "Failures in B2C Companies: Two Examples and Lessons for New Players," School of Finance and Economics, University of Technology, Sydney, Working paper, No. 113, 1–20.

Oxford English Dictionary (2012), "mash-up, *n..*" http://www.oed.com, date accessed 22 August 2012.

Palfrey, J. and Gasser, U. (2008) *Born Digital: Understanding the First Generation of Digital Natives* (New York: Basic Books).

Parkinson, B. (1996) "Emotions are Social," *British Journal of Psychology*, 87, 663–683.

Parkinson, J. (2010) *Spilling the Beans on the Cat's Pajamas: Popular Expressions – What They Mean and How We Got Them* (New York, N.Y./Montreal: Reader's Digest Association Inc.).

Patterson, L.J. (2006) "The Technology Underlying Podcasts," *Computer*, 39(10), 103–105.

Pedrinaci, C., Domingue, J. and Krummenacher, R. (2010) "On the Integration of Services with the Web of Data," The Knowledge Media Institute. http://kmi.open.ac.uk/publications/pdf/kmi-09–06.pdf, date accessed 1 April 2011.

Petty, R.E. and Cacioppo, J.T. (1981) *Attitudes and Persuasion: Classic and Contemporary Approaches* (Dubuque, IA: Wm. C. Brown).

Pickover, C.A. (2009) "Googol" in *The Math Book: From Pythagoras to the 57th Dimension, 250 Milestones in the History of Mathematics* (New York, NY: Sterling Publishing).

Poli, R. and Agrimi, E. (2012) "Internet Addiction Disorder: Prevalence in an Italian Student Population," *Nordic Journal of Psychiatry*, 66(1), 55–59.

Prahalad, C.K. and Venkatram, R. (2000) "Co-opting Customer Competence," *Harvard Business Review*, 78 (January–February), 79–87.

Preece, J. and Shneiderman, B. (2009) "The Reader-to-Leader Framework: Motivating Technology-Mediated Social Participation," *AIS Transactions on Human-Computer Interaction*, 1(1), 13–32.

Prensky, M. (2001a) "Digital Natives, Digital Immigrants," *On the Horizon*, 9(5), 1–6.

Prensky, M. (2001b) "Digital Natives, Digital Immigrants, Part II: Do They Really Think Differently?" *On the Horizon*, 9(6), 1–6.

Prensky, M. (2003) "Overcoming Educators' Digital Immigrant Accents: A Rebuttal," *The Technology Source*, May/June, Electronic version.

Press, L. (1993) "The Internet and Interactive Television," *Communications of the ACM*, 36(12), 19–23.

Press, L. (1994) "Commercialization of the Internet," *Communications of the ACM*, 37(11), 17–21.

Reagle, M. Jr., (2010) *Good Faith Collaboration: The Culture of Wikipedia* (Cambridge, MA: The MIT Press).

Rideout, V.J., Foehr, U.G. and Roberts, D.F. (2010) *Generation M2: Media in the Lives of 8- to 18-Year-Olds*. A Kaiser Family Foundation Study, January 2010. http://www.kff.org/entmedia/upload/8010.pdf, date accessed 3 October 2011.

Ridings, C. and McLure Wasko, M. (2010) "Online Discussion Group Sustainability: Investigating the Interplay between Structural Dynamics and Social Dynamics over Time," *Journal of the Association for Information Systems*, 11(2), Article 1.

Rieback, M.R., Crispo, B. and Tanenbaum, A.S. (2006) "The evolution of RFID security," *IEEE Pervasive Computing*, 5(1), 62–69.

Ritter, J.R. and Welch, I. (August 2002) "A Review of IPO Activity, Pricing, and Allocations," *The Journal of Finance*, 57(4), *Papers and Proceedings of the Sixty-Second Annual Meeting of the American Finance Association*, Atlanta, Georgia, 4–6 January 2002, 1795–1828.

Roberts, D.F., Foehr, U.G. and Rideout, V. (March 2005) *Generation M: Media in the Lives of 8–18 Year-olds*. A Kaiser Family Foundation Study. http://www.kff.org/entmedia/upload/Generation-M-Media-in-the-Lives-of-8–18-Year-olds-Report.pdf, date accessed 3 October 2011.

Rogers, E.M. (2003) *Diffusion of Innovations*, 5th edition (New York: Free Press).

Rosencrance, L. (2005) "To Apply for FEMA Aid Online, Katrina Survivors will Need IE 6," *Computerworld*, 7 September 2005. http://www.computerworld.com/s/article/104440/To_apply_for_FEMA_aid_online_Katrina_survivors_will_need_IE_6, date accessed 21 January 2011.

Rosenzweig, R. (2006) "Can History Be Open Source? *Wikipedia* and the Future of the Past," *The Journal of American History*, 93(1), 117–146.

Rosling, H. (2007) "Visual Technology Unveils the Beauty of Statistics and Swaps Policy from Dissemination to Access," *Statistical Journal of the IAOS*, 24(1–2), 103–104.

Sagolla, D. (2009) *140 Characters: A Style Guide for the Short Form* (Hoboken, N.J. : John Wiley & Sons).

Sample, N.J. (2005) *Scheduling and Resource Allocation in Autonomous Service Networks*. PhD Thesis submitted to the Department of Computer Science, Stanford University. http://infolab.stanford.edu/~nsample/pubs/njs-dissertation.pdf, date accessed 13 February 2012.

Sarvas, R. and Frohlich, D.M. (2011) *From Snapshots to Social Media – The Changing Picture of Domestic Photography* (London: Springer).

Saxenian, A.L. (1994) *Regional Advantage: Culture and Competition in Silicon Valley and Route 128* (Cambridge, MA, USA: Harvard University Press).

Schumpeter, J.A. (1934) *The Theory of Economic Development: An Inquiry into Profits, Capital, Credit, Interest and the Business Cycle*, 7th edn (Cambridge, Massachusetts: Harvard University Press, 1961).

Scott, C.E. (2008) "History of the Radio Industry in the United States to 1940" in R. Whaples (ed.) *EH.Net Encyclopedia*, http://eh.net/encyclopedia/article/scott.radio.industry.history, date accessed 29 November 2010.

Senft, T.M. (2003) "Bulletin-Board Systems" in S. Jones (ed.) *Encyclopedia of New Media: An Essential Reference to Communication and Technology* (Thousand Oaks, California: Sage Publications).

Shneiderman, B. (2007) "Web Science: A Provocative Invitation to Computer Science," *Communications of the ACM*, 50(6), 25–27.

Silver, D. (2005) "Selling Cyberspace: Constructing and Deconstructing the Rhetoric of Community," *The Southern Communication Journal*, 70(3), 187–199.

Sparrow, B., Liu, J. and Wenger, D. M. (2011) "Google Effects on Memory: Cognitive Consequences of Having Information at Our Fingertips," *Science*, 333(6043), 776–778.

Standards for the 21st-Century Learner (2007). American Association of School Librarians. http://www.ala.org/ala/mgrps/divs/aasl/guidelinesandstandards/learningstandards/AASL_Learning_Standards_2007.pdf, date accessed 28 December 2010.

Steiny, D. and Oinas-Kukkonen, Harri (2007) "Network Awareness: Social Network Search, Innovation and Productivity in Organizations," *International Journal of Networking and Virtual Organizations*, 4(4), 413–430.

Strecher, V. (2007) "Internet Methods for Delivering Behavioral and Health-related Interventions (eHealth)," *Annual Review of Clinical Psychology*, 3, 53–76.

Sunstein, C.R. (2007) *Republic.com 2.0* (Princeton: Princeton University Press).

Surowiecki, J. (2004) *The Wisdom of Crowds: Why the Many are Smarter Than the Few and How Collective Wisdom Shapes Business, Economies, Societies, and Nations?* (New York, NY: Doubleday).

Taleb, N.N. (2007) *The Black Swan: The Impact of the Highly Improbable* (New York: Random House).

Tansley, A.G. (1935) "The Use and Abuse of Vegetational Concepts and Terms," *Ecology*, 16(3), 284–307.

Tonioni, F., D'Alessandris, L., Lai, C., Martinelli, D., Corvino, S., Vasale, M., Fanella, F., Aceto, P. and Bria, P. (2012) "Internet Addiction: Hours Spent Online, Behaviors and Psychological Symptoms," *General Hospital Psychiatry*, 34, 80–87.

Treadaway, C. and Smith, M. (2010) *Facebook Marketing: An Hour a Day* (Indianapolis: Wiley Pub.).
Valaskivi, K. (2009) *Pokemonin perilliset. Japanilainen populaarikulttuuri Suomessa*, Tampereen yliopisto. Julkaisuja. Sarja A, 110 (Tampere: Journalismin tutkimusyksikkö, Tiedotusopin laitos, Tampereen yliopisto).
Van Riper, A.B. (2011) "Introduction" in A.B. Van Riper (ed.) *Learning from Mickey, Donald and Walt: Essays on Disneys Edutainment Films* (Jefferson, N.C.: McFarland).
Varadarajan, V.S. (1999) "The Apprenticeship of a Mathematician – Autobiography of André Weil," A Book Review, *Notices of the American Mathematical Society*, 46(4), 448–456.
Venkatesh, V., Morris, M.G., Davis, G.B. and Davis, F.D. (2003) "User Acceptance of Information Technology: Toward a Unified View," *MIS Quarterly*, 27(3), 425–478.
Vodanovich, S., Sudaram, D. and Myers, M. (2010) "Research Commentary: Digital Natives and Ubiquiotous Information Systems," *Information Systems Research*, 21(3), 711–723.
Walters, R. (2005) *Speed Spectrum: Hedy Lamarr And The Mobile Phone* (North Charleston, South Carolina: BookSurge, LLC).
Watts, D.J. (2011) *Everything is Obvious Once You Know the Answer* (New York: Crown Business).
Weiser, M. (1991) "The Computer for the Twenty-First Century," *Scientific American*, 265(3) 94–104.
Willmore, J. (2001) "Trends and the Profession" in. L.L. Ukens (ed.) *What Smart Trainers Know: The Secrets of Success from the World's Foremost Experts* (San Francisco, California: Jossey-Bass/Pfeiffer), 14–21.
Windrum, P. (2004) "Leveraging Technological Externalities in Complex Technologies: Microsoft's Exploitation of Standards in the Browser Wars," *Research Policy*, 33(3), 385–394.
Winograd T. and Flores F. (1986) *Understanding Computers and Cognition: A New Foundation for Design* (Norwood, NJ: Ablex Publishing Corporation).
Wu, T. (2011) "Bell Labs and Centralized Innovation," *Communications of the ACM*, 54(5), 31–33.
Zachary, G.P. (1999) *Endless Frontier: Vannevar Bush, Engineer of the American Century* (Cambridge, Massachusetts and London, England: The MIT Press).

Index

Printed in the United States
By Bookmasters